THINKING COMPREHENSIVELY ABOUT EDUCATION

While much is known about the critical importance of educative experiences outside of school, little is known about the social systems, community programs, and everyday practices that can facilitate learning outside of the classroom. *Thinking Comprehensively About Education* sheds much-needed light on those systems, programs, and practices, conceptualizing education more broadly through a nuanced exploration of

- the various spaces where education occurs;
- the nondominant practices and possibilities of those spaces;
- the possibilities of enabling social systems, institutions, and programs of comprehensive education.

This original edited collection identifies and describes the resources that enable optimal human learning and development, and offers a public policy framework that can enable a truly comprehensive educational system. *Thinking Comprehensively About Education* is a must-read for faculty, students, policy analysts, and policymakers.

Ezekiel J. Dixon-Román is an assistant professor of social policy in the School of Social Policy & Practice at the University of Pennsylvania.

Edmund W. Gordon is the John M. Musser Professor of Psychology Emeritus at Yale University; Richard March Hoe Professor Emeritus of Psychology and Education at Teachers College, Columbia University; and Director Emeritus of the Institute for Urban and Minority Education (IUME) at Teachers College, Columbia University.

THINKING COMPREHENSIVELY ABOUT EDUCATION

Spaces of Educative Possibility and Their Implications for Public Policy

Edited by
Ezekiel J. Dixon-Román and
Edmund W. Gordon

Routledge
Taylor & Francis Group

NEW YORK AND LONDON

First published 2012
by Routledge
711 Third Avenue, New York, NY 10017

Simultaneously published in the UK
by Routledge
2 Park Square, Milton Park, Abingdon, Oxon OX14 4RN

Routledge is an imprint of the Taylor & Francis Group, an informa business

© 2012 Taylor & Francis

The right of the editor to be identified as the author of the editorial material, and of the authors for their individual chapters, has been asserted in accordance with sections 77 and 78 of the Copyright, Designs and Patents Act 1988.

Library of Congress Cataloging in Publication Data

Thinking comprehensively about education : spaces of educative possibility and their implications for public policy / [edited by] Ezekiel J. Dixon-Román, Edmund W. Gordon.

   p. cm.

   Includes bibliographical references and index.

   1. Non-formal education—United States.   2. Experiential learning—United States.
3. Community and school—United States.   4. Children with social disabilities—Education—United States.   I. Dixon-Román, Ezekiel.   II. Gordon, Edmund W.

   LC45.4.T45   2012
   371.38—dc23   2011047606

ISBN 13: 978-0-415-89491-3 (hbk)
ISBN 13: 978-0-415-89492-0 (pbk)
ISBN 13: 978-0-203-12001-9 (ebk)

Typeset in Bembo
by Apex CoVantage, LLC

Printed and bound in the United States of America on sustainably sourced paper by IBT Global

CONTENTS

ACKNOWLEDGMENTS

As with any project and product, this book would not have been possible if it were not for a network and constellation of supports. This book is the final volume of four books developed as a result of the National Study Group on Supplementary/Comprehensive Education, which was financially supported by the Hewlett Foundation and the W. T. Grant Foundation and sponsored by the College Board, the Educational Testing Service, and the Institute for Urban and Minority Education at Teachers College, Columbia University. As editors, we were fortunate to have also benefited from the creative, timely, and cooperative participation of a stellar group of contributors to this final volume. We extend our appreciation to them and to Shaun Harper for introducing us to Alex Masulis and Katie Raissian of Routledge Press, both of whom were very responsive and instrumental in bringing this book to publication.

The first editor is especially grateful to Deepa Vasudevan as well as to Julianne Oothoudt, Anastasia Barron, and Carol Ross for their editorial assistance. This book would not be as sharpened and refined if it were not for their assistance. The first editor's work at the completion of this book was enabled by his faculty appointment in the School of Social Policy & Practice at the University of Pennsylvania and by an appointment as visiting scholar for the Fall 2011 semester in the Graduate School of Education at the University of California, Berkeley.

The editors acknowledge with thanks the considerable contribution to our thinking about these essays that resulted from our exchanges with members of the National Study Group on Supplementary/Comprehensive Education. Some of the members of the Study Group contributed essays to this collection. All contributed ideas and intellectual inspiration. Additional conceptual and logistical supports were provided by Ms. Paola Heincke, Executive Officer for the Study Group, and Dr. Michael Nettles, whose Policy Evaluation and Research Center at ETS hosted the Study Group. We are extremely grateful to these persons and organizations for their support, while we absolve them of any responsibility for the limitations of our work.

And, of course, *Thinking Comprehensively About Education* would not have been possible without the loving and intellectual support of our family and friends.

FOREWORD

Angela Glover Blackwell

For decades, America has been engaged in a natural experiment that has repercussions far beyond the classroom. Families with resources have consistently gone above and beyond what their average-to-great public school classrooms provide to support their children's success in school and life. These families give their children innumerable opportunities to engage in enriching experiences and provide supports to boost their sense of self and their capacity to do well in college and in chosen careers. Based on their college attendance rates (College Board, 2007), their career successes, and other indicators, this experiment has worked to the benefit of wealthier families and their children.

The parallel national experiment for poor families has had less encouraging outcomes. Poor children, expected to perform at high levels without outside enrichment supports, have had dismal levels of academic achievement and little access to good jobs and careers. Unlike their wealthier counterparts, many poor children—especially poor children of color—attend schools that are inadequately resourced, have narrowly focused curriculums, are consumed by high-stakes testing, and lack community-based supports. Inadequate, limited resources yield a disproportionate number of students of color who drop out of school or graduate high school ill-prepared for the workforce or college.

The statistics are sobering: By the end of 4th grade, Black, Latino, and poor students of all races are two years behind wealthier, predominantly White peers in reading and math; by 8th grade, they are three years behind, and by 12th grade, four years behind (Campaign for Educational Equity, Teachers College, n.d.). In 2008, the high school dropout rate for Black students was 10% and for Latinos it was 18%—compared to 5% for White students (U.S. Department of Education, 2010). Sixty-one percent of qualified White high school graduates enter 4-year colleges, compared to only 44% of Latino and 29% of African American high school graduates that are similarly qualified (Advisory Committee on Student Financial Assistance, 2001). The implications are alarming not only in terms of lost potential and diminished success but because today's young people, increasingly of color, will be the economic drivers of tomorrow.

When poor children do get access to the same resources that wealthy families provide for their children, they do well. The Harlem Children's Zone, which wraps students in healthy environments, afterschool and enrichment resources, and a strong focus on academics, has 100% of third graders at their Promise Academies at or above grade level in math, outperforming their Black and White peers in New York State and New York City, with similar results for English. Currently, over 600 of the students that participated in afterschool programs are enrolled in college (Harlem Children's Zone, n.d.). With similar resources and commitment, all children can succeed.

Thus, the solutions to our challenges are neither simple nor new. A broader concept of education is needed, one that expects all children to perform at high levels academically, graduate, and reach their full potential through higher education and fulfilling careers. Our limited notion of what it takes to educate a child must go beyond schools and incorporate resources outside of school as part of deliberate education strategy—something that wealthier parents well know. On-the-ground programs and community efforts that reflect the depth of knowledge that some neighborhoods already have about what works to prepare all children to succeed are important sources of wisdom for those seeking to build the new framework.

In my travels across the country, I have seen countless examples of neighborhoods working to address their challenges, but without policy support. Community-based organizations, places of worship, and parents often come together to provide mentoring and tutoring, arts and music opportunities, health and fitness programs, and space for critical engagement with issues that face young people. When, however, we stop short of policy change, community efforts languish and the struggle continues for funding, recognition, and priority in reform agendas.

To be effective, policy solutions must be comprehensive and must draw from what is working in local communities. We can look to examples like the Harlem Children's Zone and the federal Promise Neighborhoods initiative that it inspired as guidance. But we cannot stop at singular grant programs—rather, we need to begin thinking differently about how large-scale policy agendas and legislation, like the Elementary and Secondary Education Act, can better incorporate solutions that work. Policymakers can embed strategies into their plans that support supplementary learning, like incentives for community partnerships to align and coordinate learning opportunities and approaches that facilitate parent and guardian engagement to support children's academic and personal development. A new framework for accountability, quality, and transparency in education is also possible that is broader and less focused on standardized testing and includes out-of-school and community supports. High-quality programs can be developed and lifted up through researching promising local practices. Ultimately, it will take a coordinated, multifield effort, driven by community change advocates, to truly transform education for those who have been left behind and ensure success for all Americans not just in school but in life. This volume addresses these issues along with illustrations of the variety of settings and practices where teaching and learning transactions occur while considering the possibilities of public policy.

References

Advisory Committee on Student Financial Assistance. (2001, February 20). *Access denied: Restoring the nation's commitment to equal educational opportunity* [Report of the Advisory Committee on Student Financial Assistance, US. Department of Education]. Retrieved from http://www.ed.gov/about/bdscomm/list/acsfa/access_denied.pdf

Campaign for Educational Equity, Teachers College. (n.d.). Facts and figures. Retrieved from http://www.tc.edu/news.htm?articleID=5183

College Board. (2007). Trends in college pricing. Retrieved from http://www.career cornerstone.org/pdf/universities/tuition07.pdf

The Harlem Children's Zone. (n.d.) Our results. Retrieved from http://www.hcz.org/our-results

U.S. Department of Education, National Center for Education Statistics. (2010). *The condition of education 2010* (NCES 2010–028), Indicator 20. Washington, DC: U.S. Department of Education.

1

INTRODUCTION

Social Space and the Political Economy of Comprehensively Conceived Education

Ezekiel J. Dixon-Román

The legacy of the factory model of schooling is that tens of billions of dollars are tied up in unproductive use of time and technology, in underused school buildings, in antiquated compensation systems, and in inefficient school-finance systems.

Arne Duncan, U.S. Secretary of Education,
"The New Normal: Doing More With Less"

It should be obvious that even with schools of equal quality a poor child can seldom catch up with a rich one. Even if they attend equal schools and begin at the same age, poor children lack most of the educational opportunities which are casually available to the middle-class child. These advantages range from conversation and books in the home to vacation travel and a different sense of oneself, and apply, for the child who enjoys them, both in and out of school. So the poorer student will generally fall behind so long as he depends on school for advancement or learning.

Ivan Illich, *Deschooling Society*

We don't have after school programs when you don't want to do football, because that's pretty much the only thing that you can do in the inner-city...we're all thought of to be sports players....Is there something else for us to do?

Dragon, *Rize*

These three quotes—the first from the leading politician on U.S. education today, the second from a notable intellectual, and the final from a youth in South Central Los Angeles in 2004—bring together the core themes raised in this volume: space, education, and the co-constitutive inequality between the two. On the one hand, U.S. Secretary of Education Arne Duncan speaks to the historical and ongoing limitations of schooling while implicitly alluding to Capitol Hill's continued faith in the possibilities of educational excellence and equity in and through school re-form. On the other hand, Illich refers to the impossibility of educational equality, even with equal schooling. Moreover, both Illich and Dragon refer to the inequal-ity of educational opportunities outside of schooling, where many out-of-school resources are afforded to the children and youth of affluent communities, and to the lack of opportunities for socially and economically marginalized communities. Dragon expresses not only the dearth of educational opportunities in his social reality but also his desire for something more. The "advantages" that Illich refers to and that Dragon desires are the everyday experiences of a broader understanding of education. This understanding of education posits that the process of educa-tion is much more comprehensive than schooling and has been enabled only for those of the socially privileged spaces within society. This broader understanding of education is what the U.S. Secretary of Education seemingly overlooks in his criticisms of the legacy of federal policy on schooling.

The history of federal policy on education in the United States reveals that the nation has invested most of its reform efforts on schooling. Although school-ing is important for affirmative and adaptive human development and for build-ing competitive national economies in technologically advanced societies, school reform efforts have seldom addressed the critical social and educative conditions, resources, and possibilities, outside of schooling, in the communities and homes of learners. Current federal policy makes provisions for supplemental educational services for schools identified as "poor performing"—a posture that assumes out-of-school educational opportunities are remedial and therefore unnecessary. This assumption and narrow conceptualization of education overlooks the meaning-ful complementary, supplementary, and comprehensive education processes that occur outside of schooling. These are the very spaces at which Dragon hinted. Supplementary education refers to all of the learning and developmental experi-ences that occur outside of schooling, whereas the idea of thinking comprehen-sively about education is concerned with the deliberate and relational educative experiences in all spaces of society (not just schooling). It is in these underexca-vated spaces where rich and overlooked possibilities abound.

In the past five decades there have been gestures in federal policy to the im-portance of what goes on in complement and supplement to schooling. Some of these gestures include the development and implementation of Head Start, as well as breakfast and free or reduced-price lunch programs. Also, resources have been allocated for supplemental educational services for poor-performing schools under the No Child Left Behind Act of 2001. More recently, the Obama administration has acknowledged the educative significance of complementary and supplementary education in the development of 21st Century Community Learning Centers and the Promise Neighborhoods initiatives. Although not yet fully embraced in federal policy, each of these gestures has suggested that comprehensive approaches to education are much broader than those that occur within the four walls of schooling. These types of measures remain vital for the national endeavors of educational equity and excellence.

While substantial research exists regarding the critical importance of the educative experiences outside of schooling, the literature is mixed in its findings and not inclusive of the variety of spaces and practices of education beyond schooling. For example, little is known about the social systems that enable more relational and comprehensive processes of education, the various programs and institutions that provide equitable and deliberate pedagogical experiences, and the meaningful educational and developmental processes that are present in the everyday practices of nondominant communities. What are some examples of social systems that enable the spaces of equitable educative possibility? What are the kinds of programs and community institutions that provide the space and opportunity for education conceived comprehensively? What are the processes of comprehensive education that occur within the space and time of nondominant everyday practices, that which de Certeau (1984) suggested are tactics that cleverly maneuver through the utilization of time and heteronomy of place?

This volume seeks to bring forward the meaningful educative experiences of supplementary and comprehensive approaches to education while also offering considerations for how federal policy can enable human possibility through the broader domain of comprehensively conceived education.[1] Moreover, thinking comprehensively about education conceptualizes education as *ubiquitous* to the social process of thinking, feeling, being, and doing everyday human experiences. The examination and exploration of comprehensively conceived education is critical to enhancing the understanding of educative experiences in spaces beyond schooling and the paramount cost of not targeting the inequality of resources and processes in these spaces. Thus, this volume captures the various manifestations of comprehensively conceived education in various spaces of society while providing considerations for public policy.

Recently these concepts have been given more attention theoretically and in research, beginning with Gordon, Bridglall, and Meroe's (2005) *Supplementary Education;* in the extensive works of Heather Weiss, on complementary education; and the recent *Perspectives on Comprehensive Education,* a three-volume series with Mellen Press, edited by Hervé Varenne and Edmund W. Gordon. To help develop the educational-research and policy worlds' understanding of these meaningful processes, *Thinking Comprehensively About Education* seeks to conceptualize and capture education more broadly; capture various spaces where education occurs; feature some of the nondominant practices and possibilities of those spaces; consider the possibilities in and through comprehensively enabling social systems, institutions, and programs of education, identify and describe the resources that enable optimal human learning and development; and consider the implications for public policy that enable education to be understood comprehensively.

In this volume we seek to push the boundaries and broaden the conceptualization of education in order to capture the educative conditions, resources, and processes beyond traditional schooling. Given the social and economic marginality of many communities in the United States, and the large degree of inequality in resources between communities (Massey & Denton, 1993; Quillian, 2007; Rearden & Bischoff, in press; Sampson, Sharkey, & Raudenbush, 2008; Sharkey, 2008; Wilson, 1987), many children and youth grow up in marginalized communities, where they inherit inequitable conditions, thus making equitable education impossible. In fact, Sampson et al. (2008) found that living in a severely disadvantaged neighborhood reduces the later verbal ability of African American children on average by 4 points; the equivalent of missing a year or more of schooling. Hence, we identify and examine the various spaces and nondominant everyday practices that enable educative possibility. It is with these empirical examples in mind that we offer considerations for public policy of comprehensively conceived education.

I will frame each of the contributions to this volume by briefly discussing the idea of thinking comprehensively about education, then critically engage how (social) space complicates and affirms the idea and possibilities of comprehensive education. The theoretical mapping of social space onto the idea of thinking comprehensively about education points toward what I refer to as the "political economy of education conceived comprehensively," where the social spaces of society are organized by well-to-do and less-well-to-do spaces of social and educational resources. I will then finish this introduction with an advanced organizer of the volume.

Thinking Comprehensively About Education

In Larry Cremin's address (1975/2007) to the John Dewey Society, he stated,

> The important fact is that family life does educate, religious life does educate, and work does educate; and, what is more, the education of all three realms is as intentional as the education of the school, though in different ways and in different measures. (p. 549)

He further set forth three assertions:

> First, we have to think comprehensively about education; second, that we have to think relationally about education; and third, that we have to think publicly about education. (p. 550)

Cremin's observations and analysis challenged the existing theories of education within educational research, policy, and practice. In other words, education has been understood as a dualism between schooling and society, in which schooling has been privileged as the place, space, and time of education. Cremin pointed to this very contention in John Dewey's *Democracy and Education,* but Cremin argued that Dewey falls short of his interest of reconciling this dualistic understanding of the process of education. It is via this understanding of thinking comprehensively, relationally, and publicly about education that Cremin attempted to resolve the dualistic understanding of education and society by speaking to how one is co-constitutive of the other, how schools are related to other societal apparatuses, and how each of their relational foci is important in the equitable development of human potential.

This perspective of thinking comprehensively, relationally, and publicly about education recognizes simultaneously the relevance and limitations of schooling. While schools are still acknowledged as relevant institutions of education in society, it also suggests, as Gordon, Heincke, and Rajagopalan describe in Chapter 2, that comprehensive education is the broader domain of education, where schooling is understood as the supplement. This conceptualization has the advantage of affirming and acknowledging both the multiplicity of knowledge and ways of knowing as well as the legitimated knowledge of dominant institutions. This affirmation and acknowledgment is enabled by the understanding that education is ubiquitous in the various spaces and practices in society, not just in schooling.

For these reasons, and building upon Cremin (1975/2007), others (Gordon et al., 2005; Varenne, Gordon, & Lin, 2009) have begun to theorize, examine, and consider the various forms of supplementary and comprehensive education. They suggest that supplementary and comprehensive education might include spaces and practices such as libraries, museums, child-care centers, health education and clinics, martial arts, hip-hop, afterschool programs, athletics, parenting-practice workshops, financial-literacy programs, and prenatal services, among many others. It is via each of these institutions, programs, and practices that we find the various educational processes that Cremin asserted.

Thus, this volume supports Cremin's (1975/2007) and Varenne's (2007, 2009) notion of thinking comprehensively about education, where education is understood as *ubiquitous to being human.* By taking seriously the notion that the structures of education are rather arbitrary (Garfinkel, 2002), Varenne (2007, 2008, 2009) posited that humans are inherently ignorant, and it is the lack of knowledge that produces the desire to seek knowledge. This constant seeking of knowledge, an ongoing process of "becoming," is how humans make sense of the world in which they are situated—a process of learning how to "be" and "do" in the world as constituted by and constituting social space. In this sense, the subject is both active participator and learner of the structuring social world. As discussed in the next section, it is the social constitution and political economy of space that enables the producing and reproducing of the relations of power, inequality, and inequity. It is for this reason that the authors in this volume pay particular attention to the process of comprehensively conceived education within social space and the spatial and practical affordances for educative possibility.

Space and Educative Possibility: The Political Economy of Comprehensively Conceived Education

Although thinking comprehensively about education challenges the place-based understanding of schooling, it also makes assumptions about space and the affordances within space to enable educative experiences. For instance, how is space socially produced? How does the social production of space provide differential affordances for different spaces and for different bodies within space? In what ways might this have implications for the idea of the process of education as the lived experience? It is the exploration of these questions regarding the intersections of social space and the idea of thinking comprehensively about education that is critical for understanding the reproduction of social and educational inequality.

Space is a concept that has long been theorized and studied in philosophy, the physical sciences, and the social sciences. In fact, the early dominant approaches to the study and practical understanding of space began in the physical sciences, with astronomy and mathematics, particularly with geometry. It is for this reason that many of the social scientific approaches to the study of space have fallen short by appropriating the paradigms of the physical sciences' scientific study of space (e.g., geography). Although not conceptually agreed upon, space—understood distinctly from place—has become understood as one of the critical dimensions of human existence for the social sciences.

Theoretically, space has been conceptualized and understood in various ways in the social sciences. In *Capital,* Marx's conceptualization of space was reduced to the economic determinism of social classes. Pierre Bourdieu (1985) described social space as "a field of forces, i.e., as a set of objective power relations that impose themselves on all who enter the field" (p. 724), yet not reducible to the actions and interactions of agents in space. However, Bourdieu's conceptualization focused more on the structuring forces of space and the produced social divisions and less on the practices within space and their mediation and constitution of space. Alternatively, Michel de Certeau (1984) explained the distinction between place and space, pointing toward the practices as the primary distinction. He suggested that place is a location, whereas space is a "practiced place," determined by subjects in the history of place and the users of it. Although de Certeau gives more attention to the mediating processes of practices within space, he does not adequately account for the production and reproduction of space itself whereby we also find social divisions.

In order to account for the political economy *in* and *of* space, Henri Lefebvre (1974/1991) drew a distinction between the production of *things in* space versus the production *of* space. He posited that social space is a social product; the social production of *perceived, conceived,* and *lived* physical place and nature. Space is both produced and producing, constituted and constituting, structured and structuring. As Lefebvre stated, "social space *per se* is at once *work* and *product*" (pp. 101–102). He conceptualized the production of space as the dialectical process between spatial practice (i.e., perceived), representations of space (i.e., conceived), and representational space (i.e., lived).

Spatial practices are in dialectical interaction with space—producing space as it increasingly appropriates it. In Chapter 6, Vasudevan and Rodriguez Kerr illustrate how the practices of court-involved youth in a theater arts program socially reimagine, inscript, and reproduce the existing space for their own cultural production. The everyday practices examined in Part 3 are also the spatial practices that are constituted by and constitute the spaces of nondominant communities. It is the everyday spatial practices that are simultaneously produced by and producing the spaces of educative possibility.

The representations of space are the dominant spaces of society and, hence, associated with the relations of production of society (i.e., the social division of labor; elaborated further below). They are spaces that are conceptualized by scientists, urban planners, or policy makers with an intellectually developed system of verbal signs, codes, and knowledge. The contributions in the first section of this volume examine social systems as socially produced spaces of society. Whether in Cuban society, the Diamond Neighborhoods of Southeast San Diego, or Chinatown and Koreatown in Los Angeles, each are organized by spatial practices and compose a conceived verbal system of signs and codes that signify what educational spaces are—for what, for whom, how, and when. These were conceived of and maintained by some form of legitimated body of authority (e.g., Cuban government, community-investment group, urban planners, community organizations) and, as such, contribute to the relations of production of educational spaces. The contributions of the first section critically consider the representations of space of social systems of comprehensively conceived education.

Representational spaces are the *lived* spaces that agents occupy, interact in, and use. These are less conceptualized and more described spaces, with a less coherent system of nonverbal symbols. They are the dominated spaces of society that are more passively experienced. We introduce representational spaces throughout the volume, particularly in the third section, in which we discuss nondominant everyday practices. For instance, in Chapter 10, Nasir introduces the occupied and used spaces of youth sports settings and how to reimagine the educative possibilities in and through the activities and practices of youth sports. This section focuses reimagining the broader process of education in the various *lived* spaces of society.

Although spatial practices, representations of space, and representational space may not constitute a coherent whole, this "conceptual triad" of the production of space is an interconnected, unified system of the political economy of space. This is a political economy that produces not just things *in* space but, what is more important, the *knowledge of* space.

Following Marx's critique of political economy, the political economy of space also needs biological reproduction, the reproduction of labor power, and the reproduction of the social relations of production. Biological reproduction consists of the reproduction of the biophysical and the familial; it is that which ensures the reproduction of society from generation to generation. The reproduction of labor power maintains the existence and supply of the working class, whereas the reproduction of the social relations of production produces and sustains the social division of labor. The latter (social relations of production) becomes critically important in thinking about and understanding the political economy of space. For instance, who are the producers of the *knowledge of* the representations of space? Who is authorized to conceive of and become the architect or social engineer of the dominant spaces of society? How do these constructed dominant spaces legitimate particular spaces, symbolically exclude particular actors and communities, and co-constitute the representational spaces? These questions have direct implications for the intersections of social space and comprehensive education.

The idea of thinking comprehensively about education must be described and understood as situated within the political economy of space. Thinking comprehensively about education situates the social process of education in the spatial practices of all socially produced spaces of society. However, as observed historically in education policy in the United States, only one institution has been legitimated with the representations of educational space: schools. Moreover, the social relations of produced space not only produce social divisions in the production of space but also constitute where bodies are and can be configured in space. For instance, in postindustrial urban space we find the spatial ordering and distinctions between what is socially constituted as downtown and what is socially constituted as socially and economically marginalized communities. The former spaces of industry in the center of cities or on waterfronts have been reconfigured into communities of luxury living. The symbolic urban high-rise projects of concentrated poverty have increasingly been replaced by additional communities of luxury living, displacing and further marginalizing former residents beyond the accessibility of economic opportunity, and even the boundaries of urban space. These well-resourced luxury communities also possess libraries, out-of-school learning centers (e.g., Sylvan), dance and theater centers and programs, art classes and programs, and social organizations that provide social and academic enrichment programs (e.g., Rotary or Elks Clubs). The institutions of economically marginalized communities are generally limited to churches, corner stores, and check-cashing locations. Thinking comprehensively about education is therefore situated within this postindustrial political economy of space.

While understanding the social process of education as ubiquitous to being human posits complex and meaningful educative experiences in all socially produced spaces of society, it also suggests that even beyond schooling there *is* and *has been* a political economy of comprehensively conceived education. This political economy has and continues to organize space to enable and maintain the educational privilege and advantage for the socially and economically well-to-do. However, the structure of educational inequality is not based solely on the *place* of schooling but on all *social spaces* of educative possibility, whereby the organization and structure of out-of-school resources, institutions, and programs are spatially organized and symbolically accessible to the socially and economically privileged. It is due to the political economy of comprehensively conceived education that public policy needs a broader, more comprehensive conception of education to enable equitable educative possibility.

As models, policies are reductionistic and will always fall short of capturing the multiplicity of human possibility, but this should not constrain or limit the research, development, and implementation of policies that will maximize enabling these possibilities. As such, the authors in this volume consider the implications to public policy for comprehensively conceived education. A public-policy framework and agenda of comprehensive education is necessary to affirm and enable the spatial practices of comprehensive education in society at large, and in socially and economically marginalized spaces in particular. This framework is imperative if the democratic aims of the United States are to address the nondemocratic materiality of the reproduced social relations of production, inequality, and inequity. We provide empirical examples of social systems, programs and institutions, and spatial practices of comprehensively conceived education. As such, we offer considerations toward a public-policy agenda on comprehensive education. If the political economy's reproduced inequality of comprehensively conceived education is not addressed, the national endeavors of educational excellence and equity will continue to be an impossibility, and the children of the United States will continue to be left behind in the global community—a consequence the nation cannot afford.

Organization of the Volume

In the first three sections of this volume the authors provide empirical examples of comprehensively conceived education in three forms of produced space: social systems, programs and institutions, and nondominant everyday practices. The final section includes considerations toward a public-policy agenda that focuses on the broader domain of education and the limits of school reform.

The volume begins with a theoretically rich reconceptualization of education by Gordon, Heincke, and Rajagopalan (Chapter 2). They conceptually ground the idea of thinking comprehensively about education and discuss how the various forms of capital enable conditions for educative possibility. They posit that education is life and that schooling is the supplement, and they provide a theoretical framing for the following contributions.

In the first section we critically examine examples of the social systems of comprehensively conceived education. The out-of-school programs, policies, and practices that evolved out of the Revolution of 1959 in Cuba are ethnographically examined and critically analyzed in Chapter 3. Given the four main tenets of the revolution—the equalization of resources, the eradication of illiteracy, the universalization of education, and the universalization of health care—I describe how there existed a more comprehensive understanding of education from the beginning of the revolution. I conclude with some of the potentially rich insights that can be learned by the United States.

In Chapter 4, Zhou pushes back on the cultural values and Confucian-ideology hypotheses of Asian American high achievement. She adds to the more recent alternative narrative that suggests the development of high academic ability is a function of well-resourced and saturated communities of ethnic institutions of supplementary education. Moreover, she posits that the high levels of developed academic ability are a product of the community participant's goal socialization and engagement with the community resources. Clark and Bryan (Chapter 5) analyze a community investment model that builds in a community-member-led approach to economic sustainability and a promising alternative to the much-featured Harlem Children's Zone model. The Jacobs Center for Neighborhood Innovation is a community-run model, wherein the belief that "for change to be sustainable, residents must own the plans, process, and assets of change in their neighborhoods" socially and pedagogically empowers and addresses all members of the community. These three chapters provide examples of representations of space whereby comprehensive education can be enabled. Thus, this section offers a landscape by which to consider the various configurations of how social systems can enable comprehensively conceived education.

The second section includes examples of a program and community institution. Given the alarming statistics on the disproportionate incarceration rate of Black and Latino youth, Vasudevan and Rodriguez Kerr describe in Chapter 6 the efforts of the Insight Theater Project, which is a collaborative, arts-based program for court-involved youth. In particular, they highlight the importance of the youths' voices and perspectives as a critical social issue. The spatial and multimodal lens they employ in this chapter highlights aspects of the program and youth experience with the program that would otherwise be missed or overlooked. This analysis richly makes the chapter about youth social ontology in and through the space of the program and the embodied practices of this space.

Powell's contribution (Chapter 7) nicely relates the association of nondominant cultural practices and community institutions of comprehensive education by focusing on a Japanese cultural practice in a Japantown community institution. She discusses the historic background of San Jose's Japantown, the organization of San Jose Taiko, and Taiko, in particular, providing some social and cultural grounding to the cultural practice and institution. Both Chapters 6 and 7 show spatial practices of comprehensive education that produce the social space of the program and community institution in which they are situated.

In the third section, which focuses on nondominant everyday-spatial practices, we conceptualize from the cultural modeling of comprehensive education to the spatial practices of youth poetry. Lee (Chapter 8) employs her cultural modeling framework to pedagogically model the relational and dialectical processes of comprehensive education, with a particular focus between the home and school. She reminds us of the importance of a cultural-ecological perspective to learning and development and provides a rich conceptual framing for the following three chapters in this section. Using mixed methods, McGee and Spencer (Chapter 9) analyze the racialized social ontology and negotiations of Tinesha, an African American female, in achieving mathematics and engineering success. Additionally, this contribution adds a critical social dimension to the volume: that is, how do race, racialized constructions of the body, and racialized social ontologies have implications to education understood and conceived as ubiquitous to being human. In Chapter 10, Nasir engages a very important topic of the educative possibilities in and through youth sports from a lens of the intersectionality of identity, risk, and learning and development. The mapping of theoretical frameworks onto the analysis of the social, psychological, developmental, and learning processes in socially temporal and spatial activities and practices of youth sports creates a rich analysis and contribution. Critical literacy in and through the practice of youth poetry is the focus of Chapter 11. Jocson nicely decenters what is traditionally understood as poetry by including hip-hop, slam, and other nondominant constructions of poetry, particularly as it is defined in schooling. She discusses June Jordan's P4P program, which illustrates the possibilities of youth poetry in comprehensive education. These contributions focus on different examples of spatial practices, which point to the possibilities of comprehensive education and public policy.

The final section includes considerations toward a public-policy agenda on comprehensively conceived education. Leos-Urbel and Aber (Chapter 12) consider the challenges of designing and conducting research on complementary education. They review some of the existing evidence on the role of out-of-school influences for human learning and development and propose a policy-relevant research agenda on comprehensive education that better addresses the challenges and constraints in the field. Wells and Noguera (Chapter 13) contribute nicely to the historic, economic, social, and political complexities of educational reform in postindustrial urban space. They show that, like Baltimore, Philadelphia, or Camden, Newark is a great example of the challenges and needs of youth and families that go beyond traditional schooling to enable the kind of social, educational, and economic growth needed for a city. This contribution is based on the Broader Bolder Approach, which is a policy model that imagines how education can be thought of comprehensively and that works with the community institutions of schooling in order to provide social services, afterschool programs, and the increased capacity of schools to be responsive to the issues of social and environmental context.

In the final chapter, Gordon and Heincke (Chapter 14) argue that there are limits to what schools can do alone and what can be achieved through school reform. They call for the need to push for a national program and a Federal Office of Affirmative Development of Intellective Competence, which would focus on better enabling communities and families to support the academic and personal development of children from preconception through college. Based on the recommendations of the National Study Group on Supplementary/Comprehensive Education, they provide a framework for a public policy agenda on comprehensive education that would achieve the national endeavors of social and academic equity and excellence. They argue that these national endeavors are not plausibly attainable from school-reform efforts alone. This volume conceptually postulates and empirically demonstrates ideas and endeavors that can only be achieved *comprehensively*.

Note

1. I use supplementary and comprehensive education as inclusive of Heather Weiss's concept of complementary education. These three terms tend to be used interchangeably.

References

Bourdieu, P. (1985). The social space and the genesis of groups. *Theory and Society, 14*(6), 723–744.

Cremin, L. (2007). Public education and the education of the public. *Teachers College Record, 109*(7), 1545–1558. (Original work published 1975)

De Certeau, M. (1984). *The practice of everyday life.* Berkeley: University of California Press.

Duncan, A. (2010). The new normal: Doing more with less. Retrieved from: http://www.ed.gov/news/speeches/new-normal-doing-more-less-secretary-arne-duncans-remarks-american-enterprise-institut

Garfinkel, H. (2002). *Ethnomethodology's program: Working out Durkheim's aphorism.* Lanham, MD: Rowman & Littlefield.

Gordon, E. W., Bridglall, B. L., & Meroe, A. S. (2005). *Supplementary education: The hidden curriculum of high academic achievement.* Lanham, MD: Rowman & Littlefield.

Illich, I. (2004). *Deschooling society.* New York, NY: Marion Boyars. (Original work published 1970)

LaChapelle, D. (Producer). (2005). *Rize.* [Documentary]. Los Angeles, CA: David LaChapelle Studios.

Lefebvre, H. (1991). *The production of space* (translated by Donald Nicholson-Smith). Malden MA: Blackwell. (Original work published 1974)

Marx, K. (2010). *Capital: A critique of political economy: Vol. 1.* Seattle, WA: Pacific Publishing Studio.

Massey, D. S., & Denton, N. A. (1993). *American apartheid: Segregation and the making of the underclass.* Cambridge, MA: Harvard University Press.

Quillian, L. (2007, March). *Does segregation create winners and losers? Education and spatial segregation on the basis of income and race.* Paper presented at the Annual Meeting of the Population Association of America, New York, NY.

Rearden, S., & Bischoff, K. (in press). Income inequality and income segregation. *American Journal of Sociology.*

Sampson, R. J., Sharkey, P., & Raudenbush, S. W. (2008). Durable effects of concentrated disadvantage on verbal ability among African-American children. *Proceedings of the National Academy of Sciences, 105*(3), 845–852.

Sharkey, P. (2008). The intergenerational transmission of context. *American Journal of Sociology, 113,* 931–969.

Varenne, H. (2007). Difficult collective deliberations: Anthropological notes toward a theory of education. *Teachers College Record, 109*(7), 1559–1588.

Varenne, H. (2008). Alternative anthropological perspectives on education. In H. Varenne (Ed.), *Perspectives on Comprehensive Education Series: Vol. 1* (pp. 1–6). Lewiston, NY: The Edwin Mellen Press.

Varenne, H. (2009). Educating ourselves about education—Comprehensively. In H. Varenne, E. W. Gordon, & L. Lin (Eds.), *Perspectives on Comprehensive Education Series: Vol. 2. Theoretical perspectives on comprehensive education: The way forward* (pp. 1–24). Lewiston, NY: The Edwin Mellen Press.

Varenne, H., Gordon, E. W., & Lin, L. (2009). *Perspectives on comprehensive education series: Vol. 2. Theoretical perspectives on comprehensive education: The way forward.* Lewiston, NY: The Edwin Mellen Press.

Wilson, W. J. (1987). *The truly disadvantaged: The inner city, the underclass, and public policy.* Chicago, IL: University of Chicago Press.

2

TOWARD A RECONCEPTUALIZATION OF EDUCATION

*Edmund W. Gordon with Paola C. Heincke
and Kavitha Rajagopalan*

Introduction

There are significant limits to "school reform" as a strategy for improving the quality of academic achievement and personal development in low-income, low-status, and otherwise marginalized populations. It may be fallacious to define education as coterminous with schooling. In fact, the domain of education is life itself; schooling is but one of the educative institutions in human societies. Not only is it a limitation to consider education in terms of schooling alone, but it may in fact be erroneous to erect a kind of dualism between life and schooling, when schooling and other educative forces should be considered as a continuous process. I suggest that any effort to improve intellectual and personal development in marginalized populations must take a comprehensive approach to education, as effective education appears to be in most populations.

Thinking comprehensively about education necessitates the expansion of the definition of *education* to include a wide array of conditions and opportunities for effective teaching and learning, which enable learners to engage in life processes in a manner that promotes the development of the intellect. I define comprehensive education as inclusive of schooling and all of the family and community-based activities and learning experiences in support of academic development, which occur outside of the school, and suggest that we can actually attribute high academic achievement to exposure to these types of activities and experiences—much more so than formal academic curricula taught in schools. Several researchers have observed a significant gap in academic achievement between African American and Latino students and their White and Asian counterparts at all socioeconomic and class levels (Coleman et al., 1966; College Board, 1999). It is possible that the roots of this so-called achievement gap lie in the different ways that families and communities support the academic and personal development of their children.

In our modern, technologically advanced, global society, James Coleman's implicit challenge to the nation on education may be more appropriate now than it was when we first enunciated it almost 50 years ago. As Coleman and others of us asserted in 1966, the central challenge to education is to uncouple academic achievement from the demographic or social divisions from which children come. We felt then, as I do now, that academic achievement should not be predictable from the class, ethnicity, first language, gender, or religious beliefs of the students being served. We, members of the National Study Group on Supplementary/Comprehensive Education, believe that this challenge cannot be met effectively through our efforts at school reform alone. We embrace the assertion of James Comer (1996), that when we make this a problem of schooling alone, we are "waiting for a miracle." In this chapter, I advance a reconceptualization of education that is grounded in a little essay written by Lawrence Cremin in 1975, "Public Education and the Education of the Public," where he challenged the dualism of John Dewey's *Education and Democracy* (1916), in which Dewey advanced the notion that schools are privileged as the source of education to the neglect of life experience and other educative institutions.

Thinking Comprehensively and Relationally About Education

When I first started writing about supplementary education, my wife, Susan G. Gordon, MD, who was then president of a public school board of education, had serious reservations. She was concerned that I was pitting supplementary education, or out-of-school experiences, against the experiences of school. In doing so, she thought that we would be undercutting support for the idea of "the common school" and the society's responsibility for and commitment to support public education. Since then, my writing on the subject of supplementary and complementary education has included a concern for the complementarities between the learning and teaching that occur outside of school and the teaching and learning that occur in schools. These complementarities are what inform a comprehensive approach to education. Just as in-school experiences can be understood to enrich a person's out-of-school life, so too can out-of-school experiences be seen to enhance the effectiveness of in-school learning.

This conversation with Dr. Susan Gordon reminded me of Lawrence Cremin's friendly critique of his mentor, John Dewey, in which Cremin (1975/2007) argued that Dewey's conception of education had created an unnecessary dualism—schooling and the other educative institutions of the society. Cremin thought that the duality was inappropriate and that education is a single enterprise that should be thought of comprehensively, relationally, and publicly. Since I recently revisited Cremin's notion, I have begun to use the term *comprehensive education,* in order to make the construct more inclusive and to avoid the dualism to which Cremin was referring.

The term *comprehensive* as a qualifier for education requires that we think of education as inclusive of conditions necessary for effective teaching and learning, for opportunities to learn, and for engagement in the life processes by which learners encounter the experiences that are the grounds of the development of intellect. These conditions, opportunities, and processes are ubiquitous in life, but some institutions carry special responsibility for their delivery—family and school, for example. Effective comprehensive education is generally associated with the appropriate orchestration of these ubiquitous and redundant experiences.

Cremin's criticism of Dewey suggested that schooling and life should somehow be brought together rather than seen as two separate primary educative forces (Cremin, 1975/2007). I read this argument to mean that education must represent the complementarities between these two forces; therefore, education must be thought of comprehensively, relationally, and publicly. When we begin to think comprehensively about education, we must include concern for all the opportunities in life to learn and to teach, for the ways in which they complement each other, and for the proper orchestration of opportunities to learn, wherever they may occur. I will revisit this notion of orchestration further, and in greater detail, but I would like to emphasize that how educational opportunities are orchestrated is critical to their effectiveness in promoting intellectual and personal development in learners. The richness of these educational opportunities is very important as well, but when we think about education comprehensively, we must give particular attention to the ways in which they are knit together. Cremin (1975/2007) suggested that we think "relationally" about education, by which he meant that we must think about the ways in which different educative pieces fit together in the lives of individuals.

In general, high degrees of congruency between the values promulgated at school, at home, and in a student's immediate community are associated with high academic achievement. What may be equally critical are students' perceptions that what happens at school matters and is consistent with what parents and other family members consider important (Wilkerson, 1979). This is conveyed through expectations, physical provisions for academic pursuits, attitudes toward intellectual activity, and the models that are available for children to emulate. Participation in comprehensive education activities contributes to the development of a sense of membership in high-performance learning communities and shared values for the importance of academic achievement for personal fulfillment, community development, and social and political upward mobility (E. W. Gordon, 1999).

The values that are privileged by parents and the experiences that parents and communities provide are so critical to intellectual development and academic achievement, that an approach to comprehensive education necessitates that we place particular emphasis on teaching parents and other interested adults how to be advocates for their children's academic and personal development. I argue that it takes a well-developed adult to support the optimal development of a child. I have incorporated three related efforts in my research on comprehensive education and in the program of work that has grown out of it: (a) strengthening the capacity of families and parents to support the academic and personal development of children, (b) educating and supporting parents and other interested adults as advocates for the academic and personal development of students, and (c) better enabling parents to function as competent adults who are capable of directing and supporting the optimal development of children. In the first of these activities, the emphasis is on better enabling parents to function effectively as persons, as parents, and as supporters of academic and personal development. The second activity is more sharply focused on assisting, demonstrating, and enabling parents to interact with school people and programs and to advocate for the best interest of children. In the third set of activities, we are seeking to better enable parents to function as competent adults do—at home, at work, and in their communities. We are convinced that the absence of such competence is one of the problems faced by teenage parents. We have also observed adults trying to function as parents when their own development has been so arrested that they are incapable of providing for themselves or their children. In cases such as these, the support for the academic and personal development of children is weak. The optimal development of children requires that well-developed adults mediate and orchestrate the developmental experiences of children. Effective guidance and orchestration of learning experiences—good parenting—are obviously important components of good education; however, we recognize that a comprehensive approach to effective education entails considerably more and rests on a rich knowledge base. Several of those factors are discussed below.

Activity, Mediated Experience, Reflexivity, and the Achievement of Intellective Competence

Human behavior involves three processes referable to what people do (a) with the intention of adapting, (b) as mediated by thinking about the components of the situation in which the action occurs, and (c) what people achieve and think about the consequences of the achievement. My thinking has been influenced by activity theory (Leontyev, 1981; Vygotsky, 1978), which addresses the dynamics of action—acting, acting on, being acted upon, and being enacted. Activity theory holds that activity is a requirement of living things, that if there is no activity there is no tension in the system, and in the absence of tension, living things die. This view is not unrelated to the notion I advanced in some of my more recent work that learning might be understood as the process of human adaptation. Varenne (2007) made a similar point in his conceptualization of the nature of education, human activity in efforts at transforming one's self and one's condition. Activity could be considered to be synonymous with adaptation; as it is impossible to have an activity that is not in some ways adaptive, the two may be considered to be related within the context of learning.

Consciousness and more complex behaviors are functions of the interactions that take place during activity in human organisms. The human being's use of mind is dependent upon the prior use of senses, hands, and feet, as tools with which to do things. Michael Cole and Sylvia Scribner demonstrated in their book *Culture and Thought* (1974) that different forms of functional cognitive systems typically develop in in-school learners versus those that develop in people who learn primarily in out-of-school settings, but it seems that the common feature in learning that occurs in both settings is developed abilities as a function of the pursuit of adaptive activity. The differences between nonschool and school learning outcomes seem to be related more to the nature of the activity engaged in than to where it occurs. Following this reasoning, Dewey's (1916) assertion of a duality in education—between life and schooling—is spurious. Education is a unitary process that is manifested in different settings, sometimes for different purposes, but always involving human activity and resulting in the development of more complex adaptive behaviors, different domains and levels of consciousness, and different situationally related intentionalities.

Cole's and Scribner's (1974) notion of "functional cognitive systems" as products of human activity can be traced to Vygotsky's most famous student, A. R. Luria (1966). Following this line of reasoning, academic learning can be seen as being especially effective in the programming of the human organism for the verbal expression and symbolic reflection of one's functional cognitive–affective system. Less abstract life experience and real-time activity appear to be especially enabling of the operational nonsymbolic representational functional system. Acculturation and socialization may bridge both, but it is hard to eliminate the possible effects of schooling, since the more typical indicators of acculturation and socialization in technologically advanced societies have been documented in situations where schooling is the privileged experience (i.e., most people go to school). It is to the adaptive and functional capacities of the various functional cognitive systems that I refer in the use of the construct "intellective competence." Such competence is a reflection of the ability of the person to use these cognitive systems to access information, to create ideas and techniques, to address problems, to recognize and/ or imagine relationships, and ultimately to adjudicate relationships.

I define intellective competence as the developed abilities and dispositions to perceive critically, to explore widely, to bring rational order to chaos, to bring knowledge and technique to bear on the solution of problems, to test ideas against explicit and considered moral values and against empirical data, and to recognize and create real and abstract relationships between concrete and imaginary phenomena. In other words, intellective competence essentially reflects the effective orchestration of affective, cognitive, and situative mental processes in the service of sense making and problem solving. These achievements are less focused on what we want learners to know and know how to do, and are more sharply focused on what it is that we want learners to become and be (i.e., compassionate and thinking interdependent members of humane human communities).

I use *intellective* to distinguish my concerns—the variety of cognitive, affective, situative, and emotional processes that are integral to daily functioning and problem solving—from both *intelligent* and *intellectual* behavior. I am concerned that the term *intelligent* is too closely associated with *intelligence,* which is too often thought of as that which is measured by IQ tests. Intellectual behavior seems too easily confused with the work or habits of intellectuals and professional scholars. How then can one begin to frame the construct intellective competence? I have come to use the term to refer to a characteristic way of adapting to, appreciating, and knowing and understanding the phenomena of human experience. I also use the construct to reference the quality with which these mental processes come to be applied to one's engagement with quotidian, novel, and specialized problems. Intellective competence reflects one's habits of mind, but it also reflects the quality or goodness of the products of mental functioning.

Training, Teaching, Learning, and the Cultivation of Intellect

One of the theoretical frames that supports the idea of comprehensiveness in education is J. M. Hunt's (1961) notion of intelligence as a function of the richness of the learner's experiences. Some of those experiences are directly related to academic learning, others are enabling of it. Still others create a climate, a context out of which one's investment of effort in the pursuit of academic learning grows. Something like disposition or attitude toward learning and, ultimately, effort are products of the affective and cognitive processes that occur in the context of all human experiences. Learning, and its product, intellective competence, then is a product of experience—actual, virtual, and vicarious. What Hunt was arguing is that if we can design learning experiences that are appropriate to the learning characteristics and the learning needs of the persons we are trying to teach, the achievement of developed abilities increases. Anne Anastasi (1966) argued that "developed ability" may be what we really reference when we use the term *intelligence.* To the extent that the variety and quality of those experiences are limited, learning achievement declines. Hunt (1961) believed that if we can design appropriate matches between the characteristics of learners and the necessary learner experiences, levels of intellective development could be increased significantly. Alexander Thomas and Stella Chess make a similar point with respect to all human capabilities. In their book *Temperament and Development* (1977), they asserted that goodness of fit results when the properties of the environment and its expectations and demands are in accord with the organism's own capacities, characteristics, and style of behaving. When consonance between organism and environment is present, optimal development in a progressive direction is possible. Conversely, poorness of fit involves discrepancies and dissonances between environmental opportunities and demands and the capacities of the organism, so that distorted development and maladaptive functioning occur.

Goodness of fit is never an abstraction but is always goodness of fit in terms of the values and demands of a given culture or socioeconomic group (Thomas & Chess, 1977).

The third conceptual frame supporting this notion is found in the work of Michael Martinez. In his book *Education as the Cultivation of Intelligence* (2000), he argues that education is about the cultivation of intelligence in those who experience the process. From this perspective I think that, typically in the experience of schooling, too much attention may be given to the mastery of the specific content of the academic experience and insufficient attention to the cultivation of mental ability—the capacity to solve problems and the capacity to adaptively use the information learned. Robert Glaser (personal communication, 1980–1990) correctly reminds us that along the way to learning how to solve problems and how to use one's intellect efficiently we must also master chunks of knowledge that are part of the content of the academic experience. We interpret this to mean that if one views the academic experience being solely concerned with the mastery of academic content and not as the cultivation of intellective competence, one is missing the point. For interesting perspectives on the relationship between the study of academic content, the processes of learning, and the development of intelligence, the reader is directed to Michael Cole's and Sylvia Scribner's *Culture and Thought* (1974) and the posthumous treatment of the ideas of Richard Snow in the edited volume *Remaking the Concept of Aptitude: Extending the Legacy of Richard E. Snow* (Cronbach, 2002). From both of these works I have come to believe that the acquisition of knowledge and technique is one outcome of learning. Another outcome may be the disposition to inquire and to appreciate. Still another outcome is related to changes in the learning organism that predisposes the learner to continued inquiry and learning.

Along with Martinez's mentor, the late Professor Snow, I believe that the study of the content, processes, and techniques associated with the academic disciplines is instrumental to the development of mental ability. The development of intellect does not require academic studies, but intellective competence appears to be greatly facilitated by the acquisition of the knowledge and skills stressed in school or other systematic exposures to the academic disciplines or to the mental processes that are evoked by cognitive reflexivity.[1] The latter does not require schooling, but it does appear to be a by-product of considered experience—that is, reflexive living.

People differ greatly in their ways of learning and, to some extent, even in the capacity to learn or their capacity to learn in standard environments. The broader domain of teaching and learning that we call *comprehensive education* provides greater and redundant opportunities to learn, so that if one doesn't get it in one place, he or she will get it in another place. If the purpose of the learning experience is not served in one way, it may be served in another. The extent to which one gets the exposure, Martinez would argue, contributes to the development of intellectual capacities; the developed intellective competence of persons.

Varieties of Settings for Teaching, Learning, and Assessment

Society has developed a wide variety of educative institutions and resources from which opportunities for teaching and learning can be chosen. Some of these institutions have long histories and colloquial familiarity. Among these institutions and services are settlement houses and community centers. Established in the late 19th and early 20th centuries, settlement houses were institutions that offered social services to low-income, immigrant, and highly mobile families that lacked the resources or ability to provide the structure and supports that are associated with family life, such as health, recreation, child care, employment, personal development, and counseling. Some examples of these organizations are the British Association of Settlements and Social Action Centers (BASSAC) in the United Kingdom, the Hull House in Chicago, and the University Settlement House in New York. Other examples include the following:

> **Faith-based institutions:** Churches, synagogues and mosques emerged very early as institutions concerned with teaching and learning. Initially, they ran educational activities directed at the development of their leaders. Most of the efforts went into the religious training of followers. For a long time, faith-based institutions have sponsored K–16 education. In many communities, the colloquial perception that faith-based institutions provide social structure and moral education and promote excellence has made them the preferred choice. In addition to more formal settings for academic learning, faith-based institutions have become major sources for the incidental learning of attitudes, habits, mores, and values that are associated with beliefs propagated by these institutions.
>
> **Youth development services:** There is a wide array of organizations that offers different kinds of learning experiences for the development of young people. The following are some examples:
>
> **Prevocational education:** Prevocational education includes a variety of organized experiences designed to introduce and orient learners in a knowledge base required to live and work in a given profession. Children are introduced to vocational education early in their lives. Some examples of childhood vocational education experiences are 4H, Future Farmers of America, and Future Teachers of America.
>
> **Scouting (the Scout Movement):** Scouting is a worldwide youth movement with the stated aim of supporting young people in their physical, mental, and spiritual development so that they may play constructive roles in society.
>
> **Big Brothers Big Sisters:** This national mentoring organization's mission is to help and support children ages 6 through 18 years living in underserved communities across the country reach their potential through professionally supported one-to-one relationships with mentors. It has demonstrated a measurable impact on the youth it serves.

Apprenticeships: Apprenticeships are supervised learning experiences that involve engagement in the activities of a craft, skill, or profession, usually under the supervision of an expert who acculturates the learning person in the tacit knowledge associated with the area of expertise.

Coaching, mentoring, and tutoring: Mentoring and tutoring are more widely recognized as academic resources than is coaching, but all three place their emphasis on individualization, customization, and personalization. In mentoring, the relationship between the teaching person and the learning person is sometimes thought of as primary, and the content of the experience tends to focus on socialization and psychological development. The nature, structure, and intention of the tutoring relationship vary depending on whether tutoring takes place in a commercial or volunteer-based context and setting, and whether the goal of the tutoring is remedial, developmental, or enrichment. We associate the coaching function with the learning and honing of a particular skill or set of skills, while the tutoring function is often dominated by a purpose of academic content and academic skill development. However, the product of each of the three functions is the development in the learner of competences comparable to those of the teacher and achievement in the novice that often surpasses the achievement of the expert.

Many of the characteristics of successful coaching may contribute to more effective instructional strategies to promote academic learning, especially for young people who are academically successful but at risk of academic failure. If we revisit activity theory (Leontyev, 1981), we find a useful framework for understanding this phenomenon. The central focus in the study of coaching strategies is the trustful relationships (Bryk & Schneider, 2002) that coaches create and nurture in order to inspire their athletes to high performance. This trustful relationship seems to be the basis of successful learning. The coach–athlete relationship includes several other aspects, which are also applicable to academic learning, such as motivation and inspiration; the role of challenge and competition; clear understanding of excellent performance; intrinsic rewards for diverse modes of demonstrating mastery; collaboration, team work, and a place to belong (Nasir, 2008; also see Chapter 10 of this volume); self-regulation and integration of body and mind and spirit through mindful practice; and close alignment of training (instruction) with task, specificity, perseverance, and time on task.

In U.S. society, tutoring is often thought of as an intervention to be introduced only after a learner runs into a problem or if a school is thought to be inadequate, but in many societies around the world—including India, Korea, and France—tutoring is a part of an existing approach to supporting education through out-of-school learning. Although these approaches may not reflect the entirety of a whole comprehensive education theory and practice, they do offer some insights, and draw attention to the fact that what I am proposing as a program of comprehensive education has some existence and precedent in other parts of the world.

In some cases, the effect of these types of arrangements has begun to draw research attention. Hsi-Chi Hsiao, Ming-Chao Lee, and Su-Ling Yang (2010) published a study to investigate whether or not attending out-of-school care centers affects the learning attitudes of elementary school pupils. They note that Taiwanese parents are increasingly enrolling their children in afterschool care centers, which take care of pupils, instruct in homework, offer different talent classes, and help with schoolwork. With in-depth interviews of fifth- and sixth-grade teachers, they examined the impact of out-of-school learning, which differs from formal, in-school learning in terms of teaching style, environment, and approaches, on student attitudes towards class learning, interaction with peers, teacher–pupil relationships, and parent–child relationships.

To some extent, these practices may be found in certain immigrant and racial or ethnic minority communities and may offer some explanation of relatively high levels of academic achievement in the students from these communities compared with their classmates in under-resourced and low-quality schools here in the United States (see Chapters 4 and 5 of this volume). This is not to draw generalizations about academic achievement as a derivation of belonging to certain racial or ethnic groups. All racial and ethnic groups, including groups with high levels of academic achievement, are heterogeneous. It may be that some of the groups that contribute the greatest numbers of high-achieving, highly intelligent people are not only heterogeneous but they also do not typically favor intellectualism or orient themselves toward intellectual achievement. Individuals in the middle class who privilege intellect and study may not be typical of their communities—this privileging may in fact be a motile characteristic. One clear observation, based on existing research, is that high achievement is pursued in different ways in different communities.

In the *East Ramapo High School Achievement Study* (E. W. Gordon, Everson, & Meroe, 1993), Everson, Meroe, and I set out to explain the marked differences in academic achievement between Caribbean-born and American-born students of African descent. Although the students attended an underresourced school, the students of Afro-Caribbean descent achieved at much higher levels, on average, than their African American classmates. Similarly, schools in low-income, underserved neighborhoods in Brooklyn with predominantly Caribbean student bodies had achievement patterns similar to schools in much better served neighborhoods. Although it cannot be said that high academic achievement is typical of all Caribbean people, the approach to and strategies for supporting high achievement seem to yield greater success in Afro-Caribbean communities than in African American communities of comparable socioeconomic status.

Following is a list of several specific programs and projects that capture or reflect these different types of interventions and strategies, which were identified by the Study Group:

> **The Posse Model for Admission to and Success in College:** This is a unique program of selection and support for admission to and completion of college

for culturally diverse and low-income students who might otherwise be less likely to be admitted to highly selective colleges.

The Black Star Project Parent and Student Development: This program provides educational services that help preschool through college-age low-income Black and Latino students in Chicago succeed academically and become knowledgeable and productive citizens with the support of their parents, families, schools, and communities.

Boarding families and boarding schools: These are an alternative for families who want to offer their children the out-of-home life experiences that they consider appropriate for their development.

The Fifth Dimension: This is an educational activity system that offers school-aged children a specially designed environment in which to explore a variety of off-the-shelf computer games and gamelike educational activities during the afterschool hours.

The Folk School Movement: This is an organization of schools lead by laypersons and communities with a primary focus on life skills and academic studies.

We are deliberately excluding from this inventory formal school settings where teaching and learning are given priority. However, there is emerging a set of institutions that are called *schools,* which incorporate into their missions a broader range of experiences than those that are typically available in schools. Two specific illustrations follow, along with an overview of the community schools movement:

The Harlem Children's Zone: This project has a unique, holistic approach to building and rebuilding the Harlem community in order to improve its ability to help its children stay on track through college and to successfully enter the job market.

The Eagle Academy for Young Men: This public school was founded in 2004 and is designed to optimize the academic and social success of Black and Latino young men.

Community Schools: A Community School is a school that combines best educational practices with in-house youth development, health, and social services to ensure that children are physically, emotionally, and socially prepared to learn.

Places of Learning—Places of Joy: In most of these settings for learning, the opportunity to privilege the "for fun" aspects of the activity is greater than in more formal academic learning situations where, typically, greater emphasis is placed on accountability or mastery of a particular skill or content.

Essential Features of a Comprehensive Approach to Education

There is a wide range of activities and experiences that we associate with a comprehensive approach to education. This includes maintaining health through food and nutrition; conversation; reading (encouraging children to read as well as reading with and to children); the provision of enriching experiences through travel, sightseeing, and museum and library visits; and the kinds of interactions and experiences that take place in churches and community-based organizations. In short, thinking comprehensively about education leads us to consider the educative value of everything that people do in life, or, to consider education as life itself. Some of the programs listed previously are likely to be merely ritual in nature, but some carry particular educational weight. Which aspects of living, among the wide range of activities and experiences that characterize a child's life, seem to be critical to intellectual development and high achievement?

Internalization and Personalization

Recent theoretical and empirical literature indicates that effective learning occurs in personalized learning environments that emphasize high academic standards, rigorous and relevant curriculum and teaching, and continued professional development for administrative and teaching staff. But what exactly is personalized learning, and how do we create it, particularly when this conceptualization includes various definitions that depend on the learning context, condition, and population? For example, this construct can refer to students' engagement in and attachment to a learning environment, usually the school, and their effort in mastering the concepts taught. It also refers to a reflexive and deliberate structuring of the learning environment so that progressively rigorous exposure to curriculum results in student mastery of concepts and ultimately academic excellence. The implication is that learning environments that are sensitive to their students' cognitive styles, temperaments, sources of motivation, identities, and cultures are more likely to have students who are engaged in and have positive relationships to school.

Personalization thus includes (a) the individualization of teaching and learning transactions, (b) the casting of academic learning in the context of the relationship between teacher and learner, (c) the internalization of the content and product of the learning, and (d) the learner's ownership of the material learned and the process by which it is learned. In the conceptualization represented in *a* and *b,* personalization is a pedagogical technique that is used on the student's behalf by the instructor. However, in the conceptualization implicit in *c* and *d,* personalization is an achievement of the learner, or something that the learner does for herself or himself. The literature on the subject is much richer in reference to this construction as a pedagogical technique than as a pedagogical product or learner achievement. Personalization as a customizing pedagogical technique was described half a century ago by George Kelly (1955), who denominated it personal construction theory (PCT).

The key message of PCT is that the world is "perceived" by a person in terms of whatever "meaning" that person applies to it, and the person has the freedom to choose a different meaning of whatever he or she wants. In other words, as suggested by George Kelly, the original proponent of the theory, the person has the freedom to choose the meaning that he or she prefers or likes. He called this *alternative constructivism.* In simple words, the person is capable of applying alternative constructions (meanings) to any events in the past, present, or future. One is not a prisoner of one's "biography or past" and could liberate oneself from the misery of "miserable" events if one desires by reconstruing (reinterpreting and redefining) them. The theory rejects the existing schism between affect, cognition, and action and recommends that they be construed together for developing a fuller understanding of human behavior.

In the same period that concern with Kelly's PCT was prevalent, John Flanagan (1971) advanced notions concerning personalization and individualization through his project PLAN. It was Flanagan's idea that learning experiences should be matched to the characteristics of learners, and to achieve this, a dynamic "plan" should be created for each child. The plan was to be dynamic in that it should change with the changing needs of the learner and used as the framework for the teaching and learning experiences of the learner. Flanagan (1971) anticipated the advent of the electronic computer, which would be needed to manage the vast amount of information and instructional material that would be necessary to implement hundreds of plans in each school. Bolvin and Glaser (1968) encountered the same problem with his efforts at individually prescribed instruction (IPI). In IPI classrooms, teaching assistants helped teachers produce and manage the voluminous files of instructional materials from which the teacher could choose. Flanagan (1971), Bolvin and Glaser (1968), Kelly (1955), and others who sought to customize teaching and learning encounters in consideration of the specific characteristics and needs of the learner did not emphasize personalization, but the underlying assumption was that individualization made it easier for the learner to identify with and take ownership of experiences and materials that were so adapted. Thus, individualization was often used synonymously with personalization.

The use of personalization to refer to an achievement of the student has received more implicit attention in the literature and in practice. The learning process is individualized in part to gain greater learner identification with what is to be learned. The teacher–learner relationship is used as a vehicle for encouraging learner engagement with and internalization of the content and process. In general usage, the term *personalization* suggests an identification with and ownership of the object or stimulus that is being personalized. Personalization refers to the dynamic interaction between learner and elements of the learning situation, which results in a sense of ownership, empowerment, and gratification for the learner.

From my perspective, personalization is a trifocal phenomenon that references the extent to which

1. the teaching and learning process is adapted to or fits with the characteristics of the learner;
2. the processes by which teachers and students relate in transforming what is being learned into the learner's data; and
3. the learner's identification with and ownership of products of the learning transaction.

Thomas and Chess (1977), whom I referenced earlier in this chapter, as well as Bryk and Schneider (2002), also referenced earlier, and Bennett et al. (2004) emphasized the importance of trustworthy relationships and environments as the contexts for identifying with and taking ownership of learning processes and learning products. Gardner (2006), E. W. Gordon (1992), Greeno (2005), Kornhaber (1994), and Sizer (1973) emphasized the internalization of the learning experience and the products of that experience as habits of mind and intellective character. Similar to the complex construct we call *culture,* our use of the construct personalization encompasses all of these notions referable to the processes and products of human learning. Like culture, personalization is both a determinant and consequence of particular learning behaviors.

Education-Relevant Forms of Capital That Enable Education

Those who are familiar with the sociological literature will recognize Pierre Bourdieu (1986) in association with the idea that education is enabled by the learner's access to certain forms of capital, which have powerful impacts on human development and achievement. Most famously, he described social, economic, and cultural capital. Coleman et al. (1966), Miller (1995), and E. W. Gordon and Meroe (1989) have built upon these ideas to develop a list of what I call *education-relevant forms of capital*:

- *Cultural capital:* The collected knowledge, techniques and beliefs of people
- *Financial capital:* Income and wealth along with family, community, and societal economic resources available for human-resource development and education
- *Health capital:* Physical-developmental integrity, health and nutritional condition, and so forth
- *Human capital:* Social competence, tacit knowledge, and other education-derived abilities as personal or family assets
- *Institutional capital:* Access to political, educational, and socializing institutions
- *Pedagogical capital:* Supports for appropriate educational experiences in home, school, and community
- *Personal capital:* Dispositions, attitudes, aspirations, efficacy, and sense of power
- *Polity capital:* Societal membership, social concern, public commitment, and participation in the political economy
- *Social capital:* Social networks and relationships, social norms, cultural styles, and values

Miller and Gordon (1974) added to Bourdieu's list the technological and informational capitals, defined as the access to the capabilities and instrumentalities by which people communicate, by which people collect information, by which people process that information and exchange it in technologically advanced modern societies.

I cannot stress too much the importance of these resources to developmental outcomes, including linguistic competence, habits of mind, dispositions, acquired skills, information, and identity and purpose to which they are related. Health and nutrition are of crucial importance; children can function and survive in the presence of ill health and poor nutrition, but impairments in these domains take their toll on the efficiency with which humans function and on the quality of the human effort invested in learning. Poor health and nutrition impede attention, attendance, and energy deployment. Some conditions so compromise the integrity of the organism that they interfere with learning.

One of the most intriguing of these various forms of education-relevant capital is the conception of *polity capital,* which Miller (1995) introduced in *An American Imperative: Accelerating Minority Educational Advancement.* I later elaborated upon the term in my own work, using the term to refer to the sense of membership in and by the social order as reflected in social commitment, concern, and participation. In other words, if I do not feel that I belong in the group, I am not likely to take the group's standards and values seriously. If the group does not consider that I belong, it is not likely to take my needs or my development seriously. Banks and McQuarter (1976) make a telling point in research that suggests that when one sees inappropriate behavior in a person considered to be like-minded or related to the observer, the cause of the behavior is attributed to the context or environment. When the same behavior is observed in one who is considered "other than me" or "unlike me," the cause of the negative behavior is attributed to the nonbelonging person. This reciprocal sense of membership—polity capital—is an often-ignored but critically important resource for learning and survival. Unfortunately, all children do not have easy access to this important resource.

Building on Bourdieu's (1986) core notion that access to the many forms of education-relevant capital influences one's way of life, attitudes, behavior tendencies, and disposition to act in certain ways, I argue that educated people are more effectively and efficiently educated if they have access to these forms of capital. In essence, it is access to these forms of capital that enables schooling to work. Further still, we might even argue that it is not simply access to capital alone but rather active participation in an environment that has resulted from access to education-relevant forms of capital that enables education. To illustrate this, we might observe subsets of the population within which access to material expressions of capital have not proven sufficient to enable schooling to effectively and efficiently promote high levels of achievement, such as in the African American middle class. Here, I am recontextualizing data and observations I presented at the beginning of this chapter, demonstrating that African Americans and some Latino populations seem to perform at significantly lower levels than their White and Asian American counterparts, even in the middle and professional classes.

If a population's access to social capital is abbreviated, distorted, or compromised, it is possible that the derivations of such access also become compromised. This may explain underproductivity among the Black middle class, which has access to material capital but not to other forms of education-relevant capital. Edmund T. Gordon (2004), in his research on Black male identity, wrote that, since it may be more difficult for Black males to achieve respectability, many have a tendency to settle for reputation instead. Reputation, being a shortcut, deprives them of the instrumental features of respectability that are rewarded in modern, technologically advanced societies. My student Ezekiel J. Dixon-Román (2007) suggested that "intergenerational exposure" to certain ways of thinking about the world enables some populations to better engage with the social capital available to them than others. Dixon-Román draws from Bourdieu's (1977) conceptualization of habitus in order to theoretically situate his notion of the social inheritance of intergenerational inequality in educational achievement. Inheritance, he observed, "is a social process of the acquisition or (re)appropriation of symbolic systems" (Dixon-Román, 2010, p. 103). He goes on to observe that inheritance produces a "scheme of dispositions," which is transposable and can be restructured with new experiences and information. Such dispositions lead individuals and communities to interiorize social difference and exteriorize actions and practices, which in turn constitute and reproduce social structures; this, says Dixon-Román (2007), is what Bourdieu referred to as *habitus*.

Habitus can be predicated by degree of access to various forms of education-relevant capital, and it is the forms of capital that regulate or determine the kinds of pedagogical experiences that are meaningful and conferred by dominant institutions (Bourdieu, 1986; Dixon-Román, 2010; E. W. Gordon & Bridglall, 2005; Miller, 1995).

The comprehensive-education approach seeks to compensate for the fact that access to these forms of capital is unequally distributed. All people don't have access to these forms of capital, so the programs we propose within comprehensive education either make these forms of capital available to underserved or marginalized communities, or find alternatives for them. If these forms of capital are what effective education must depend upon, then one cannot think of an adequate education or an adequate system of education that does not address them.

Access, Guidance, and Orchestration

Access to opportunities to learn is an essential feature of comprehensive education. An approach to comprehensive education must first begin with access to opportunities and experiences that support, enable, and reinforce academic development. Academic development can be redefined as the development of intellective competence, which I define as developed abilities and dispositions to perceive critically, to explore widely, to bring rational order to chaos, to bring knowledge and technique to bear on the solution of problems, to test ideas against explicit and considered moral values and against empirical data, and to recognize and create real and abstract relationships between concrete and imaginary phenomena.

In my discussion of intellective competence in a chapter I contributed to an edited volume on affirmative development (E. W. Gordon, 2006) I noted that there are different routes to the development of intellective competence. One of the features of comprehensive education is guidance in how to progress on different paths. This guidance, undertaken by a more sophisticated adult to put different activities, experiences, materials, and networks together in a meaningful educative program, is what we refer to as *orchestration*. In essence, intellective competence essentially reflects the effective orchestration of affective, cognitive, and situative mental processes in the service of sense making and problem solving. These achievements are less focused on what we want learners to know and know how to do, and are more sharply focused on what it is that we want learners to become and be (i.e., compassionate and thinking interdependent members of humane human communities). We therefore assert that, not only must the learner have access to learning opportunities, but these opportunities must also have breadth, variety, and richness. Most important, the learner must also have access to guidance in how to use the materials and concepts he or she encounters and engages with in these learning activities and experiences.

The learning situation is guided by intentionality, in which one is either trying to teach or learn something. The design of that learning experience must reflect that learning behavior consists of the dynamic blending (Esposito, 1971) of a variety of experiences as well as the learner's interpretation of those experiences, and the educator must be aware of and able to blend these variables in a way that is appropriate to the anticipated outcome.

I liken the idea of orchestration to the role of the conductor in a symphony orchestra. As a good orchestra tunes up, as each artist attempts to tune his or her individual instrument, there is a great deal of confusion and dissonance. Then the conductor, who has orchestrated the event, brings these various pieces together in ways that serve the particular intent. This is what must take place in a program of comprehensive education.

One of the primary challenges for children from marginalized or disadvantaged populations is that the orchestration may be accidental, unsystematic, or lacking in clear intent. In the absence of parents or societies that may provide access to an array of varied and rich learning experiences, and orchestrate them in such a way as to allow the development of intellective competence, a program of comprehensive education must compensate for this absence.

Engagement, Effort, and Redundancy

In the late 1950s, John Carroll first introduced his notion that aptitude could well be a function of time spent on task, which was meaningfully related to the material to be learned (Carroll, 1993). Lauren Resnick (1999) later used this idea as the basis for the emphasis she placed on learner effort. Several years ago, I started writing about the importance of attention given to learner behaviors, among which I claim are (a) time spent on task, (b) deployment of effort, and (c) resource utilization. As I reflect on the emergence of these notions in my consciousness, I am aware of the centrality of learner effort and engagement, so much so that I currently argue that where there is modest engagement and low-level effort, learning is likely to be impaired, as opposed to the results of high levels of engagement, which I see as reflecting the three learner behaviors noted. Thus, comprehensive education includes not only the varieties of opportunities to learn and to have one's learning experiences supported but also engagement and effort by the learner.

We should be careful to make the distinction between *intentional* and *incidental* engagement, or active versus passive engagement. Certainly, there are exceptions to the idea that engagement and learner effort form a central component in any approach to comprehensive education. Learning often occurs even in the absence of motivation, effort, or engagement on the part of the learner. One can observe differential effects of different levels or kinds of engagement. When a learner is intentionally, or actively, engaged in learning, the goals of learning are likely to be more explicit. When the exposure or engagement is incidental, or less a part of the learner's consciousness, learning does occur, but its content and processes may not be as explicit for the learner.

Most complex systems that achieve effectiveness and stability are characterized by redundancy—that is, systems in which all critical mechanisms have back-up alternative components in case of failure in the primary system. We routinely see such redundancy in biological, electronic, and mechanical systems. It is possible that the educative systems of human societies also require redundancy—multilayered mechanisms by which the developmental tasks of human learning are engaged, supported, and mastered. At best these compensate or take over when one mechanism or another fails. Supplementary education just may be a part of that ubiquitously redundant system concerned with motivating, preparing, enabling, mediating, facilitating, consolidating, and ensuring that high levels of academic learning and personal development are achieved.

Challenge, Activity, and Support

A recurring problem in all education concerns the relationship between time on task, engagement, and persistence, or perseverance—in other words, the idea that formal learning requires a learner to be engaged in the learning experience for a long period of time and to persevere until the completion of the task. Earlier in this chapter I introduced John Carroll's (1993) research into time on task as well as the importance of engagement in the act of learning. In order for time to be spent on task, a learner must be engaged in the subject and the task at hand, and for learning to occur in formal settings, the learner must remain on task until it is completed. Comprehensive education may provide greater opportunities to be responsive to this problem, because the wide range of things we include in comprehensive education gives learners many more modalities and avenues from which to choose, by which special interests or special abilities of the learning person may be engaged.

One way to approach the issue of engagement is to envision it almost as a problem of match between what the learner is bringing to the task and what the learning task requires. Where those kinds of natural complementarities or congruence are not the case, we know that human beings tend to be attracted by the challenge of incongruence, especially when the lack of congruence is within what Vygotsky (1978) has called the zone of proximal development, or when the absence of fit, the thing that does not quite match, is just beyond the level or space of one's development. The programmed learning movement of the middle of the last century was based upon this notion. Students were presented with problems that were just beyond their reach in the context of material that they could handle. We take from this the possibility that the content of comprehensive education needs to be challenging to the learner, within the learner's reach, and accessible in a context that is supportive of the learner's engagement and mastery. To be challenging, it is our judgment that the experience must be perceived as standing in the path of something intended or desired and to be achieved by the learner.

I have discussed the circumstance wherein learners must know how to seek help (Sternberg, 1999), but the critical point I wish to emphasize is that a comprehensive approach to education must include multiple possibilities, several approaches to engaging learners. This idea leads me back to the importance of relationships, which I also discussed under my earlier discussion of engagement. When one is presented with a challenge that is perceived to be out of one's reach, but support is available, it is imperative to have relationships between the learning and teaching persons that enable or encourage the asking for support and the utilization of support. Education more broadly defined may ultimately require the legitimization of help seeking as a learning strategy, although the tradition in teaching and learning for academic purposes has focused on just the opposite. Students are penalized for turning to a neighbor for help or using a book as a resource. In less formal, comprehensive, and cooperative learning settings, help seeking, in which students are also encouraged to learn how to access and utilize the resources needed to accomplish the learning task, is a part of the experience, and students are rewarded for doing it. Lauren Resnick (1987) has observed that a number of the things we discourage in traditional schooling are actually rewarded in real life, such as problem solving in teams and being able to work cooperatively. What is called distributive knowledge in the workplace is often penalized in the classroom. Many educators in academic contexts are beginning to warm to the idea that this is an aid to learning and not to be penalized, but as long as formal education rewards individual learning, it is hard to know what is a product of group effort.

A program that meets all of these requirements—a challenging activity that offers a match between the learning person and the task at hand, that requires perseverance and time on task but in which the learning person is encouraged to utilize available forms of support, is Outward Bound, a nonprofit education program that provides active learning experiences for varyingly challenged target populations. Outward Bound expeditions engage learners in a set of challenging activities, and supports personal development both through cooperative learning in a group setting and at the guidance of a trained educator who acts as a resource person. The program offers an activity that is challenging, supported by a peer group, and guided by a resource person, meeting all the criteria for an effective comprehensive education program.

As E.W. Gordon and Bridglall (2007) discussed in *Affirmative Development: Cultivating Academic Ability,* early and progressive exposure to rigor is facilitative of learning, but this exposure must always be accompanied by access to supports that help the learner meet the challenge posed by rigorous activity. In a comprehensive education setting, learners must not only actively and intentionally engage with an activity and exert effort, but they must also know how to seek help and to utilize resources that are available to them in their effort to meet a challenge. Sternberg (1999) described one form of intelligence as the capacity to seek out, recognize, and use available resources.

Mediation and Scaffolding

Comprehensive education rests on "the scaffolding that caring members of our families and communities create around the mainstream of society that enables our children to move up" (Blackwell, 2006, p. 28). The essence of what we call supplementary, complementary, or comprehensive education is as much about the ethos of caring and concern, and the acts of enablement, nurturance, and protection, as it is about the institutions, resources, and services that should be available for families and communities. The à la carte, or supplemental, components of education include attitudes and expectations. Included are the demands, the routine provisions, the things that are done for fun, and even things that are forced under duress in the effort to ensure that optimal development and effective education are achieved.

In the contexts advanced by such scholars as Brice-Heath and Mclaughlin (1993), Rebell and Wolff (2008), Stenberg (1999), Weiss, Caspe, and Lopez (2006), Weiss, Dearing, Mayer, Kreider, and McCartney (2005), Varenne (2007), and myself (E. W. Gordon, Bridglall, & Meroe, 2005), emphasis is given to family–home, school and community, but comprehensive education is not coterminus with these institutions. It also occurs in peer and intergenerational relationships. It is ubiquitous to one's personal and public efforts at making sense of the world. It is a function of commercial enterprise, gang life, political participation, fun seeking, and making love. It happens in the solitary practice of shooting baskets on the basketball court. One of my students cautions that we are ignoring the learning involved in epistemic games, social computing, and the electronic exchange and transformation of information.

Trust and Trustworthiness

I have discussed the importance of rigor in a comprehensive education program, but here I must emphasize that comprehensive education seeks to enable the development of the learner as a whole person. Bloom (1976) wrote that rigor is important but argued that it must be accompanied by joy, by pleasure, by satisfying human encounters. The joy of such encounters is often provided by the relationship with the adult, resource person, or person providing instruction, just as a young child gets pleasure out of pleasing his or her parents, or the student finds pleasure in the supportive and reinforcing relationship with the teacher, or the team member puts in the extra effort because of the satisfying relationships with other team members whom he or she wants to please or certainly does not want to let down.

It was some years after Bloom that Bryk and Schneider (2002) described the relationship between trust and school achievement. Based on work in the Chicago public schools, he found a higher degree of the variance in school achievement to be associated with variance in the levels of trustworthiness perceived by students between themselves and other students, and between themselves and instructional staff. In fact, Bryk and Schneider also reported a positive impact of sense of trust between the instructors themselves. Thus, it is that in the learning situation in which the people who are doing the teaching trust each other and trust their students, and in which students trust each other and trust the people who are teaching, Bryk and Schneider argued, that achievement levels go up.

Personal Data and the Data of Others

When Tiedeman (1965) distinguished between other people's data and one's personal data as competing concerns of school learners, he was referring to the tension between our concentration on the mastery of the academic content of schooling and the pressing learning demands of peer relations, dating, pursuit of reputation, athletic and social competition, and the adjudication of the relationships in family as well as community politics. Schooling privileges teaching and learning related to the demands of academic knowledge and process mastery, but it competes with the learning and teaching related to learning to live and survive. Thinking comprehensively about education requires that we privilege both and the ways in which the two are conjoined and dialectically related. Following Cremin (1975/2007), logic requires that these processes be thought of as a whole and that they be thought of publicly (i.e., as in the public domain and as part of the public responsibility for education). If there is validity to the Tiedeman (1965) concern, academic learning may be advanced when we can map the demands of learning in academic settings as well as the content of academic learning to the compelling agendas of those who would learn. My anthropologist son claims that he was finally able to engage the demands of schooling after he was able to map on to his own agenda at least some of what he was doing and learning in school. Personal data and concerns may be easier to incorporate with the demands of learning in the more flexible and obviously relevant context of learning to play ball; to observe and create art; to play, read, and talk with grandma; or to observe artifacts in the museum. Attending to idiosyncratic interests or special needs or individual sources of motivation may likewise be simpler to address in such settings.

Medical Care and Public Health: A Delivery Model

The very best of instructional and managerial systems, combined with the excellence of teachers and their teaching, together with orderliness and safety, are necessary components of good education and should be demanded in our schools, but such ideal educational institutions may fall short of achieving excellence in academic achievement in ways similar to the failure of excellent hospitals and medical schools in this country to achieve excellence in health maintenance. These institutions have contributed to the improvement of health care and medical service in the United States, but it is actually the improvements in provision for public health and attention to public-health issues that are thought to account for the nation's major strides forward in health maintenance. Modern systems of garbage and sewage removal; the elimination of stagnant swamps and other mosquito breeders; the availability of potable water and nonpolluted air; improvements in personal hygiene; changes in diet to favor health-producing nutrients and the exclusion of health-demeaning foods along with the recognition of the importance of exercise are all now recognized as major contributors to health maintenance. One of my students (Bridglall & Gordon, 2004) has suggested that education borrow from the field of public health a concern for a focus on changes in health-maintenance attitudes, behaviors, and dispositions, and parallel attention to controlling the anti-intellectual, distracting to academic learning, and nonsupportive life conditions of students. Improvements in the quality of teachers and schools are imperative but may not be sufficient to offset the deleterious effects of the nonsupportive lives of many of our children. A public health approach to education may be indicated.

The Human Capital Requirements of Education, So Broadly Conceived

When we begin to think of human learning as being, in large part, the result of human activity and the mediation of its meanings in other people, or as the product of human engagement with things and symbols of things, we return to the concept of activity theory, which I discussed earlier in this chapter. Here, I build on this concept using the work of J. M. Hunt (1961), as reflected in his book *Intelligence and Experience*. I think of experience as being (a) actual, in which I have engagement with or in an experience in reality; (b) virtual, in which I hear or read about an experience; and (c) vicarious, in which I have some simulation of the experience, often mediated by someone else. If we think of learning as being constituted of these three experiential domains, it is important to recall that a learner is surrounded by other humans who provide or guide either an actual or vicarious experience. It is no accident that intelligent behavior is believed more likely to be found in persons who have been exposed to other intelligent people. People are more likely to develop abilities if they are exposed to other people who are proficient in those abilities. Humans tend to mimic and benefit from the experiences of others. It can be said that humans and other animals tend toward docility, in that we are inclined to mimic and learn from the behaviors of others.

Some time ago, an undergraduate student of mine, who was of Korean descent, wrote her senior essay, which included an observation that, among Korean families in the New York area, Korean men tended to marry "up," choosing to marry women who were more intelligent than they, and that these women were frequently kept at home after marriage. Her assessment was that these women were not kept at home out of patriarchal imperative but rather because there was a community belief that intelligent people should raise children, in other words, that the intelligence of children may be raised by the intelligence of their caretakers—female or male.

Following this line of reasoning, in a population of academically underdeveloped people, where the adults have not had successful academic experiences, it is unrealistic to expect them to provide the examples and experiences necessary to advance the academic development of their children. It follows that higher levels of academic achievement are to be found in well-resourced families, in part because many of the experiences children have in school were also experienced by their parents, and the experiences of the subsequent generations—whether implicitly or explicitly shared—are influenced by the forms of human and social capitals that were the source of comparable experiences that their parents encountered.

It is therefore ludicrous to simply say that academically underdeveloped or otherwise underresourced and undercapitalized (to return to our list of education-relevant capital) populations need to support their children better. These populations need assistance in how to provide appropriate and effective supports. In conversation with single mothers who were recipients of welfare (E. W. Gordon & Wilkerson, 1966), I soon realized that they almost universally had high aspirations for their children's education and careers but simply lacked the know-how to translate those aspirations into effective practices and supports for high levels of achievement.

In the Comprehensive Education and Parents' Resource Center, my colleagues and I are developing a model for delivering comprehensive education resources and support skills to low-income, low-status, marginalized, or academically underdeveloped populations, we place a heavy emphasis on parent education. Some of our programs focus on how to provide and support academic development in children, but some focus on life-skills development for parents. Some of these parents started having children early in their own lives, before they had completed their own processes of personal and academic development. Although some of these parents may have had the opportunity to develop life skills as a result of fortuitous encounters and experiences, many more have not had the access or opportunities for access to such experiences. One of the interventions that must be included in any effective program of comprehensive education is the development of life skills and other academically related abilities in the adults of the population in which the program is being introduced.

There is an association between parents' position in the labor force and the level of academic achievement in their children (Conley & Yeung, 2005). Children whose parents have higher levels of decision authority in their work tend to do better in school. This finding suggests that the correlation might result from the fact that people who have more decision authority tend to be better educated than others lower in the employment hierarchy. But there is still another possibility to consider. If a large part of learning is incidental to one's exposure to people who themselves have well-developed ability, it may be that these decision-making, active adults are in fact demonstrating to children how to be decisive and actively engaged in life—or how to be intentional rather than incidental in engagement with learning experiences—and this exposure becomes a part of the children's vicarious experiences. Populations whose labor force is lower in the employment hierarchy, and who are relatively lacking in opportunities to make decisions at work, may need interventions that demonstrate to parents in that population how to make active decisions that will affect the decision-making process toward and within the learning experiences their children employ. This suggestion arises from the concept of human agency, which I define as disposition and capacity to act on one's own interest; the ability to make decisions that act in one's favor. Agency is typically acquired by acting and observing other people acting with agency. To transfer a sense of agency to subsequent generations of a population that is low in agency, it may be necessary to develop interventions that impart a sense of agency to the adults in that population.

In my work with a group of parents in the Harlem neighborhood of New York City, whose children were enrolled in a program for gifted students, I encountered several parents who complained about what they felt were unreasonable demands on their children (E. W. Gordon, 1982); one of the mothers expressed concern that her child was given 1 hour's worth of homework each night. The parents of the children in that program did not understand that not only was that requirement fairly minimal, but it was also nowhere near enough to stimulate high levels of academic development. Another group of parents I observed in Nyack, just north of New York City, felt that they had done their part to support their children's education by paying high taxes, sending them to good schools, and keeping them properly fed and clothed. But informed parents will say it is not enough to get your children to school, but that you, as parents and family members, must supplement what happens in school.

It is this domain to which I am referring when I discuss the human capital requirements of a program of comprehensive education—that effort must be made to give access and develop the human capital of parents. Adults and people who provide access to and advocate for a learner's education must themselves be equipped with adequate amounts of education-relevant capital. This is not to suggest that academically underdeveloped people cannot be supportive of education. In his autobiography *Gifted Hands: The Ben Carson Story,* neurosurgeon Ben Carson (1996) described his early education under the guidance and supervision of his grandmother, who cared for him while his mother worked. She helped him with his homework by encouraging him, reviewing his work, and sitting with him while he worked out problems, and she was actively engaged in his schoolwork; he did not realize until he had reached junior high school that she was illiterate. As inspiring as this story is, I cannot help but think about how much more help and support she could have provided Carson if she had been literate or academically advanced herself. Perhaps a learner who was less intelligent than Carson, who required more orchestration or mediation of his learning experience, would have been significantly handicapped by the fact that the adult overseeing his learning experience was herself academically underdeveloped.

Access to schooling is widely protected, even required in the United States, as a matter of public policy, yet access to academic coaching, remediation, and tutorial services remains ubiquitous in more affluent families and underutilized in under-resourced families. There is good reason to believe that the access that children from affluent families have to such services and other forms of complementary–supplementary education is the "hidden curriculum" associated with serious differences in the patterns of academic achievement seen in high-status and low-status children. I fully embrace Robert Moses's claim that access to education of high quality is a civil right, and I argue that access to coaching, remediation, and tutoring should be included in that basic right that citizens have to education.

In some more affluent and culturally attuned communities, formal opportunities for complementary–supplementary education are plentiful. In less affluent and some ethnic-minority communities, such opportunities are scarce. As a matter of policy, government will need to create and support community-based centers for professional development, information resources, and technical assistance for families, faith-based institutions, and community agencies concerning comprehensive education.

The program of the Comprehensive Education Resource Center is informed by a public-health approach to education through which we seek to think comprehensively and relationally about education—comprehensively and relationally in the sense that all of the education-relevant forms of necessary capital are considered in their dialectical interactions, each with the other. As in modern approaches to public health, the Resource Center will promote the orchestrated availability and utilization of these various forms of education-relevant resources in the lives of children and their families. We propose to create an education center that will guide communities and families in the development of an approach to education that is both comprehensive and relational, and is supplemental to excellent public schools.

To better enable and ensure that less affluent communities and their families are able to create Resource Centers and complementary–supplementary services, I have proposed that a federal Comprehensive Education Development Bank be created and charged with providing the investment capital and seed money for the creation and initial support of comprehensive–complementary–supplementary education agencies and services in communities where they do not exist, and where the resource base makes it less likely that they will emerge. Long-term loans should be available at reduced interest rates. Preference should be given to the cooperative and not-for-profit sectors, but for-profit enterprises should not be excluded.

Note

1. Cole and Scribner (1974) have investigated the differential manifestations of intellect that are associated with exposure to school and other settings for learning.

References

Anastasi, A. (1966). *Testing problems in perspective.* Washington, DC: American Council of Education.

Banks, W. C., & McQuarter, G. V. (1976). Achievement motivation and black children. *IRCD Bulletin, 11*(4), 1–8.

Bennett, A., Bridglall, B. L., Cauce, A. M., Everson, H. T., Gordon, E. W., Lee, C. D., ... Stewart, J. K. (2004). All students reaching the top: Strategies for closing academic achievement gaps. *Report of the National Study Group for the Affirmative Development of Academic Ability.* Naperville, IL: Learning Point Associates, Central Regional Educational Laboratory.

Blackwell, A. G. (2006). Ensuring broad access to affordable neighborhoods that connect to opportunity. In T. Smiley (Ed.), *The covenant with black America* (pp. 97–101). Chicago, IL: Third World Press.

Bloom, B. S. (1976). *Human characteristics and social learning.* New York, NY: McGraw Hill.

Bolvin, J., & Glaser, R. (1968). *Developmental aspects of individually prescribed instruction.* Pittsburgh University, PA Learning Research and Development Center. Sponsor Agency: Office of Education (DHEW). Washington, DC: Bureau of Research.

Bourdieu, P. (1977). Cultural reproduction and social reproduction. In J. Karabel & A. H. Halsey (Eds.), *Power and ideology in education.* New York, NY: Oxford University Press.

Bourdieu, P. (1986). *The form of capital.* In J. G. Richardson (Ed.), *Handbook of theory and research for sociology of education* (pp. 241–258). New York, NY: Greenwood Press.

Brice-Heath, S. B., & Mclaughlin, M. W. (Eds.). (1993). *Identity and inner city youth: Beyond ethnicity and gender.* New York, NY: Teachers College Press.

Bridglall, B. L., & Gordon, E. W. (2004). The nurturance of African American scientific talent. *Journal of African American History, 89*(4), 331–347.

Bryk, A. S., & Schneider, B. (2002). *Trust in schools: A core resource for improvement.* New York, NY: Russell Sage Foundation.

Carroll, J. B. (1993). *Human cognitive abilities.* Cambridge, UK: Cambridge University Press.

Carson, B. (1996). *Gifted hands: The Ben Carson story* Grand Rapids, MI: Zondervan.

Cole, M., & Scribner, S. (1974). *Culture and thought.* New York, NY: John Wiley & Sons.

Coleman, J., Campbell, E., Hobson, C., McPartland, J., Mood, A., Weinfeld, F. D., & York, R. L. (1966). *Equality of educational opportunity.* Washington, DC: Department of Health, Education and Welfare.

College Board. (1999). *Reaching the top: A report of the National Task Force on Minority High Achievement.* New York, NY: The College Entrance Examination Board.

Comer, J. P. (1997). *Waiting for a miracle: Why schools can't solve our problems—And how we can.* New York, NY: Dutton.

Conley, D., & W.-J. J. Yeung. 2005. Black-White differences in occupational prestige: Their impact on child development. *American Behavioral Scientist, 48*(9): 1229–1249.

Cremin, L. (2007). Public education and the education of the public. *Teachers College Record, 109*(7), 1545–1558. (Original work published 1975)

Cronbach, L. (Ed.). (2002). *Remaking the concept of aptitude: Extending the legacy of Richard E. Snow.* Mahwah, NJ: Erlbaum.

Dewey, J. (1916). *Democracy and education.* New York, NY: Macmillan.

Dixon-Román, E. (2007). *The mystery of inequity: Modeling the influence of intergenerational access on intellective competence.* Doctoral dissertation, Department of Psychology, Fordham University, New York.

Dixon-Román, E. (2010). Inheritance and an economy of difference: The importance of supplementary education. In L. Lin, E. W. Gordon & H. Varenne (Eds.), *Educating comprehensively: Varieties of educational experiences: Vol. 3. Perspectives on comprehensive education series* (pp. 95–112). Lewiston: The Edwin Mellen Press.

Esposito, D. (1971). Homogeneous and heterogeneous groupings: Principal findings and implications for more effective educational environments. *Review of Educational Research, 43*(2), 163–179.

Flanagan, J. C. (1971). The plan system for individualizing education. *NCME Measurement in Education, 2, 2.*

Gardner, H. (2006). *The development and education of the mind: The selected works of Howard Gardner.* New York, NY: Routledge.

Gordon, E. T. (2004). Academic politicization: Supplementary education from black resistance. In E. W. Gordon, B. L. Bridglall, & A. S. Meroe (Eds.), *Supplementary education: The hidden curriculum of high academic achievement* (pp. 88–103). Lanham, MD: Rowman & Littlefield.

Gordon, E. W. (1982). Culture and ethnicity: Implications for development and intervention. In M. D. Levine, W. B. Carey, & A. C. Crocker (Eds.), *Developmental-behavioral pediatrics.* Philadelphia, PA: Saunders.

Gordon, E. W. (1992). *Implications of diversity in human characteristics for authentic assessment.* Los Angeles: University of California, National Center for Research on Evaluation, Standards, and Student Testing (CRESST).

Gordon, E. W. (1999). *Education and justice: A view from the back of the bus.* New York, NY: Teachers College Press.

Gordon, E. W. (2006). The affirmative development of academic ability: In pursuit of social justice. In A. Ball (Ed.), *National Society for the Study of Education Yearbook 2006.* Ames, IA: Blackwell.

Gordon, E. W., & Bridglall, B. L. (2005). The challenge, context, and preconditions of academic development at high levels. In E. W. Gordon, B. L. Bridglall, and A. S. Meroe

(Eds.), *Supplementary education: The hidden curriculum of high academic achievement.* Lanham, MD: Rowman & Littlefield Publishers.

Gordon, E. W., & Bridglall, B. L. (2007). *Affirmative development: Cultivating academic ability.* Boulder, CO: Rowman & Littlefield.

Gordon, E. W., Bridglall, B. L., & Meroe, A. S. (Eds.). (2005). *Supplementary education: The hidden curriculum of high academic achievement.* Lanham, MD: Rowman & Littlefield.

Gordon, E. W., Everson, H., & Meroe, S. A. (1993). *East Ramapo high school achievement study.* New York, NY: The College Board.

Gordon, E. W., & Meroe, A. S. (1989). Common destinies—Continuing dilemmas. *Psychological Science, 2*(1), 23–29.

Gordon, E. W., & Wilkerson, D. (1966). *Compensatory education for the disadvantaged: Programs and practices, preschool through college.* New York, NY: College Entrance Examination Board.

Greeno, J. G. (2005). Toward the development of intellective character. In E. W. Gordon & B. L. Bridglall (Eds.), *Affirmative development: Cultivating academic ability* (pp. 17–47). Lanham, MD: Rowman & Littlefield.

Hsiao, H.-C., Lee, M.-C., & Yang, S.-L. (2010). The learning attitudes of pupils attending out of school care centers. *International Journal of Learning, 16*(11), 157–168.

Hunt, J. M. (1961). *Intelligence and experience.* New York, NY: Ronald.

Kelly, G. (1955). *The psychology of personal constructs.* New York, NY: Norton.

Kornhaber, M. (1997). *Seeking strengths: Equitable identification for gifted education and the theory of multiple intelligences.* (Doctoral dissertation). Cambridge, MA: Harvard Graduate School of Education. Solicited by ERIC for reproduction at Level 1 (paper, microfiche, and electronically), February 1999.

Leontyev, A. N. (1981). *Problems of the development of the mind.* Moscow, Russia: Progress.

Luria, A. R. (1966). *Higher cortical functions in man.* New York, NY: Basic Books.

Martinez, M. E. (2000). *Education as the cultivation of intelligence.* Mahwah, NJ: Erlbaum.

Miller, L. S. (1995). *An American imperative: Accelerating minority educational advancement.* New Haven, CT: Yale University Press.

Miller, L. S., & Gordon, E. W. (1974). *Equality of educational opportunity: Handbook of research.* New York, NY: AMS Press.

Nasir, N. S. (2008). Everyday pedagogy: Lessons from basketball, track, and dominoes. *Phi Delta Kappan, 89*(7): 529–532.

Rebell, M., & Wolff, J. (2008). *Moving every child ahead.* New York, NY: Teachers College Press.

Resnick, L. B. (1987). Learning in and out of school. *Educational Researcher, 16*(9), 13–20.

Resnick, L. B. (1999). From aptitude to effort: A new foundation for our schools. *American Educator, 23*(1), 14–17.

Sizer, T. (1973). *Places for learning, places for joy: Speculations on American school reform.* Cambridge, MA: Harvard University Press.

Sternberg, R. J. (1999). The theory of successful intelligence. *Review of General Psychology, 3*(4), 292–316.

Thomas, A., & Chess, S. (1977). *Temperament and development.* New York, NY: Brunner/Mazel.

Tiedeman, D. V. (1965). A symposium on existentialism in counseling: Prologue. *Personnel and Guidance Journal, 43,* 551–552.

Varenne, H. (2007). Difficult collective deliberations: Anthropological notes towards a theory of education. *Teachers College Record, 109*(7), 1559–1587.

Vygotsky, L. S. (1978). *Mind in society: The development of higher psychological processes.* Cambridge, MA: Harvard University Press.

Weiss, H., Caspe, M., & Lopez, M. E. (2006). *Family involvement makes a difference: Family involvement in early childhood education.* Cambridge, MA: Harvard Family Research Project.

Weiss, H., Dearing, E., Mayer, E., Kreider, H., & McCartney, K. (2005). Family educational involvement: Who can afford it and what does it afford? In C. Cooper, C. García Coll, W. Bartko, H. Davis, & C. Chatman (Eds.), *Developmental pathways through middle childhood: Rethinking context and diversity as resources* (pp. 17–40). Mahwah, NJ: Erlbaum.

Wilkerson, D. (Ed.). (1979). *Educating all our children: An imperative for democracy.* Westport, CT: Mediax.

Wolf, M. M. (1966). The measurement of environments. In A. Anastasi (Ed.), *Testing problems in perspective* (pp. 491–503). Washington, DC: American Council on Education.

Social Systems and the Produced Spaces of Comprehensively Conceived Education

3

PRODUCTS OF THE REVOLUTION

The Social System of Comprehensively Conceived Education in Cuba

Ezekiel J. Dixon-Román

> Finally, a revolutionary government would undertake the integral reform
> of the educational system, bringing it into line with the projects just men-
> tioned with the idea of educating those generations which will have the
> privilege of living in a happier land.
>
> Fidel Castro, *La Historia Me Absolverá*

This quote is from Fidel Castro's famous speech, *La Historia Me Absolverá* (History Will Absolve Me). He gave this speech as he legally defended himself during the trial of what became known as the 26th of July Movement in 1953, the beginning of the Revolution of 1959. Much of the 70-page speech described the ongoing social and economic injustices and U.S. exploitation of Cuba prior to the revolution as well as what Castro imagined as a revolutionary society. This revolutionary society was an ideal Cuba where health, education, and social equality were central. Almost 60 years later, Cuba is consistently evaluated by the global community as to whether history has absolved Fidel Castro.

In 1998, the Latin American Laboratory for Assessment of Quality in Education (LLECE) of the United Nations Educational, Scientific and Cultural Organization (UNESCO) published the first comparative study of language, mathematics, and associated factors of primary school in 13 Latin American countries. Results of this report overwhelmingly suggest that Cuban students meaningfully outperform all other Latin American nations in academic achievement (LLECE, 1998). In fact, Martin Carnoy (2008) estimated that, on average, Cuban students would meaningfully outperform students of the United States if they were participants in one of the international assessment programs.[1] These results suggest that the education system of U.S. embargoed Cuba has done much to accomplish their revolutionary goals in education.

Given the results of the LLECE study, Carnoy, Gove, and Marshall (2007) conducted a focused examination of education in Cuba, attempting to identify the meaningful characteristics of schooling that contribute to their high levels of academic achievement. Although both studies provide meaningful data on the factors of schooling that contribute to the academic advantage of Cuban education, neither looks at the overwhelming historical and current existence of supplementary and comprehensive education in Cuba. How is education conceived of in Cuba? What is the social system of supplementary and comprehensive education in Cuba? How has this social system evolved out of the Revolution of 1959? What are some of its limitations? Is it plausible that the high levels of achievement by Cuban youth are enabled by the social system beyond schooling?

In this chapter, I explore and provide an initial description of the social system of supplementary and comprehensive education in Cuba. That is, I describe the structure and the social system and the various organizations and institutions that contribute to comprehensive education while situating them within their historical trajectory of the revolution. These organizations and institutions include, but are not limited to, the campaign for literacy, day-care centers, culture centers, family doctors, and social workers. Without the exploration of these questions we will continue to have a narrow conception and understanding of education in Cuba. Moreover, our understanding of the meaningful contribution of supplementary and comprehensive education on high levels of equitable learning and development will continue to be misinformed.

The social revolution of 1959 enabled the possibility for the needed equitable distribution of the various resources that theoretically underpin supplementary education, that is, social, cultural, health, economic, and polity capital. Each of these forms of capital is important in order to enable the development of human potential. Cuba has made serious efforts to equalize each of these necessary forms of resources, but not without complications and limitations. Many of these efforts were outcomes of the revolution and compensations of revolutionary state crisis (Calder, 1988; Skocpol, 1979/2007).

The study discussed in this chapter is part of an ongoing program of research on youth culture and comprehensive education in Cuba. As such, much of the data discussed in this chapter are based on continued ethnographic research, interviews, and the analysis of existing academic and policy literature from both the United States and Cuba. This work has included visits and observations of an urban day-care center and rural primary- and secondary-education schools, as well as art museums and a community project in Havana for primary school youth, Casa del Niño y La Niña. I also met with members of the Cuban Teacher Union, where much was discussed about the Cuban education system, the campaign for literacy, social workers, and the Federation of Cuban Women. I also visited and participated in several Culture Centers and the community Committee for the Defense of the Revolution, as well as interviewed staff at most locations.

In addition, the information learned from my observations and interviews was corroborated and added to with various existing academic sources.

I begin this chapter by briefly discussing the background of education and supplementary education in Cuba and the sparse research literature on Cuban education. I then critically discuss the structure of the social system of supplementary and comprehensive education in Cuba, including a description of the various organizations and institutions that contribute to comprehensive education. Following the presentation of the Cuban social system of comprehensive education, I discuss some of the major drawbacks and limitations. I now turn to a discussion on the background and research on Cuban education.

Background and Research on Cuban Education

Following the 26th of July movement from 1953 to 1959, a Communist government replaced the previous Fulgencio Batista Regime. The economic exploitation that occurred during the Batista regime made Cuba the bastion of the Caribbean for gambling, prostitution, and drugs. As a consequence, this also resulted in extreme social and economic inequality, high levels of poverty, and over 23% of the population being illiterate. This new Communist government came with four main commitments: to equalize income; provide mass, high-quality education; provide universal, high-quality health care; and enable universal adult literacy.

In education, in particular, Cuba immediately dissolved all private schools into the greater educational system and made serious efforts to equalize education in urban and rural areas and among urban neighborhoods. These efforts moved alongside other policies, programs, and structural changes, such as "schools to the countryside," "school in the countryside," the creation of elite secondary schools, curricular reforms, placing secondary school dropouts in the military, and reducing class size to 20 students in primary schools and 15 in lower secondary schools (Carnoy et al., 2007). Due to the equalization of income, teaching also became a high-status profession until the *special period*. The special period was the largest economic crisis of the revolution and was a product of the fall of the Soviet Union in 1988. Prior to the fall, Cuba had enjoyed very strong political and economic relations with the Soviet Union. The fall of the Soviet Union weakened relations and brought about much famine and increased levels of poverty and malnutrition in Cuba. In order to survive these dire times, Cuba turned to tourism in 1993 in order to survive. This ultimately had profound effects on education and the structure of the labor market (discussed further in the Critical Reflections section).

In addition to the school-related endeavors, education was also an endeavor outside of schooling. In 1961, Cuban rural illiteracy was 42%. In that year, Fidel Castro implemented an intense adult literacy program. The Cuban school year ended early in 1961 in order to concentrate on the development of literacy in all areas of Cuba, including rural, countryside, and small, impoverished towns. School did not resume in the fall until the national literacy campaign was completed in

December. Through the Central Organization of Cuban Workers, 30,000 workers were mobilized to help the campaign without hurting production (LaBash, 2007). When visual impairment was identified as an issue, corrective lenses were provided in order to decrease any obstacles to literacy development. By December 1961, Cuba became the first country in the Western hemisphere to eradicate illiteracy and, in 2005, Cuba had an adult literacy rate of 99.8%, second in the world to Georgia, which was 100% (United Nations Development Programme, 2008). This was one of the first of many nation-state–funded programs of supplementary and comprehensive education.

It is, in part, because of these efforts that, despite the consumption per capita in Cuba being low, poverty, as it is understood in the United States, does not have the deleterious effects on learning and development in Cuba as it does in the United States. In fact, Carnoy et al. (2007) stated that "few Cubans are 'in poverty,' in the sense that they cannot get housing, food, health care, and education" (p. 28). Thus, many of the factors that are known to be associated with poverty in the United States that have negative effects on learning and development (e.g., quality health care, malnutrition, homelessness or high residential and school mobility, unequal quality of education and resources) are not issues or as deleterious in the development of human potential in Cuba.

It is, in part, these socially equitable reasons that enable the emphasis on mass high-quality education to be effective in Cuba. As the UNESCO Latin American Laboratory for Assessment of Quality Education found, Cuban student performance was far superior to all other Latin American nations in language and mathematics (LLECE, 1998). It was also found that Cuban students take less time to complete a grade than each of their Latin American counterparts, and that gender differences were nonmeaningful (LLECE, 2002). LLECE (2002) found that parent participation with children in reading and in school had meaningful effects. Moreover, the study found that school-related factors accounted for nearly two-thirds of the variation in student achievement across all Latin American countries, but only around 15% of the variation was accounted for within schools. Carnoy et al. (2007) also found meaningful effects of teacher–school characteristics (e.g., students having a language textbook, teacher education, principal autonomy) and social context (e.g., preschool attendance, classroom fights, school socioeconomic factors, students working outside the home, students working in the home). Each of these associated factors attribute to the high levels of achievement in Cuban schools.

Although both studies focus on and refer to the meaningful influence of schooling and its associated factors in the high levels of achievement in Cuba, neither speaks to the potentially meaningful processes of out-of-school learning, and both overlook the indicative evidence in their own studies. Both studies found family characteristics such as parents reading with children, parents helping with homework, and/or the number of books in a household to have meaningful effects on achievement. The Carnoy et al. (2007) study found that the number of students who work outside the home is larger than the number of students who work inside the home, and both groups are meaningfully larger than students who do not work. This suggests the importance of work-related, out-of-school-type experiences. While Leiner (1974) and Kozol (1978) do consider day care, the community, and the family, they do not analyze this as a social system or with a more comprehensive conception of education. Moreover, both Leiner and Kozol's works predate many of the programs and policies that came in the 1980s, particularly with the special period. It is due to these limitations and un-mined indicative findings as well as Cuba's existing history of education beyond schooling that I focus on the social system of supplementary and comprehensive education in Cuba.

The Social System of Supplementary and Comprehensive Education in Cuba

The social system of supplementary and comprehensive education in Cuba is a manifestation of the state's conceptualization of education. Given the Cuban Revolution's commitment to and politicization of education, many policies, programs, and institutions evolved beyond schooling in order to meet the educational and cultural needs of the people and the revolution. These evolved policies, programs, and institutions are products of the revolution.

I will distinguish these products between outcomes and compensations of the revolution. I will define *outcomes* of the revolution as policies, programs, institutions, and structural changes that unfold as part of the commitment of the revolution, such as the equalization of income or the turning of private and Catholic schools into public schools. In contrast, *compensations* refer to "material benefits, usually distributive in character, extended to support groups exerting strategic political efforts on behalf of the grantor" (Calder, 1988, p. 159). These material benefits usually develop as a result of various crises of the revolution although not as direct commitments of the revolution. For example, the U.S. trade embargo on Cuba created a growing shortage of key textbooks, especially for the university level. Thus, the state sent professors from the Department of Philosophy at the University of Havana abroad to purchase single copies of key textbooks in order to reprint them illegally in Cuba, an endeavor Cuba referred to as *piracy* (Kapcia, 2008). These texts were reprinted under the auspices of the *Ediciones Revolucionarias* (Revolutionary Publications) and disseminated for free to university students. Reprints of great world literature were also cheaply sold to the increasingly literate population. This is an example of state compensation in a moment of crisis, as a result of the revolution.

Of course, outcomes and compensations of the revolution are not mutually exclusive; both are co-constitutive products, directly or indirectly, of the revolution. That is to say, compensations need and are constituted not only by crisis but also by the necessity of outcomes as commitments of the revolution that enable the very context and possibility for crisis; whereas outcomes need and are constituted by not only the commitments of the revolution but also by the need for compensations to the inevitable crises of the revolution. In part, state compensations have maintained the endurance of the revolution despite the economic crises of the fall of the Soviet Union in 1988 and the onset of the special period.

Thus, I will discuss the products of the revolution as outcomes or compensations, given the historical evolvement out of the revolution. I will note how they enable the possibilities of education comprehensively and their limitations. These products include the Campaign for Literacy, Federation of Cuban Women (FMC), Committee for the Defense of the Revolution (CDR), day-care centers, adult education, culture centers, the national library system, community computer centers, community centers, family doctors/polyclinics, and social workers. Given that the evolvement and practice of these programs and institutions is a manifestation of the dominant educational philosophy in Cuba, I will begin with a discussion of the Cuban conceptualization of education as set forth by the Cuban Ministry of Education (Ministerio de Educación, 1995).

Conceptualization of Education in Cuba

The conceptualization of education in Cuba places great importance on the family, schools, and the community in the comprehensive education of the child. That is, the Cuban Ministry of Education understands that the learning and development of the human organism occurs in multiple, interacting contexts.

The family is posited to be the first and basic form of education. This is why the ministry places importance on teachers knowing and studying the family. In fact, teachers visit the homes of each of their students on a monthly basis to discuss the child's academic performance and behavior, to observe the home environment, to identify additional needs, and to become acquainted with the parents and home front. Teachers also work regularly with social workers and the family doctors in order to address the social and educational needs of the family. Cuba sees the family as constructing the basic cell of the society, biologically and socially. It functions as a microsystem within the ecology of the society for the child. Families are the bearers of ideology, norms, and customs that they characterize. They are the primary field where the first social rules of conduct and behavior are interiorized.

The Ministry sees the family as the first social group that the child encounters at birth. These first social contacts coincide with a period of the lifespan when the child is the most permeable and adaptable. Through the communicative process, the family transmits the accumulated experiences, habits, norms, customs, and modes of behaving. This communicative process of the family is what the Ministry of Education refers to as *familial communication*. Familial communication is the multiple interactions between parents and children of multidirectional form. Given the spongelike capacity of the child, they are able to assimilate—and, much later, reflect—everything their family, of voluntary or involuntary form, offers.

Likened to Pierre Bourdieu's (1972/1977) *habitus,* the familial communication becomes valuable and essential, not only through knowledge, habits, and attitudes, which the family transmits and educates, but because of agreement with their structure and style of life, the family creates a psychological climate that influences the stability and mental health of the child. This becomes complemented with the pedagogic actions the school develops.

Figure 3.1 depicts the Ministry of Education's purported structure of the home–school–community ties of education. You will see in Figure 3.1 that the school is not alone. Each student occupies his or her place within a system of influences: besides the teachers' relationship with them, the students occupy parent–child relationships, the relationships with other family members, with other children, and with other social groups. The Ministry of Education posits that the

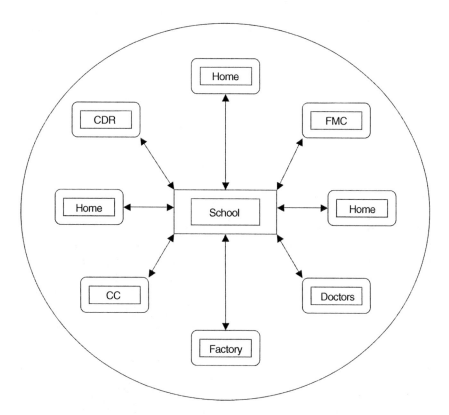

Figure 3.1 Diagram of the Cuban Ministry of Education's conceptualization of education.

Note: CDR = Committee for the Defense of the Revolution, FMC = Federation of Cuban Women, CC = Casas de Cultura (Culture Centers). Adapted from *La Escuela, la Familia y la Educación Para la Salud: Para la Vida* (p. 13), by Ministry of Education, 1995, Havana, Cuba: Editorial Pueblo Y Educación.

school and the family must complement each other if each one attempts to achieve effectiveness at guiding the education for the welfare of children and youth. The school, through its guiding role within the Communist education system, occupies the central place in the formation of the personality of the next generation during the 11 or 12 years of school life. The family, through being the basic cell of the society, permanently affects the education of the children.

Similar to Dewey (1916/1966), while the family plays a major role, schools are still central to the education of the child, particularly for inculcating the values and morals of Communism. Moreover, the Cuban conceptualization of education also posits the process of education within place rather than as ubiquitous to the social process of being human. In addition, the inculcation of the values and morals of the revolution, alongside the high levels of social censorship (even in the classroom) also raises concerns for the limited and narrow pedagogical experience. (The concern for social control and censorship is discussed further later in this chapter.) Although Cuba's dominant conceptualization of education continues to center schooling as the educative institution, it continues to place much value and importance on education outside of the school. It is to these supplementary educational institutions and programs that I now turn.

Cuban Supplementary Educational Institutions and Programs

Campaign for Literacy

The Campaign for Literacy was the first major supplementary education program of the revolution. Because of the high illiteracy rate in Cuba prior to the revolution (over 23%), especially in the rural areas (over 41%), and the need for literate people in order to raise revolutionary consciousness, literacy was one of the major commitments of the revolution. This outcome of the revolution began in January 1961 and did not end until December 22, 1961. Inspired by Jose Martí, who stated that Cubans had to open schools for teachers and then send them out, schools were closed in order for the nation to concentrate its efforts on eliminating illiteracy. By December 22, 1961, Cuba was declared the most literate country in the Americas (96.1%), which was confirmed by a 1964 United Nations investigation.

The campaign enlisted people young and old to participate as teachers. If they could read, they could teach; if they couldn't read, they learned. The organized brigade of literacy teachers included a popular literacy program in the cities and a brigade of volunteer students who wore uniforms and were known as the *literacy brigade,* who stopped studying and went to the countryside to teach. They were joined in August 1961 by salaried workers, when it appeared that the goal was a substantial challenge. In total, 271,000 people were mobilized—including 35,000 professionals, 136,000 volunteers, and 100,000 young *brigadistas* between the ages of 12 and 14 years and some of whom were younger (Kapcia, 2008).

Literacy teachers were provided 2 weeks of preparatory training, a manual they called *Alfabeticemos* (We Teach Literacy), a notebook called *Venceremos* (We Will Conquer), and a lantern, which became the symbol of the campaign. Where vision was an obstacle to literacy, people were provided with corrective lenses. The curriculum used national and international events, employing composite analysis in progressive and repetitive format. The expectation was to read and write and give the alphabet in Spanish, a first-grade level of literacy.

Additional literacy campaigns unfolded following the 1961 Campaign for Literacy. The second campaign was the Battle for the Sixth Grade, in 1962, in which 96% of the general population achieved competency in sixth-grade literacy. The third campaign was the Battle for the Ninth Grade, in which 67% of the general population achieved ninth-grade literacy by 1985. The Battle for the Ninth Grade campaign emphasized the importance of higher education so that people who were now literate knew the importance of higher education. For these campaigns, classrooms were open and used on weekends and week nights. All campaigns were found to be very successful.

Although Cuba no longer has a domestic literacy campaign because of their already existing majority literate population (99.8%), they have created a method (called "Yes, I Can") to teach how to read and write for people in Latin America, Africa, and New Zealand. This program prepares a specialist in Cuba over 6 months. These specialists generally have an MA or PhD in the languages. Inspired by Paulo Freire, the program also makes use of audio-visual mediums. With the "Yes, I Can" method, Cuba has collaborated with 26 different countries. For example, the "Yes, I Can" method was used in Bolivia and Venezuela and was able to eliminate illiteracy in just 1 year.

The extraordinary literacy rate in Cuba has diminished the amount of obstacles in the home front for parents to support their child's education. In fact, the piracy practices of the revolution were, in part, to respond to the growing hunger the people had for books and information. The importance and emphasis on literacy often manifests itself in lively discussions and debates in spaces such as the streets, regarding the writings and philosophical thought of thinkers such as Karl Marx, Jean Paul Sartre, and Malcolm X, or in the lyrics of musical forms such as hip-hop. The high rate of literacy marks not only the revolution's commitment to education but also the revolutionary consciousness. The selection of and access to of text is constrained to those in the spirit of this revolutionary consciousness; a consciousness that reflects a Marxist-Leninist ideology. This constraining includes the surveillance of the Internet (which few have access to) and books brought into the country. These latter issues and more will be discussed in the Critical Reflections section.

Federation of Cuban Women (FMC)

In 1959, Fidel Castro asked Vilma Espín (later, the wife of Raul Castro) to organize and become the head of the women's federation in order to address the needs for gender equality. On August 23, 1960, the Federation of Cuban Women (FMC) was founded. While pushing for gender equality in the labor market and in the homes with the government-instituted Family Code of 1975 (Kapcia, 2008), the FMC also realized the need for other social and educational programs for women. Thus, *círculoi infantiles* (day-care centers) were created by the FMC in order to enable women's participation in the labor market (Azicri, 1989; Kapcia, 2008). In order to support the *círculo infantiles,* the FMC established and advanced programs such as the Women's Improvement Plan, the Schools for Directors of *círculo infantiles,* the Ana Betancourt School for Peasant Girls, and the Schools for *círculo infantiles* workers (Azicri, 1989). Each of these programs helped to enable greater gender equality in homes and in the labor market.

In order to meet the professional and educational needs of the women, the FMC created several programs. *Círculo familiar de lectura* (family reading circles) were designed to work on the literacy development for women who remained illiterate after the 1961 campaign for literacy (Azicri, 1989). In addition, the FMC offered courses in health care and personal hygiene, crash courses on agricultural techniques, clerical skills, handicrafts, cooking, and physical education in order to prepare women for the labor force (Azicri, 1989). Women now make up more than 64% of the labor force and, although not equal to men in proportion or decision-making power, women occupy 43% of the positions in the National Assembly (Kapcia, 2008).

Despite the tremendous efforts of the FMC, gender discrimination and social and political hierarchies still exist. These gendered dynamics can be heard in social discourse and in the assumptions that are made about the male and female roles in society as well as observed in practice on the streets and in public. The machismo ideology of masculine domination continues to manifest itself in a high prevalence of domestic violence, something that I have witnessed on more than one occasion in public spaces. Although these social issues continue to exist, the FMC, an outcome of the revolution, has still been able to enable and create many programs, policies, and resources for the affirmative development of both women and children beyond schooling.

Círculo Infantil: Day-Care Centers

Day-care centers, or *círculo infantil,* were established by the Federation of Cuban Women to serve the early-child-care needs of working mothers with children from 1 to 5 years of age. In the first year of the child's life the government provides the mother with 1 year of maternity leave. This outcome of the revolution enabled greater gender equality in labor participation as well as meeting the socioemotional and academic developmental needs of the child. In addition, the day-care centers also serve as one of the first institutions socializing the values, morals, and history of the revolution.

Day-care centers are in every part of Cuba and open from 6 a.m. to 6 p.m., Monday through Saturday year round (closed only on holidays), providing breakfast, lunch, and two snacks. The facilities have kitchens that serve traditional Cuban food such as *morros y cristianos* (black beans and white rice), eggs, and *boniatos* (a kind of sweet potato) for the children. The cost is generally free, but depending on how much the family makes they may pay a minor fee.

The curriculum consists of teaching the children different values and heroes of Cuba, language skills, reading, mathematics, science, physical education, music, dance, and health/nutrition. Children learn about medicine and have different kinds of medical instruments, such as stethoscopes or IVs. The facility may be decorated with all kinds of educational and revolutionary images as well as a fabricated market where there might be an ice-cream cart, bread store, meat store, and so forth. There could also be a nonfunctional TV with a picture on the front and a nonfunctional computer, for children to begin to become acquainted with the computer. Despite the lack of resources, all the materials were made by the teachers with recycled material.

All of the teachers are professional teachers with teacher certificates and diplomas in different areas. They are all trained in the arts, physical and social sciences, and language skills that are important for preschool children, at the *Escuela de Educadoras* (Leiner, 1989). The teachers work one of two shifts, morning or afternoon. In addition, social workers and speech pathologists come to the day care to help students with mental health or language needs. Special-needs children go to different day cares with specialists. Children with special needs also include children of parents with alcoholism. Thus, the day-care centers provide the physical and cognitive nourishment for comprehensive education.

Committee for the Defense of the Revolution (CDR)

The Committee for the Defense of the Revolution (CDR) was established in September 1960 by the revolution, in order to identify dissidents of the revolution for the state's internal security apparatus (Dominguez, 1993). Located on every city block or village, CDRs now offer social programs in education and health and keep the vicinity clean and crime-free (Kapcia, 2008). While the CDRs today serve more of a role of providing social programs to the community and enabling the possibilities for comprehensive education, they also represent the symbolic gaze of the revolution, a gaze of revolutionary consciousness, and anything anti-revolutionary comes under the purview of state censorship and social control.

Adult Education

Adult education has been an intricate outcome and critically political component of the revolution beginning with the campaign for literacy. It nurtures and provides the opportunity to develop the highest level of human capital for the nation. Adults can go to the university to study as well as work. There is also a university for the elderly. This is to improve quality of life and for them to learn about different topics. The quality, accessibility, and wide use of adult education create a more equalized home context of parental competencies and skills in order to enable the possibility for more equitable comprehensive education of children.

Casas de Cultura (Culture Centers)

In the early 1960s, another revolution was brewing over the role of culture, within the current social revolution. This enabled the creation of a National Culture Council. The debate on culture led to three public meetings with leading intellectuals, artists, and government representatives. On June 30, 1961, as part of a speech at one of the public meetings, Fidel Castro laid out the first cultural policy of the revolution by stating (a) "within the Revolution, everything [would be allowed], against the Revolution, nothing"; and (b) that every Cuban had the right and ability to acquire cultural skills, to learn to dance, sing, act, paint, sculpt, or play an instrument (Kapcia, 2008). The censorship of the earlier statement (along with the popularization of the latter) instilled fear into many Cuban artists, which led to many of them choosing to leave. In terms of the latter, he called for the creation of *instructores de arte* (cultural teachers) to teach these skills to the Cuban population in the same manner as the literacy workers, going into schools, factories, and fields (Kapcia, 2008). Although it did not receive the same widespread valorization as the Campaign for Literacy, it later began the *movimiento de aficionados* (amateur movement). It was this movement that created *casas de cultura* (culture centers) in every municipality in order to enable Cubans to learn and practice art in various forms. Thus, *casas de cultura* became one of several compensations by the state that were developed as responses to the earlier debates about the role of culture in the revolution (or Cultural Revolution).

Casas de cultura teach all children and adults of the municipality art, dance, music, and theater. Children of all ages attend the culture center, which is open from 7 a.m. to 8 p.m. every day. For instance, they may participate in dance classes with professional dance instructors or voice lessons with a professional singer and instructor.

The culture center in Viñales had a restaurant and bar that served the community and provided different forms of entertainment such as dancing and live music at night. The culture centers also have art galleries and host conferences, such as the annual Hip Hop Symposium, organized by the Cuban Rap Agency, and concerts and shows for the community.

Although free and in every municipality, the casas de cultura are in prerevolution mansions and are not always in the greatest conditions. Resources for instruments and other equipment are not available and, as such, the students have to supply their own. This can often marginalize a student from learning an instrument because of the cost of the instrument being beyond their means. In spite of these limitations, the casas de cultura is one product of the Cultural Revolution that takes culture outside of the ivory tower to the people, developing the creative intellect in all Cubans. A plaque in the casas de cultura of the municipality of Viñales sums this up with the following quote: *"Donde lo Cubano se hace Arte"* ("Where the Cuban Makes Art").

Joven Club: Community Computer Centers

In the 1980s, with the fast development of computers, Fidel Castro developed community computer centers known as *joven club* (youth club). These computer centers offer youth and adults the opportunity to learn how to use computers, and learn new computer software. Many of the youth use the centers to play video games or work on homework assignments. Unfortunately, this outcome of the revolution does not have the tremendous impact that it could because of the youths' restricted access to the Internet and lack of new and innovative software due to the embargo.

Casa Comunitarias

One of the more recent and unique endeavors are the community centers, *casas comunitarias*. These were developed to respond to the many social and educational needs that evolved out of the special period. These centers were modeled after a community project in the community of Cayo Hueso in Havana, *La Casa del Niño y la Niña* (House of the Boy and Girl). Children of the community go to the center to learn acting, dancing, and the arts, and receive help with homework and school projects. They are open 7 days a week and serve all of the children in the community. These community centers are usually very small, have few resources, and are limited in the kind of social and educational services they are able to provide. The casas comunitarias are one product of the revolution that was inspired by a nongovernment-sponsored or nongovernment-initiated endeavor, but they provide for community needs.

Family Doctors/Polyclinics

Polyclinics are physician-dominated local medical facilities in Cuba. They house physicians that are responsible for all families within a defined neighborhood (Ubell, 1989). Thus, every community has its own family doctor. The family doctor is usually familiar with the patient's medical history and family, which means their patients' medical records are always at hand for immediate avail (Ubell, 1989). These facilities are open to the public from 9 a.m. until late in the afternoon. The family doctors also deal with the patients' social issues and work with teachers and social workers. Polyclinics are one of the most prominent features of the Cuban health-care system, which was developed as one of the commitments of the revolution to help enable the development of health capital.

Trabajadores Sociales (Social Workers)

Known as the "army of the healers of the soul," social workers develop relation-ships with the local families and neighborhood people and through these close relationships work to evaluate their needs. They work with schools, families, psychologists, and family doctors in serving the social, behavioral, and mental health needs of the person. They also pay special attention to children under 15 years, looking for nutritional problems and providing nutritional counseling and intervention as well as target interventions for other population subsets, such as schools for children who exhibit conduct–behavioral difficulties; people ages 16 to 29 years; people with disabilities, seniors, those in prison, and truant children. They also work specifically with schools to strengthen the family–school partner-ship. Approximately 74% of the youth have been visited by social workers.

Social work is a relatively young profession in Cuba. Fidel Castro instituted this profession as a way to maintain solidarity toward the revolution, especially for youth after the special period. Thus, much of their work is to socially manage and maintain the revolutionary ideology and spirit. Acts of deviance are constituted as anything not of the revolution and further labeled as counterrevolutionary. As a compensation of the revolution, Cuban social workers respond to the social, behavioral, and mental health needs of the people while also socially policing the boundaries of the revolution and constraining possibility.

These are a few of the many programs, institutions, and structures that have evolved out of the revolution that enable a more comprehensive approach to education in Cuba. Some other examples not discussed here are Cuba's national library system and public education television. The Cuban social system of com-prehensive education provides social and educational equity beyond schooling and appears to educate the whole person throughout the lifespan. Despite the constraints of over 40 years of a U.S. trade embargo, it appears that Cuba has been able to redistribute resources in order to enable equity in affirmative human development. The degree of inequality was reduced—as indicated by a Gini co-efficient that went from 0.55 to 0.22 from 1953 to 1986 (del Carmen Zabulla Argüelles, 1999)—to where every person has been provided some degree of eco-nomic capital. The Cuban health-care system—in particular, family doctors—provides the necessary health capital for everyone in the country. It appears that the regular monthly visits by teachers and the collaboration and communicative relationality with social workers, family doctors, psychologists, other specialists, and parents enables a large degree of social capital. In fact, Cuba has a profession known as *social communications,* where one of the main functions is to enable the communication and networks of the various institutions in communities. Further, the collectivism, communalism, and inclusivity of Cuban culture create strong social networks among the members of each community. The small degree of social and economic inequality, the high amount of social capital, and the exist-ence of culture centers makes the cultural capital of dominant institutions more accessible to all Cubans. More important, the state tries to ensure every citizen's access and membership within the political economy and greater polity. However, as does any system, the Cuban social system of comprehensive education has its limitations.

Critical Reflections on the Cuban Social System of Comprehensive Education

The previously discussed institutions and programs each provide the spatial and practical opportunities for the possibilities of equitable supplementary and comprehensive education. However, each are either sponsored by the state or under the panoptic purview of the hegemony of the revolutionary ideology. This is a hegemony that emphasizes social egalitarianism in and through the inculcation of Marxist–Leninist philosophy while also controlling and censoring anything against these philosophical ideals. Social and political expression becomes constrained to "for the Revolution, everything; against the Revolution, nothing" (Kapcia, 2008, p. 31).

These mechanisms and practices of social control and censorship constrain the social, political, and pedagogical possibilities. Much of the process of education is about not knowing, questioning, exploring, and learning about new or alternative information, phenomena, and processes. Under these hegemonic conditions of social control and censorship—which are both embodied in institutional policies and practices, and in the dispositions and everyday practices of the people—these new and alternative possibilities become constrained and stifle the development of the individual and society. Although Cubans, in general, and youth, in particular, find their moments and spaces of critical questioning and expression, one does wonder how much greater the intellectual development may be if these practices were enabled by the State.

While the revolution provides social egalitarianism and the possibilities in and through education, the Cuban society has also lost a substantial amount of capital in its moral economy, especially post–special period (Kapcia, 2008). Prior to the special period, the economy of Cuba was well resourced and healthy. Their economic and political relationship with the Soviet Union maintained a substantial amount of national income and resources, despite the U.S. embargo on Cuba. During these times, the top two professions were doctors and teachers. There were good reasons to go to college and to contribute to the revolution, because the revolution was providing for the people. However, when the Soviet Union fell in 1988, these forged relationships broke, and so did the national resources. The economy dropped and the government had to turn to tourism in order to save the country. Unfortunately, tourism gave workers in the tourist industry access to currency beyond what they were paid by the government. This began to shift the valued occupations in the labor market, and the country began to see many doctors and teachers leaving their respective professions to work in tourism.

Hotel staff and taxi drivers began to make more money than doctors or teachers, which began to put into question the necessity of higher education for many people.

The turn toward tourism also came with spatially segregated practices that have become known as *tourism apartheid* (Espino, 2000). Tourism apartheid refers to both legal and cultural practices, as well as the symbolic organization of space, in order to protect, privilege, and comfort the tourist of the island at the cost of and in contrast to Cuban nationals. In the early days of the turn toward tourism, these legal practices included Cubans not being able to have contact with tourists or being allowed to enter or use hotel facilities. While the former legal practice was ended in 1997 and the latter was ended in 2006, they both have structured cultural practices in which doormen of hotels and police will question and ask for identification from Cubans, particularly those racially constructed bodies that are constituted as deviant and potential thieves. This has also translated into the protection and restoration of social spaces of tourism at the cost of the continued deterioration of nontourist social spaces. This is most stark in Old Havana, where the spaces of tourism have been under major restoration efforts since 1982 and the nontourist spaces, particularly of residential living, have not received much attention at all. These stark differences within and between neighborhoods can also be seen in more well-resourced communities, such as Nuevo Vedado and Miramar, where many high-ranking government and military officials reside. The stores, institutions, and schools within these communities are also more aesthetic and well maintained. This kind of inequality in social space is recognized by the people and has had direct implications on the social structuring of the Cubans' lived experience.

In addition to the implications of the shifts toward tourism, other policies have existed since the beginning of the revolution that contributed to the lack of a moral economy. For instance, it has been almost impossible for any Cuban citizen to leave the country unless they are a particular kind of professional, government official, artist, or athlete. In addition, no matter what the profession, Cubans are paid the same amount their whole life. There are almost never raises in salaries, unless it is done nationally. Thus, there are very little economic incentives to become exceptional, and many of the Cuban youth I have interviewed have expressed this. One youth spoke about ceilings in Cuba (and the glass ceiling for women in the United States); that in Cuba, the ceilings are only so high: "You want to grow higher and expand horizons, but your growth is stunted by the low ceiling" (i.e., the government control, etc.).

These constrained possibilities have had direct implications on the Cuban social system of comprehensive education. One of the meaningful implications has been with respect to the stifled development of the national economy (despite the embargo) and the lack of national resources to fully support many of the previously discussed institutions and programs of supplementary education. Moreover, when questioning, creativity, and expression are constrained, it also limits the possibilities of human development and social change.

Despite these limitations Cubans, in general, and youth, in particular, do find their moments and spaces of critical social, cultural, and political expression. One example of this can be found in Cuban hip-hop (Baker, 2011). These Cuban-society-constituted moments, spaces, and spatial practices of deviance need to be studied further for their richness and complexity in pedagogical processes, what I have referred to in other work as *indigenous cultural capital* (Dixon-Román, 2009). What's more is that, in the face of the U.S. economic embargo and limited national resources, Cubans have continued to be relatively responsive to the comprehensive social, cultural, health, and educational needs of the people. They have maintained their commitment to providing a socially egalitarian society that enables equitable and affirmative human development in and through their social system of comprehensively conceived education.

Conclusions: Potential Insights for the United States

Foucault might have referred to each of these institutions and programs as heterotopic; that is, the "real places—places that do exist and that are formed in the very founding of society—which are something like counter-sites, a kind of effectively enacted utopia in which the real sites, all the other real sites that can be found within the culture, are simultaneously represented, contested, and inverted" (1967/1986, p. 24). Each of these programs and institutions are products of the Cuban revolutionary society and simultaneously represent the hegemonic ideology of the revolution while also enabling the possibilities of contesting and inverting that same hegemonic structure. Thus, I suggest that these institutions and programs enable the heterotopic moments of equitable comprehensive education. It is not the place that enables heterotopia, but the socially produced space. As such, these spaces are very much a product of spatial practices and are situated in time. There is nothing fixed or essential about them. Analogous socially produced spaces could exist in the United States.

Despite the differences of nationalized schooling and a socialist economy, the Cuban social system has several institutions, programs, and practices that can be very insightful to the United States. A variation of the culture centers could be considered in the United States, especially with the peeling away of arts education in U.S. public schools. The closest the United States has come to the day-care centers is Head Start, though it is not nearly as universalized or close in quality of service. It would also benefit from government-supported 1-year maternity leaves. Universalized health care would, at minimum, make health care more accessible and substantially improve the nation's health capital. The regular monthly teacher visits to each home would be beneficial for teachers, in order for them to learn more about the whole student, not just the person in the classroom. While there are school social workers in the United States, social workers, in general, do not work with as many youth or in as many ways in the United States as they do in Cuba. The emphasis, encouragement, and availability of adult education are tremendous in Cuba. It is clear that Cuba does not see education as stopping after secondary schooling. These commitments to continued education will only help build the nation's human capital. Last, illiteracy in one of the wealthiest nations in the world is an embarrassment. If Cuba can eliminate almost 20% of illiteracy in less than a year, then the United States should be able to do the same and be willing to make such a commitment.

Conversely, we don't know in what ways and how much Cubans, in particular, youth, fully engage and participate in many of these programs and institutions. How effective are these programs and institutions in providing meaningful educative experiences? How do these programs/institutions vary from the countryside versus urban areas? What do youth think about many of these programs/institutions? How do they experience them? What are Cuban youths' everyday practices beyond these spaces and schooling? What are the various moments, spaces, and spatial practices in which youth engage in open and critical social, cultural, and political expression? These potential future research questions are important in order to get a better understanding of how the Cuban social system of comprehensive education effectively functions.

As Gordon, Bridglall, and Meroe (2005), Cremin (1975/2007), and Varenne (2009) remind us we need to think, examine, and implement education comprehensively, not just in the narrow sense of schooling, as is currently understood in education policy in the United States. Although the United States has not actualized this assertion in social and educational policy and practice, it can gain insights from other nations, such as Cuba, that have achieved high levels of equitable human development through its potentially already-existing social system of comprehensively conceived education.

Acknowledgments

This research was supported by a University Research Foundation Grant from the University of Pennsylvania. I am grateful to Zunzún Education Services of British Columbia, Canada, for their exceptional tour and travel services early on in this project as well as Edmund W. and Susan G. Gordon for their research support. I must also acknowledge the tremendous research assistance of Megan Basham. All correspondence should be sent to Ezekiel J. Dixon-Román, Penn School of Social Policy & Practice, University of Pennsylvania, 3701 Locust Walk, Philadelphia, PA, 19104–6214, ezekield@sp2.upenn.edu.

Notes

1. Based on the overlap of the seven Latin American countries that participated in the Program of International Student Assessment and UNESCO's 2006 Second Regional Comparative Study, Carnoy (2008) estimated what Cuban 15-year-olds would have scored on the PISA 2006 tests in mathematics and reading, had they taken them. While

there are several psychometric issues of equating and score estimation, this is probably the best comparative estimate of Cuban students' performance, on average, on an international assessment that included the participation of the United States.

References

Azicri, M. (1989). Women's development through revolutionary mobilization. In P. Brenner, W. M. LeoGrande, D. Rich, & D. Siegel (Eds.), *The Cuba reader: The making of a revolutionary society* (pp. 457–471). New York, NY: Grove Press.

Baker, G. (2011). *Buena vista in the club: Rap, reggaetón, and revolution in Havana* (Refiguring American Music Series). Durham, NC: Duke University Press.

Bourdieu, P. (1977). *Outline of a theory of practice.* New York, NY: Cambridge University Press. (Original work published 1972)

Calder, K. (1988). *Crisis and compensation: Public policy and political stability in Japan.* Princeton, NJ: Princeton University Press.

Carnoy, M. (2008, June 25). Are Cuba's schools better than ours? *The Huffington Post.* Retrieved from http://www.huffingtonpost.com/martin-carnoy/are-cubas-schools-better_b_109280.html

Carnoy, M., Gove, A. K., & Marshall, J. H. (2007). *Cuba's academic advantage: Why students in Cuba do better in school.* Stanford, CA: Stanford University Press.

Castro, F. (2001). *La historia me absolverá* [History will absolve me]. Havana, Cuba: Editorial de Ciencias Sociales. (Original work published 1953)

Cremin, L. (2007). Public education and the education of the public. *Teachers College Record, 109*(7), 1545–1558. (Original work published 1975)

Del Carmen Zabulla Argüelles, M. (1999). Does a certain dimension of poverty exist in Cuba? In J. B. Lara (Ed.), *Cuba in the 1990s.* Havana, Cuba: Editorial José Martí.

Dewey, J. (1966). *Democracy and education.* New York, NY: Free Press. (Original work published 1916)

Dixon-Román, E. (2009, April). *Deviance as pedagogy: A critical perspective on indigenous cultural capital.* Paper presented at the annual meeting of the American Educational Research Association, San Diego, CA.

Dominguez, J. (1993). Cuba since 1959. In L. Bethell, *Cuba: A short history* (pp. 95–148). New York, NY: Cambridge University Press.

Espino, M. D. (2000). *Cuban tourism during the special period.* Proceedings of the Annual Meetings of the Association for the Study of the Cuban Economy (ASCE), Volume 10.

Foucault, M. (1986). Of other spaces, heterotopias (Jay Miskowiec, trans.). *Diacritics, 16*(1), 22–27. (Original work published 1967)

Gordon, E. W., Bridglall, B. L., & Meroe, A. S. (2005). *Supplementary education: The hidden curriculum of high academic achievement.* Lanham, MD: Rowman & Littlefield.

Kapcia, A. (2008). *Cuba in revolution: A history since the fifties.* London, England: Reaktion Books.

Kozol, J. (1978). *Children of the revolution: A Yankee teacher in the Cuban schools.* New York, NY: Dell.

LaBash, C. (2007). Cuba teaches the world to read. *Workers World.* Retrieved from http://www.workers.org/2007/world/cuba-0111/

Latin American Laboratory for Assessment of Quality in Education (LLECE). (1998). *First international comparative study of language, mathematics and associated factors for students in the third and fourth grade of primary school.* Santiago, Chile: UNESCO.

Latin American Laboratory for Assessment of Quality in Education (LLECE). (2002). *First international comparative study of language, mathematics and associated factors for students in the third and fourth grade of primary school* (2nd Report). Santiago, Chile: UNESCO.

Leiner, M. (1974). *Children are the revolution: Daycare in Cuba.* New York, NY: Penguin.

Leiner, M. (1989). Cuba's schools: 25 years later. In P. Brenner, W. M. LeoGrande, D. Rich, & D. Siegel (Eds.), *The Cuba reader: The making of a revolutionary society* (pp. 445–456). New York, NY: Grove Press.

Ministerio de Educación. (1995). *La escuela, la familia y la educación para la salud: Para la vida* [The school, the family and education for well-being: For life]. Havana, Cuba: Editorial Pueblo y Educación.

Skocpol, T. (2007). *States & social revolutions: A comparative analysis of France, Russia, & China.* New York, NY: Cambridge University Press. (Original work published 1979)

Ubell, R. N. (1989). Twenty-five years of Cuban health care. In P. Brenner, W. M. LeoGrande, D. Rich, & D. Siegel (Eds.), *The Cuba reader: The making of a revolutionary society* (pp. 435–445). New York, NY: Grove Press.

United Nations Development Programme. (2008). *Human development report 2007/2008.* Retrieved from http://hdr.undp.org/en/media/HDR_20072008_EN_Complete.pdf

Varenne, H. (2009). Educating ourselves about education—Comprehensively. In H. Varenne & E. W. Gordon (Eds.), *Perspectives on Comprehensive Education Series: Vol. 1. Theoretical perspectives on comprehensive education: The way forward* (pp. 1–24). Lewiston, NY: The Edwin Mellen Press.

4

THE ETHNIC SYSTEM OF SUPPLEMENTARY EDUCATION

Lessons From Chinatown and Koreatown, Los Angeles

Min Zhou

The extraordinary educational achievement of the children of Asian immigrants has attracted a great deal of media and scholarly attention. Quantitative data show that children of Asian immigrants do significantly better in school than children of other racial minorities and reach parity to (and, in some key outcome measures, surpass) non-Hispanic White children. Moreover, Asian Americans fare significantly better than Whites in school outcomes such as grade-point average, while Blacks and Hispanics fare significantly worse, even after controlling for family and demographic characteristics. What is more striking is that young Asian Americans—not only the children of foreign-born physicians, scientists, and engineers but also those of uneducated, low-skilled, and poor immigrants and refugees—have repeatedly shown up as high school valedictorians and academic decathlon winners and have enrolled in prestigious colleges and universities in disproportionately large numbers. Why do Asian Americans generally fare better in education than members of other ethnic minorities? Why does the ethnicity variable yield varied effects on children's educational outcomes in statistical models? What is embedded in ethnicity—superior cultural values or privileged social-class resources? Based on findings from my ethnographic research on Chinese and Korean immigrant communities in Los Angeles, in this chapter I examine what gives the children of Chinese and Korean immigrants a competitive edge in the educational arena. I argue that what explains the educational achievement of Asian Americans is not cultural values per se, but rather the collective ability to actualize these values on the individual.

Theoretical Background

For a long time, educators and researchers have sought to explain the unequal educational outcomes of different ethnic minorities by focusing on either cultural

factors—an ethnic group's traits, qualities, and behavioral patterns—or on structural factors—an ethnic group's special historical encounters of domination and
subjugation, socioeconomic backgrounds, immigration selectivity, labor-market
conditions, and residential patterns (Fordham, 1996; Ogbu, 1974; Wilson, 2009).
These values and norms in turn lead to a set of self-defeating behavioral problems,
such as labor-force nonparticipation, out-of-wedlock births, welfare dependency,
school failure, drug addiction, and chronic lawlessness (Lewis, 1966; Wilson, 1996,
2009). But such cultural explanations are often shunned as blaming the victim.

Other studies, in contrast, have found that low-income families of racial/ethnic
minorities tend to concentrate in poverty-stricken and unsafe inner-city neighborhoods. Parents who lack human capital (e.g., education, professional job skills,
and English proficiency for immigrants) have few options other than to send
their children to dilapidated urban schools that have inadequate facilities and
resources, poorly trained and inexperienced teachers, and large proportions of
low-achieving students, hence putting children at a much higher risk of school
failure (Suarez-Orozco & Suarez-Orozco, 2001; Telles & Ortiz, 2008). These explanations emphasize the enduring effects of historical legacies of ethnic groups
in contact with mainstream America but tend to overlook the possible intersection between group-level socioeconomic characteristics and behavioral patterns
emerged from structural advantage or disadvantage, which have profound implications for community formation at the neighborhood level. For example, some
ethnic communities have the capacity of creating or fostering certain social environments that are endowed with tangible resources conducive to education while
others do not. Coethnic (of same ethnicity) members and non-coethnic members are likely exposed to different social environments even though they share
the same neighborhood. Many urban neighborhoods, indeed, consist of multiple
communities and social environments shaped by ethnicity. Here the segmented
assimilation theory is most relevant.

The segmented assimilation theory is a middle-range sociological theory. In
contrast to the classical assimilation perspective, which assumes that immigrant
group members must shed their ethnic baggage to become assimilated into a
White, middle-class mainstream, it conceptualizes the American mainstream shaped
by the system of racial and class stratifications and exclusive of the marginal segments of the American population (Portes & Zhou, 1993; Zhou, 1997). While
rejecting the classical vision of an undifferentiated, unified, and White middle-
class core to which *all* immigrants assimilate, the segmented assimilation theory
points out three discernible patterns of adaptation among contemporary immigrants and their offspring. The first is the time-honored upward-mobility pattern: acculturation and economic integration into the normative structures of
mainstream middle-class America. The second is the downward-mobility pattern
of acculturation, leading to integration into the margins of American society, a
pathway of adapting to native, or constructing hybrid (native and foreign mixed),
subcultures associated with being trapped at the bottom rungs of the host society's

mobility ladder. The third pattern involves socioeconomic integration into mainstream America with lagged or selective acculturation *and* deliberate preservation of the ethnic community's values and norms, social ties, and institutions. This is the pathway of deliberately reaffirming ethnicity and rebuilding ethnic networks and ethnic social structures for socioeconomic advancement into middle-class status. This nuanced theory predicts divergent outcomes and explains why some national-origin groups are more likely than others to move ahead into the mainstream society or to get trapped on the margins of the host society. More specifically, it places the process of becoming American, in terms of both acculturation and socioeconomic incorporation, in the context of a host society consisting of segregated and unequal segments and considers this process to be multidirectional, leading to varied outcomes of convergence as well as divergence.

Into which segment of the host society immigrants assimilate is the crux of the matter. The segmented assimilation theory diverts from the classical framework with regard to the effects of observable socioeconomic and acculturation factors, such as family income, parental education, residence, length of time since immigration, and English language skills. It instead assumes that these two sets of determinants are significant by default and focuses instead on interaction between the two. From the segmented assimilation perspective, varied outcomes are determined by group-specific contexts of exit and reception (Portes & Rumbaut, 1990). The context of exit entails a number of factors, including the social-class status already attained by the immigrants in their homelands, premigration resources that immigrants bring with them (such as money, knowledge, and job skills), and immigrants' means of migration, motivation, aspirations, and practices. The context of reception includes the national-origin group's positioning in the system of racial stratification, government policies, labor-market conditions, public attitudes, and the strength and viability of the ethnic community in the host society. Particular contexts of exit and reception can create distinctive ethnocultural patterns and strategies of adaptation, social environments, and tangible resources for the group and give rise to opportunities or constraints for the individual, independent of individual socioeconomic and demographic characteristics. While contexts of exit and reception give rise to distinct modes of incorporation for immigrant or refugee groups, different modes of incorporation in turn explain variations in the *contexts* within which individuals strive to "make it" in their new homeland.

In the segmented assimilation framework, the ethnic community is conceptualized as a crucial site for the formation of tangible and intangible resources influencing children's adaptation. This is especially relevant for ethnic group members from low family socioeconomic status (SES) backgrounds.

If growing up in poor neighborhoods has adverse social consequences for native-born minority children, how, then, do the family and ethnic community steer children away from negative influences associated with poverty and move them out of the inner city? Ethnicity and social class are not all that count; just as important is the intersection between the two that creates a unique ethnic social

environment conducive to education and adaptation, a point enlightened by segmented assimilation, to which I now turn.

Urban Neighborhood Versus Ethnic Community

Urban neighborhoods are inherently unequal by ethnicity and social class. Contemporary urban neighborhoods in major immigrant gateway cities have grown
increasingly multiethnic. In Los Angeles, there are more urban neighborhoods
inhabited by racial or ethnic minorities than in the past because of the out-
migration of the White middle class, or White flight, and mass international migration. But very few of these minority–majority neighborhoods are dominated
by a single ethnic or national origin group. Moreover, not all native minority
neighborhoods succeeded by new immigrants suffer from further decay; some
experience growth (Zhou & Kim, 2003). These new patterns of neighborhood
changes emerge not because of accelerated White flight, or because of natural
reproduction of native minorities, but rather because of the rapid influx of new
immigrants from diverse ethnic and social-class backgrounds.

Los Angeles is a new gateway metropolis, attracting mostly immigrants from
Mexico, El Salvador, Guatemala, China, Taiwan, Korea, the Philippines, and
Southeast Asia. As a result, minority populations of Asian and Latin American origins grow rapidly. In the 2000 census, the population in Los Angeles County was
made up of 31% non-Hispanic White, 10% non-Hispanic Black, 35% Mexican,
10% other Hispanic, and 13% Asian (compared to 53%, 12%, 22%, 6%, and 10%,
respectively, in 1980). Not surprisingly, inner-city Los Angeles reveals a pattern of
diversity in origins and socioeconomic backgrounds that clearly intersects with
ethnicity. In Chinatown and Koreatown, or example, three demographic patterns
stand out: minority dominant, foreign-born dominant, and low-SES dominant. In
1960, non-Hispanic Whites dominated Koreatown and had a significant presence
in Chinatown, but their numbers had shrunk to less than 7% in Koreatown and
4% in Chinatown by 2000. Even though Chinese continued to dominate Chinatown (55% in 2000), they were no longer uniformly Cantonese as they once were,
and many came from other regions of China as well as from Southeast Asia (Zhou,
2009b). In Koreatown, Koreans made up less than one-fifth of the population,
while other Asian populations (mostly Chinese, Filipinos, and Southeast Asians)
made up about 12%. In contrast, Hispanics in Koreatown formed the majority
(57%), with Mexicans accounting for a third, and Salvadorans and Guatemalans
accounting for nearly a quarter. Both Chinatown and Koreatown are immigrant
neighborhoods in the fullest sense of the word, as foreign-born persons comprise
more than two-thirds of the neighborhood's total population. This characteristic
of course does not make these neighborhoods unique; in fact, it is something they
share with many other neighborhoods in immigrant Los Angeles. Among the
foreign-born who lived in these neighborhoods, many were recent arrivals (post-
1990 arrivals accounted for about 40% in Chinatown and 52% in Koreatown).

Residents in Chinatown and Koreatown also demonstrated low levels of human capital and economic resources. In 2000, nearly 60% of adults in Chinatown had not completed a high school education, and less than 10% had college degrees. In Koreatown, the average level of educational attainment was much higher, but still much lower than the county's average level. Median household incomes, ranging from $18,000 in Chinatown to $22,000 in Koreatown, were also much lower than the county's average ($42,200). Poverty rates were high, 27% in Chinatown and 31% in Koreatown, compared to 15% for the county as a whole.

Chinese and Koreans in Los Angeles have different histories and patterns of migration and settlement. The Chinese are one of the oldest immigrant groups resettling in Los Angeles. Chinatown is an enclave that emerged from Chinese exclusion and has developed and consolidated ethnic social structures in response to legal exclusion. New arrivals in Chinatown came mostly from low SES backgrounds. Many lacked English language proficiency and education or job skills but share the same dialect—Cantonese. High SES Chinese immigrants and Mandarin speakers tend to resettle in Los Angeles's eastern suburbs, or Chinese *ethnoburbs* (ethnic suburbs).[1] Comparatively, Koreans are a much more recent immigrant group, and they establish Koreatown as an ethnic enclave with high visibility of ethnic businesses rather than as a residential enclave. Even though most of the Asian immigrants living in Chinatown and Koreatown are poor and work at low-wage jobs, a significant proportion hailed from urban and middle-class backgrounds prior to migration. Also, the majority of Asian immigrants have legal status. Like Asians, Mexicans, and Central Americans converged in Los Angeles's Chinatown and Koreatown primarily through longstanding migration networks of family, kin, and friendship. Unlike Asians, however, most of the Mexican and Central American immigrants living there are of low SES backgrounds, and a substantial number have undocumented status.

Diverse origins and socioeconomic backgrounds underscore the varied contexts of reception of different ethnic groups, suggesting varied mechanisms by which immigrants and their children negotiate the urban space. In the inner city, the space outside the home is often plagued by common urban problems—such as crimes, drugs, gangs—which are unsafe for children's well-being and disruptive for educational achievement. Chinatown and Koreatown are no exception. The space inside the school is also problematic. Inner-city schools are inadequate and understaffed, and they concentrate low-income and low-achieving minority students. Many immigrant parents want their children to do well in school but lack the human capital and financial resources necessary to support their children's education. Oftentimes, parental cultural practices of child rearing are considered deficient and are even stigmatized as "the culture of poverty" by the school and other mainstream institutions (Lewis, 1966). Low SES and societal prejudice function to weaken parental authority, lower educational expectations, and exacerbate school failure. In fact, public schools in inner-city Los Angeles concentrate very high percentages of English learners (formerly called limited English proficiency) and students enrolled below grade levels or with low achievement and motivation, and have high rates of turnover and dropout. But these schools are not equipped with sufficient institutional resources to meet the special needs of immigrant students.

The prospect of school success for inner-city immigrant children is daunting. Even though almost all the parents I interviewed said that education was very important for their children and that they wanted their children to do well in school, the collective ability to actualize that value varied by ethnicity. Next, I examine the formation of an ethnic system of supplementary education rooted in the inner city that enables some, but not all, children living in the same neighborhood to succeed in school.

The Ethnic System of Supplementary Education as Part of the Ethnic Enclave Economy

Supplementary education is described as the "hidden curriculum for high academic achievement" (Gordon, Bridglall, & Meroe, 2005). It involves a wide range of structured afterschool programs, activities, and practices that function to enrich children's and youth's educational experience and promote personal growth (Bridglall, Green, & Mejia, 2005). Supplementary education is institutionalized, readily available for, and routinely utilized by middle-class families but is often beyond the reach of low-income families, especially those living in inner-city neighborhoods. However, urban neighborhoods consist of multiple ethnic communities. Some ethnic communities are better organized and have greater capacity to mobilize or generate resources to support education than others, despite similar geographic locations. But the availability and access to ethnic educational resources in urban neighborhoods are exclusive of non-coethnic members, rendering local social environments unequal, as illustrated in Los Angeles's Chinatown and Koreatown.

Formal institutions serving children and youth exist in America's urban neighborhoods, often in the form of nonprofit, community-based organizations (CBOs). The numbers and types of nonprofit CBOs do not vary drastically across urban neighborhoods. Many of these nonprofits depend primarily on public funds or on a combination of funds from various levels of government, private foundations, and individual or organizational donations. The functions and services of nonprofit CBOs are similar across Los Angeles's urban neighborhoods (Zhou, 2009c). For example, the Chinatown Service Center routinely offers Chinese language classes, afterschool tutoring, cultural activities, youth volunteer opportunities, and employment referrals, and cosponsors special cultural events, such as the Chinese New Year parade, mid-autumn festival celebration, and street cultural fairs. The Korean Youth and Community Center in Koreatown offers various language classes, crime/gang prevention programs, family counseling, tutoring and tutor referral services, job training, and music and recreational activities.

CBOs in Los Angeles's inner city form the most important source of institutional support for immigrant children. Some of these CBOs, such as LA Arts Corps, Teen Smart, and Teen Council, which pair college students or suburban high school students with local school-age children, are remarkably successful (Loukaitou-Sideris & Hutchinson, 2006). However, due to the mandates from funding agencies and limited operating funds, nonprofits can serve only a small proportion of the local population, especially those identified as the poor, low-income, or "at risk." Given the overwhelmingly high demand for services, these nonprofits are often underfunded and understaffed, and their ability to provide quality services for those in need is severely constrained. Further, these CBOs usually have few coethnic participants from affluent families or from middle-class suburbs, and thus unintentionally reinforce class segregation.

Private enterprises serving children and youth are an outgrowth of the ethnic enclave economy. They emerge in the neighborhood to directly respond to the educational demand but also serve to compensate for the shortage of publicly funded programs and services (Zhou & Kim, 2006). While middle-class families in suburban communities have relatively easy access to private education institutions, such as Kaplan, Princeton Review, and a range of private tutoring services, these kinds of supplementary education are either nonexistent in many inner-city neighborhoods or beyond the reach of the low-income families living there, with Chinatown and Koreatown as exceptions. As part of the ethnic enclave economy, there has been a growing visibility of private enterprises targeting children and youth over the past 20 years. Table 4.1 provides a detailed description of private child- and youth-targeted institutions in Chinatown and Koreatown. As shown, there is a fairly wide range of private establishments serving children and youth that exist in these two low-income immigrant neighborhoods. Almost all of the private educational institutions are owned by coethnics (Chinese in Chinatown and Koreans in Koreatown). The non-Asian owners there are mostly non-Hispanic Whites. In fact, some mainstream standardized test preparation institutions, such as the Princeton Review, offer regular classes in Chinatown and Chinese ethnoburbs in the San Gabriel Valley and Koreatown that attract Chinese and Korean youths.

In Chinatown, the presence of various types of private enterprises serving children and youth is visible, but the density level is moderate compared to that in Koreatown. This moderate density is largely due to Chinatown's close proximity to Monterey Park (an ethnoburb with Asian majority) and other Chinese ethnoburbs in the San Gabriel Valley,[2] an area heavily settled by middle-class Chinese immigrants with a fast-growing ethnic enclave economy (Zhou & Kim, 2003). Monterey Park is a suburb just east of Chinatown, only 10 minutes away by car or a 20-minute bus ride. Easy access to Chinese ethnoburbs such as Monterey Park enables Chinatown families and children to tap ethnic resources outside Chinatown that few other immigrant groups living in the inner city are able to do.

In Monterey Park and other neighboring suburb cities east of Los Angeles, the development of Chinese language schools has paralleled the development of a

Table 4.1 For-profit educational institutions in Chinatown and Koreatown, Los Angeles

Type	Chinatown			Koreatown		
	Chinese	Other Asian	Non-Asian	Korean	Other Asian	Non-Asian
Academic						
Afterschool tutoring	+★★			+★★★		+★
Academic enrichment	+★			+★★★		+★
College preparation	+★			+★★★		+★
Preschool academies	+			+★★★		
Extracurricular/recreational						
Music studios/classes	+★			+★★★	+	
Dance studios/classes	+★		+	+★★	+	+
Art studios/classes	+★	+	+	+★★	+	+
Martial arts studios	+★	+		+★★★	+	+
Golf schools/clubs				+★★		
Other sports schools/clubs	+★			+★★★		+
Vocational training						
Technical	+★			+★★★		+
Administrative/clerical	+★			+		+
Real estate/finance	+★	+		+★★		+
Personal services	+★	+			+	+
Health services	+★	+		+★	+	+

Note: +Presence of type; ★3–5 per type; ★★6–8 per type; ★★★more than 8 per type. Data are from neighborhood phone directories, 1995–2004; ethnographic field observations, 1998–2000, 2003–2004. Adapted from "How Neighborhoods Matter for Immigrant Children: The Formation of Educational Resources in Chinatown, Koreatown, and Pico Union, Los Angeles," by M. Zhou, 2009, *Journal of Ethnic and Migration Studies, 35,* Table 4. Copyright 2009 by Taylor & Francis Group.

wide range of private enterprises serving children's and youth's educational needs since the late 1980s, such as *buxiban* (academic tutoring),[3] early childhood educational programs, academic enrichment programs, college preparatory centers, arts studios, karate or kung fu studios, and sports clubs, some of which are lodged in nonprofit Chinese language schools. For example, the 2004 *Southern California Chinese Consumer Yellow Pages* (Chinese Consumer Yellow Pages, 2004) listed 90 Chinese schools, 135 academic afterschool tutoring establishments, including buxiban, 50 arts schools/centers, and 90 music/dance schools, mostly located in Los Angeles's suburban Chinese community in Monterey Park and the neighboring suburbs. Students enrolled in these afterschool institutions are almost exclusively Chinese from immigrant families but of varied SES backgrounds. Daily programs run from 3 to 6 p.m., drawing students who live nearby while weekend programs draw students not only locally but also from areas across greater Los Angeles.

Driving around the commercial core of Monterey Park, one can see flashy bilingual signs of these establishments, such as Little Harvard, Ivy League School,

Little PhD Early Learning Center (a preschool), Stanford-to-Be Prep School, IQ180, and Hope Buxiban. Major Chinese language media, such as the *Chinese Daily News, Sing Tao Daily,* and *China Press,* publish weekly editions with educational news and commentaries and numerous advertisements of these private afterschool institutions (Zhou & Cho, 2010; Zhou & Kim, 2006). These child- and youth-targeted institutions have sprung up to join the existing Chinese language schools to constitute a comprehensive system of supplementary education. The core curricula of these various ethnic institutions are supplementary to, rather than competing with, public school education. Many of the Chinese youths I interviewed agreed that going to a Chinese school or a Chinese-run buxiban had been a common experience of being Chinese American, even though they generally disliked the fact that they were made to attend these ethnic institutions by their parents.

Unlike the Los Angeles Chinese immigrant community, which now centers in Monterey Park and branches out into the San Gabriel Valley rather than in Chinatown, the Korean immigrant community anchors in Koreatown, even though the ethnic population is much more spread out across the metropolitan region beyond the Los Angeles County line.[4] In contrast to Chinatown, the level of diversity and density of private enterprises serving children or youth in Koreatown are exceptionally high, and the return of suburban coethnics is unusually regular for an inner-city neighborhood. In 2004, the *Korean Business Directory* of greater Los Angeles lists 209 private *hagwon* (academic tutoring).[5] Thirty-six of them offer just SAT I & II intensive preparatory courses for high school students, and the rest offer basic subjects such as math and English for younger students in addition to the SAT, PSAT, SSAT, and AP for teenagers. In addition to hagwon, the directory lists a large number of private afterschool establishments, including 116 Korean-run art and music schools and 145 Tae Kwon Do or karate Korean martial arts studios. The concentration of these private enterprises in Koreatown is high. In the commercial core of Koreatown, for example, there are a handful of Korean language schools lodged in Korean Christian churches; more than 30 hagwon; numerous college preparation institutions; 30-plus music, dance, and arts studios; and more than 20 karate and sports clubs, along with a visible number of vocational training facilities. Korean children who live in the neighborhood have easy access to a wide variety of hagwon and private tutoring in the homes, college-preparation classes, enrichment and recreational programs, and vocational training offered by Korean private businesses (Bhattacharyya, 2005; Zhou & Kim, 2006). These enrichment programs not only aim to help prepare high school students with well-round portfolios for college applications but also offer instruction for preschool, elementary, and middle-school students.

Like those in Chinatown and Chinese ethnoburbs, private enterprises serving children and youth in Koreatown constitute an ethnic system of supplementary education. Hagwon enterprises are owned by Koreans but are taught by both Korean and non-Korean teachers. They have eye-catching names like "Harvard

Review, Yale Academy, Princeton Academy, Smart Academy, IVY College, and UC Learning Institute. Even the non-Korean-owned private supplementary schools such as Prep Center and Princeton Review have branches set up in or near Koreatown and in ethnoburbs that have a large Korean population. They are advertised in Korean newspapers with promises of helping students excel in school, score high on the standardized tests, complete the college application process, and get into the college of their choice. Students enroll at very young ages and receive help in order to get into magnet programs, honors classes, and advanced-placement courses in their respective public schools or school districts. These efforts are taken from early ages to increases their chances of getting into highly competitive colleges. A private tutor whom I interviewed at a Korean hagwon put it wryly, "The Korean goal is narrow: Harvard, Princeton, Yale ... Harvard, Princeton, Yale ... as if other universities nonexist. Chinese parents are more relaxed. They are happy if their kids get into a U.C. school."

The development of the ethnic system of supplementary education allows for coethnic, cross-class relationships, creating channels for information exchange between coethnic middle-class suburbanites and low-SES enclave residents, hence easing the negative consequences of social isolation associated with inner-city living. For example, non-English-speaking Korean parents in Koreatown are able to obtain detailed information about high school and college requirements, school and college rankings, scholarship and financial aid, and other education-related matters through their casual contacts with a more informed group of middle-class coethnics who attend the same church, restaurants, beauty salons, and other ethnic institutions, and through the ethnic-language media. Parents can find tutors and afterschool programs from a wide range of options and prices offered by for-profit institutions advertised in ethnic-language newspapers. The ethnic-language media also routinely announce and honor their own children and youths who win national or regional awards and competitive fellowships, get accepted into prestigious colleges, and score exceptionally well on SAT and other scholastic standardized tests. Thus, Chinatown and Koreatown constitute multiple social environments that vary by national origins. For example, for Korean residents, Koreatown is not merely a place to live but also an ethnic community with many tangible and intangible educational resources.

Even though Chinatown and Koreatown contain institutional resources to support education, many of the educational resources are owned and run by ethnic entrepreneurs that benefit coethnic members to the exclusion of non-coethnic members living in the same neighborhood. In both Chinatown and Koreatown, the Mexican presence is substantial, but there are no private educational institutions owned by Mexicans and other Hispanics, and few Mexican and other Hispanic children participate in Chinese-owned or Korean-owned institutions in their neighborhoods. Such ethnic exclusion is due not only to low SES of Hispanic families but also to language and cultural barriers. As a result, Mexican and other Hispanic children sharing the same neighborhood are kept out of these local resources because of language and cultural barriers and the lack of human capital and economic resources needed to develop a similar ethnic system of supplementary education. Thus, it is the availability of and access to for-profit educational institutions, or an ethnic system of supplementary education, at the local level that appear to make a significant intergroup difference in educational outcomes.

Social Capital Formation Through Coethnic, Cross-Class Interaction in Ethnic Enclaves

Various types of local institutions that support education in Chinatown and Koreatown are shown in Table 4.1. Access to local institutional resources is unequal, but the formation of social capital that is conducive to education is also unequal. The organizational structure of local institutions in immigrant neighborhoods is bounded by coethnicity, which in turn shapes the patterns of interpersonal relationships and hence social-capital formation. Local institutions in Chinatown and Koreatown include both nonprofit CBOs and for-profit private enterprises serving children and youth. At nonprofits, interpersonal interactions among coethnics may sometimes involve non-coethnics, but these interactions are largely constrained by social class. Among Chinese and Korean residents, however, interpersonal interactions at the local level are not limited to nonprofits but extended to for-profit institutions offering ethnic-specific goods and services as well as serving educational needs. The development of the ethnic-enclave economy along with the system of supplementary education creates sites and opportunities for interpersonal interactions and allows for intraethnic (among coethnic members) and cross-class interaction because of the presence of nonresident middle-class coethnics in ethnic private institutions.

Among Mexican and other Hispanic residents in Chinatown and Koreatown, in contrast, interpersonal interactions tend to be interethnic among different Spanish-speaking ethnic groups, such as Salvadoran and Guatemalan, but seldom cross class lines because these ethnic places have less to offer to middle-class Hispanics than to Chinese and Koreans. The main reason is twofold: on the one hand, the local institutions in which they participate are mostly CBOs either serving immigrants' survival needs or serving the low-income and at-risk with no participation of middle-class families; and on other hand, the development of local ethnic businesses primarily serves the immediate needs of local residents without much attraction to lure the return of a coethnic middle-class clientele on a regular basis. In fact, my systematic field observations in local CBOs and private institutions in Chinatown or Koreatown found few interpersonal interactions among Hispanics that cut across ethnic and class lines.

It is well-documented in existing literature that one of the key factors for the decline of inner-city neighborhoods and the consequential social isolation has been the flight of the middle class along with their social institutions (Wilson,

1987). Inner-city neighborhoods such as Chinatown and Koreatown are undesirable settling grounds for immigrant families because of poor housing conditions, unsafe streets at night, and inadequate schools. Under these adverse conditions, middle-class immigrants rarely reside in the inner city, and they have no particular demands for services offered by local institutions of the inner city. Nonetheless, middle-class coethnics are present in their respective ethnic neighborhoods, although their institutional participation varies, depending largely on how the community is organized and whether social and economic developments enable routine return of the suburban middle class. In these urban neighborhoods, middle-class coethnics are commonly found in two types of local institutions: nonprofits, as leaders or service providers, and for-profit establishments, as owners or managers; but nonresident middle-class Chinese and Koreans are visible in Chinatown and Koreatown also as customers and clients of private institutions (Zhou, 2009c).

Inner-city neighborhoods can become attractive to middle-class customers in two significant ways: through the development of a tourist industry, with a unique historical or cultural symbolism and a range of exotic goods and services, such as ethnic restaurants and souvenir or trinket shops, catering to both coethnics and non-coethnics, and through the development of a diverse array of upscale retail, trade, and professional services (Lin, 2011). Chinatown and Koreatown are both tourist attractions, identified in popular and official guidebooks. Upscale restaurants in both neighborhoods draw visible crowds, of coethnic and non-coethnic professionals who work nearby during weekday lunch hours, and of tourists over weekends. Upscale retail malls in Chinatown and Koreatown also tend to draw coethnic middle-class crowds over the weekends. Middle-class coethnics seldom cross the enclave boundaries, however. Suburban, middle-class Chinese families who frequently go to Chinatown to eat and shop would rarely venture into Koreatown, or vice versa. Due to business developments that target affluent coethnics, a considerable middle-class presence is observed in other businesses, such as for-profit educational institutions, beauty salons and spas, golf ranges, and other ethnic recreational facilities, as well as in churches, ethnic institutions, and public libraries (Zhou, 2009c).

The high density and variety of ethnic businesses in an ethnic enclave create more space and opportunities for coethnic cross-class interactions, which has profound implications for the formation of social capital conducive to education in the inner city. In my face-to-face interviews, I have found that education is highly valued in both Asian and Hispanic families. Most parents reported that they believed in education as the best and only way for their children to move ahead in society, that they wanted their children to succeed in high school and go on to college, that they knew education was the most effective for their children to move ahead, and that they had high hopes for their children to do what they were unable to achieve occupationally. My interviews with youth also revealed similar educational values. A Mexican high school senior who arrived in Los Angeles at age 16 responded to our question regarding her view on education by saying,

"Yes, education is the best *herencia* one can have. If you study, you can *defenderse* (get along) in life."

However, having strong values is one thing, and being able to reinforce the value or being able to turn these values into aspirations and realize them is quite another (Zhou, 2009c). There are main intergroup differences, however. Asian parents generally have much higher expectations for their children than Hispanic parents do. Going to college is "a nonissue." A Korean teenager said in an interview, "If a Korean high school kid wasn't thinking about going to college most of the time, he would appear very strange. For us, the question is not whether you are going to college, but what college. You must go to a good college, and you would feel it when you are around other Koreans." For many Hispanic parents, the issue is how to get their kids through high school. To the parents, a high school diploma is a big leap forward and a celebrated family achievement. School counselors, speaking at the parent council meetings in a local high school (with more than 80% Hispanic enrollment), also put much more emphasis on how to make sure the child finishes high school than how to get this child into college. This is by no means suggesting that Asians have stronger educational values and higher aspirations than Hispanics do, but it does imply that Asian kids grow up in a very different social environment, where there is a generally accepted norm and associated behavioral patterns in regard to educational achievement, and where there is an ethnic system of supplementary education to support this norm.

Another main difference between Asian parents and Hispanic parents living in Chinatown and Koreatown appears to be that Asians are much better informed about the educational system and more knowledgeable and articulate about specific strategies for getting ahead in school. Data from interviews with immigrant youth show that Korean adolescents in Koreatown had a more sophisticated understanding of the educational system and were more informed about college options than were their Hispanic peers living in the same locale. For example, Korean respondents had concrete knowledge about what specific paths lead to higher education, such as which middle school was a feeder school to a better high school, which high school offered AP courses, how to prepare for AP and SAT tests, when to take these standardized tests, and how to make their college applications competitive. Many reported that they had to take SAT tests early so that they had time to retake them if necessary. They also mentioned repeatedly the names of prestigious colleges, such as Harvard, Princeton, California Institute of Technology, and Stanford, and had concrete remarks about how these colleges were ranked. Those who were high school seniors reported that they had surfed the websites of many colleges. Most of the Korean respondents reported having attended structured afterschool academic or recreational activities in Korean-owned or operated institutions. In responding to the question about their plans beyond high school, most said that not going to college was not an option in their families. Korean adolescents also reported that taking more AP tests, having higher SAT scores, or playing a musical instrument makes them "look good on college applications," that participating in afterschool activities could connect them to those who "know about college admission and financial aid stuff," or to those who "can write your recommendation letters for college," and that volunteer work in the community could help them "make up [for] bad grades in school." A Korean low-achiever responded, when asked why he got involved in a local service club, "Well, I like to help people, but mostly it's for college, because my grades aren't too good. They [colleges] like to see some of that extra stuff."

Thus, Asian immigrant children generally fare better than Latino immigrant children living in the same neighborhood and attending the same school largely because they have better access to neighborhood-based resources. An educator working in a neighborhood school reiterated the point in an interview: "When you think of how much time these Chinese and Korean kids put in their studies after regular school, you won't be surprised why they succeed in such a high rate." Unfortunately, the resources created at the neighborhood level for one ethnic group do not necessarily serve to benefit non-coethnic residents living in the same neighborhoods.

The ethnic system of supplementary education has a downside. It creates tremendous pressure to achieve that often takes a financial toll as well as an emotional toll on both parents and children. Families have to spend a substantial amount of money sending children to afterschool programs, and they are under tremendous pressure to do so. The ethnic system of supplementary education has a wide range of private enterprises, with a wide spectrum of fees, ranging from those that rival Kaplan or Princeton Review on one end to low-cost mom-and-pop operations on the other. For low-income families, however, children's afterschool programs represent a substantial household expenditure, and community pressure renders it nonnegotiable. A Chinatown mother, a sewing machine operator, said matter-of-factly in an interview, "I am sewing for my daughter's piano lessons, but she does not always appreciate that." When asked why she spent most of her wages to pay for something that her daughter did not enjoy doing, she replied that it was because most of her friends "are doing the same thing to their children," and that "someday, she will understand why I do this for her. I just don't want her to miss any opportunity now because I am poor." At the emotional level, parents are drawn into an unspoken, highly stressful competition for their children's educational achievement. If their children get into a good college, they would be saving "face" (the respect of others); otherwise, they would lose face. So they put pressure on the children to achieve, which is often at the core of intense parent–child conflict (Zhou, 2009a). Children often dislike going to afterschool programs. They want more time doing what they want to do and what their school friends often do, namely, having fun. They also want to look and act cool, and doing the school thing is not so cool. And, they don't want to look different. "This is in America. I just want to be like everybody else. But my mom never gets it," said a Chinese teenager whom I interviewed.

Tremendous parental pressures for achieving and behaving in the ethnic way can lead to intense intergenerational conflict, rebellious behavior, withdrawal from school, and alienation from the networks that are supposed to help. Alienated children fall easy preys to street gangs. Even children who do well in school and hope to make their parents happy and proud are at risk of being rebellious. A high school student said, "But that [doing well to make parents happy] never happens. My mother is never satisfied, no matter what you do and how well you do it." This remark echoes a frustration felt by many other Chinatown youths, who voiced how much they wished not to be compared with other Asian children and how much they wished to rebel.

Conclusion

As I have shown, organizational structures in urban neighborhoods are bounded by class and ethnicity. It appears that the availability and accessibility of ethnic institutions in the inner city—both nonprofit and for-profit—serving immigrant children and youth are crucial for building a social environment that is conducive to education. However, access to neighborhood-based resources is unequal and ethnically exclusive. Los Angeles's Chinatown and Koreatown each present a slightly different organizational structure specifically relevant to immigrant children's education—one connected outwardly to the ethnoburb and the other anchoring in the inner city—but both ethnic communities have developed a fairly elaborate system of supplementary education through the ethnic enclave economy. The reason to explain why Chinese and Korean immigrant children generally fare better than Hispanic immigrant children living in the same neighborhood and attending the same school is beyond family values on education. Cultural values need structural support. Asian immigrant families can actualize their educational value on children because they benefit from tangible resources and social capital generated by their own ethnic communities.

My study implies that the mobilization of educational resources at the neighborhood level has a lot to do with immigration selection and group-specific contexts of exit and reception. In particular, variations in SES and legal status of different national-origin groups can reproduce advantages and disadvantages in the inner city in ways that influence cultural practices with regard to education. The institutional developments in Koreatown and Chinatown underscore the important role of the ethnic-enclave economy in community building and social-capital formation.

This ethnographic study only begins to unfold the ways in which each national-origin group organizes its members and affects the life of the second generation. Thus, significant intergroup differences in educational outcomes such as standardized test scores, grade-point averages, high school graduation rate, and college attendance are rooted in the social structures of ethnic communities rather than in group-specific cultural traits or individual characteristics. The Chinese and Korean cases may be unique, but their institutional developments underscore the importance of socioeconomic resources in community building and the role of the ethnic community in mobilizing resources and facilitating cross-class interaction. For ethnic groups with low SES, public intervention may aim at two targets: to build community rather than meet the basic needs of the individual and to bridge cultural gaps between ethnic communities lodged in the same neighborhoods to open up local ethnic resources to non-coethnic members.

Notes

1. *Ethnoburb* is a term coined by Wei Li to refer to multiethnic middle-class suburbs (see Li, 1997).
2. The San Gabriel Valley is a vast suburbia to the east of the city of Los Angeles, including Monterey Park, an Asian-majority city with 41% Chinese, 21% other Asian, 30% Hispanic, and 7% White.
3. *Buxiban* is a Chinese term that literally translates into English as "tutoring class." Some large buxiban run arts, recreational, and leadership programs as well.
4. The Korean population (195,000, or 2% of LA total) is much smaller that the Chinese population in Los Angeles (372,000, or 4% of LA total), and it is more spread out, with fewer ethnoburbs.
5. *Hagwon* is a Korean term that literally translates into English as "study place" and is generally referred to as afterschool tutoring for the purpose of reviewing or previewing material for regular school classes and exams.

References

Bhattacharyya, M. (2005). Community support for supplementary education. In E. W. Gordon, B. L. Bridglall, & A. S. Meroe (Eds.), *Supplementary education: The hidden curriculum of high academic achievement* (pp. 249–272). Lanham, MD: Rowman & Littlefield.

Bridglall, B. L., Green, A., & Mejia, B. (2005). A taxonomy of supplementary programs. In E. W. Gordon, B. L. Bridglall, & A. S. Meroe (Eds.), *Supplementary education: The hidden curriculum of high academic achievement* (pp. 151–188). Lanham, MD: Rowman & Littlefield.

Chinese Consumer Yellow Pages. (2004). *Southern California Chinese consumer yellow pages.* Rosemead, CA: Chinese Consumer Yellow Pages.

Fordham, S. (1996). *Blacked out: Dilemmas of race, identity, and success at Capital High.* Chicago, IL: University of Chicago Press.

Gordon, E. W., Bridglall, B. L., & Meroe, A. S. (Eds.). (2005). *Supplementary education: The hidden curriculum of high academic achievement.* Lanham, MD: Rowman & Littlefield.

Lewis, O. (1966). The culture of poverty. *Scientific American, 215*(4), 19–25.

Li, W. (1997). *Spatial transformation of an urban ethnic community from Chinatown to Chinese ethnoburb in Los Angeles.* Unpublished doctoral dissertation. University of Southern California, Los Angeles.

Lin, Nan. (2011). *Social capital: Critical concepts in social sciences.* Vol. 4. London: Routledge.

Loukaitou-Sideris, A., & Hutchinson, J. (2006). Social networks and social capital: Latinos in Pico-Union. In P. Ong & A. Loukaitou (Eds.), *Jobs and economic development in minority communities* (chapter 10). Philadelphia, PA: Temple University Press.

Ogbu, J. U. (1974). *The next generation: An ethnography of education in an urban neighborhood.* New York, NY: Academic Press.

Portes, A., & Rumbaut, R. (1990). *Immigrant America: A portrait*. Berkeley: University of California Press.

Portes, A., & Zhou, M. (1993). The new second generation: Segmented assimilation and its variants. *The Annals of the American Academy of Political and Social Science, 530,* 74–96.

Suarez-Orozco, C., & Suarez-Orozco, M. M. (2001). Children of immigration. *Harvard Educational Review, 71*(3), 599–602.

Telles, E. E., & Ortiz, V. (2008). *Generations of exclusion: Mexican Americans, assimilation, and race*. New York, NY: Russell Sage Foundation.

Wilson, W. J. (1987). *The truly disadvantaged: The inner city, the underclass, and public policy*. Chicago, IL: University of Chicago Press.

Wilson, W. J. (1996). *When work disappears*. Chicago, IL: University of Chicago Press.

Wilson, W. J. (2009). *More than just race: Being black and poor in the inner city*. New York, NY: Norton.

Zhou, M. (1997). Segmented assimilation: Issues, controversies, and recent research on the new second generation. *International Migration Review, 31*(4), 825–858.

Zhou, M. (2009a). Conflict, coping, and conciliation: Intergenerational relations in Chinese immigrant families. In N. Foner (Ed.), *Across generations: Immigrant families in America* (pp. 21–46). New York: New York University Press.

Zhou, M. (2009b). *Contemporary Chinese America: Immigration, ethnicity, and community transformation*. Philadelphia, PA: Temple University Press.

Zhou, M. (2009c). How neighborhoods matter for immigrant children: The formation of educational resources in Chinatown, Koreatown, and Pico Union, Los Angeles. *Journal of Ethnic and Migration Studies, 35,* 1153–1179.

Zhou, M., & Cho, M. (2010). Noneconomic effects of ethnic entrepreneurship: Evidence from Chinatown and Koreatown in Los Angeles, USA. *Thunderbird International Business Review, 52,* 83–96.

Zhou, M., & Kim, R. (2003). A tale of two metropolises: Immigrant Chinese communities in New York and Los Angeles. In D. Halle (Ed.), *Los Angeles and New York in the new millennium* (pp. 124–149). Chicago, IL: University of Chicago Press.

Zhou, M., & Kim, S. (2006). Community forces, social capital, and educational achievement: The case of supplementary education in the Chinese and Korean immigrant communities. *Harvard Educational Review, 76*(1), 1–29.

5

SAN DIEGO'S DIAMOND NEIGHBORHOODS AND THE JACOBS CENTER FOR NEIGHBORHOOD INNOVATION

Andrea Yoder Clark and Tracey Bryan

Challenges in urban communities, often related to poverty (Anyon, 1997), have persisted for decades. As the United States is facing one of the worst economic crises in recent memory, the mental and physical health needs of students are rising as they return to homes where parents are battling unprecedented economic challenges. Unemployment reached record levels in San Diego, 11% at its peak, in response to the national collapse of the housing market (Tintocalis, 2010). The current economic reality has increased the relevance of social and economic connections to learning. As the cost of meeting students' needs rises for schools (Wong, 1992), school funding is being cut at record levels. In fiscal year 2009–2010, over $98 million was cut from San Diego Unified School District's budget alone (Tintocalis, 2010). Cuts to public education funding often have a greater impact in center-city neighborhoods, like the Diamond Neighborhoods of southeastern San Diego, where state funding can be the primary source of revenue for public schools.

In this chapter, we will review the connections between the social and economic realities of urban communities and the success of their schools. A comprehensive community led urban revitalization project implemented by the Jacobs Center for Neighborhood Innovation (JCNI) in the Diamond Neighborhoods of San Diego, California, will be explored. Despite the challenges of the recent economic downturn, JCNI has partnered with communities to produce sustained economic growth and improved quality of life through strengthening and connecting existing cultural assets within the communities of southeastern San Diego.

The goal of JCNI's partnership with residents is to improve the social well-being of the community. The Diamond Neighborhoods are located about 5 miles east of downtown San Diego. Originally a vibrant, middle-class community in the postwar economic boom times of the 1950s, during the 1960s and 1970s less economic investment and increases in crime (Caldwell, 2004) became the norm as residents and businesses fled (Moran, Magill, Monteagudo, & Gao, 2007). Since 2007, the area has undergone dramatic economic revitalization as a result of the communities' partnership with JCNI; however, JCNI realizes its partnership with residents of the Diamond has only just begun. Today, despite multiple years of consistent economic growth, 20% of area residents continue to live below the poverty line (www.jcni.org).

In 2008, economic effects related to the collapse of the national housing market shook the very foundation of the Diamond Neighborhoods and their partnerships with JCNI. Granting agencies and investment firms were forced to dramatically reduce their support for the Diamonds' community revitalization efforts (www.jcni. org). In 2010, cuts in state funding to local governments and school districts were felt deeply. From 2006 to 2010, over $400 million dollars have been cut from San Diego Unified School District's budget. Since 2003, the City of San Diego has suffered budget deficits ranging from $10.3 to $35.9 million (Haynes & Tevlin, 2008). City budget woes have been felt in the Diamond as public safety services have declined. Since the 1980s, patrols of public safety officers in the southeast San Diego region have been cut in half (Caldwell, 2004), despite resident-reported increases in crime (www.jcni.org). Unfortunately, there is no end in sight to area financial concerns, as fiscal year projections for 2011–2012 in San Diego Unified School District anticipate as of this writing a $123 million budget deficit (www.sandi.net) and the City of San Diego faces a projected budget shortfall of $179 million.

Economic stresses manifest in additional psychosocial challenges for families, often creating obstacles to school success (Wong, 1992). Historically, less than half of all ninth graders entering city schools graduate from high school (Fossey, 1996). Recent data collected from the California Department of Education reports a 20% dropout rate for the state in the 2007–2008 school year (www. cde.ca.gov), with over 60% of these dropouts from African American (34.7%) or Latino (25.5%) ethnic groups. San Diego Unified demonstrates similar challenges with dropout statistics slightly higher than the state average at 22%, albeit a bit lower than other large urban districts (Tintocalis, 2008).

Decades of reform initiatives have attempted to address the challenges of schools in center-city communities, most of which have failed to produced long-term sustainable improvements in urban districts (Anyon, 1997; Comer, 1980; Jehl & Kirst, 1993). The 1990s focused on school-culture–based reforms, with the goal of producing change in the school as a unit through district decentralization practices (Lieberman, 1995; Sizer, 1992), small-school initiatives, learning community programs (Comer, 1980), and restructuring school decision-making bodies to reflect democratic principles (Darling-Hammond, 1996; Hess, 1995; Lieberman, 1995). While such reforms have produced small successes, systematic district-wide reform has continued to remain elusive.

More recently, comprehensive school-reform efforts have begun to recognize the central role of schools in communities. Chicago public schools have achieved good results following school decentralization practices in addition to the implementation of elected parent-majority school councils that have resulted in extensive partnering between teachers, parents, and community-based organizations (Woestehoff & Neill, 2007). This approach brings the voice of the community to school governance. In this model, school sites are also linked to "wrap around" social services, connecting mental and physical health resources, afterschool care, out-of-school-time organizations, and other social resources to the school site, both physically and organizationally. In Chicago, large gains over long periods have been produced as a more holistic model of reform has been implemented.

The Harlem Children's Zone (HCZ) represents another successful holistic school-reform model with promising results (Jean-Louis, Shoemaker, & Gordon, 2009). Geoffrey Canada, the CEO of HCZ, worked to establish a preschool-to-college pipeline through the creation of "baby colleges," charter schools, and the addition of wrap-around services at school sites and the larger community with the goal of supporting entire families to ensure that the social, physical, and emotional needs of youth were met.

While these models have demonstrated great success, limitations remain. The HCZ goes far in addressing the core issues of multigenerational poverty, yet the model's reliance on outside funds limits its capacity, resulting in a large number of students being left out of the preschool-to-college pipeline. Although high-quality out-of-school-time experiences and social services have been extended to other neighborhood youth, the core educational experience for those in traditional public schools continues to be dramatically different than those at HCZ schools. Finally, the expense of maintaining this system is dependent on a long-term funding source to supplement the cost of such services. In Chicago, existing social-service agencies and nonprofits have been relocated to school sites, allowing them to connect with schools and build capacity through leveraging the services of existing programs. In this way, many community needs have been addressed without additional funding dollars. However, while this model has increased the overall health of these communities, the root causes that led to underinvested communities continues to plague residents and act as barriers to students' educational progress. Chicago Public Schools have done wonders to address the symptoms of poverty in communities; however, the long-term economic causes of poverty remain untouched.

As the United States slowly begins to climb out of the worst recession in recent memory, underinvested communities continue to fight against overwhelming challenges. As central-city residents combat high unemployment rates, crumbling civic infrastructure, eruptions of violence, and languishing schools, it becomes more important than ever to work toward holistic community-wide efforts directed at root causes of poverty. In this chapter we will examine one unique model, the Jacobs Center for Neighborhood Innovation (JCNI), that is specifically designed as a long-term community partnership with the goal of addressing root causes of poverty in the community as a whole with the expectation that educational and social improvement will follow. After 16 years of partnership with San Diego's Diamond Neighborhoods, JCNI has demonstrated consistent results that have contributed to a revitalization of the neighborhood.

Investing in Communities: The Jacobs Center for Neighborhood Innovation

After entrepreneur Joseph J. Jacobs Jr. grew his business, the Jacobs Engineering Group, from his garage to a multi-billion-dollar Fortune 500 company, he and his family decided to use their resources to help others access the same opportunities. Joe, his wife Vi, and their three social-justice-minded daughters created the Jacobs Family Foundation in 1988, with the goal of strengthening families and communities. The foundation began its work as a grant maker in Pasadena, California, where Joe and Vi lived, but in recent years they have focused all of their philanthropy in San Diego's Diamond Neighborhoods, one of San Diego's most culturally diverse communities.

The Diamond Neighborhoods of southeastern San Diego, named for their diamond-shaped business-improvement district, are home to over 88,000 residents. The Diamond Neighborhoods are primarily Hispanic (43%) and African American (30%), with significant Caucasian (11%) and Asian (11%) populations as well as smaller populations of Somalis, Samoans, Sudanese, Laotians, and Chamorro. Close to 60% of the population is non-English speaking, with over 20% of residents' incomes falling below the poverty line. Almost 40% of the region's residents are under the age of 18, making youth a key target population in this community.

The Diamond Neighborhoods are characterized by significant assets. One of the greatest strengths of the Diamond Neighborhoods is the large number of single-family housing units (23,763), reducing the density of the region and increasing the potential for urban renewal. Additionally, there is a significant population of African American middle-class families that have remained within the community over time. The average household size is also low, at 3.53 people per household. The area also has a low-vacancy rate, hovering at just 3%. The community itself has retained a strong sense of pride, with a long history of community organizing work adding to its strength. The great residential assets of this neighborhood have added to its stability. The Jacobs family recognized the potential of these neighborhoods, which are supported by historic community resources such as the Malcolm X Library, the Elementary Institute of Science afterschool science center, and the Tubman-Chavez Center, which houses the office of the local city council representative and serves as a center for community organizing. Today, the future of the Diamond is being shaped by the residents' vision and the Jacobs Foundation's commitment to resident-led ownership and community change. Together, the partnership is working to transform 45 to 80 blighted and underutilized acres into a vibrant "cultural village" with a connected set of residential, commercial, social, educational, and cultural projects benefitting the community.

JCNI's work in the Diamond Neighborhoods began in 1995, when declines in regional income (average family income was only $35,000), deteriorating community safety, and abandoned properties had decreased the quality of life in the area (www.jcni.org). At this time, the Jacobs Family Foundation began to work toward a holistic vision of community redevelopment, with the goal of producing long-term sustainable progress for neighborhood residents. Led by this vision, the family created the Jacobs Center for Neighborhood Innovation the same year. JCNI's leadership believed that if economic prosperity was restored to the area and community safety returned, the residents' quality of life would improve as well. With a mission of "resident ownership of neighborhood change," JCNI set out to partner with the community to develop resident ownership of the plans, change process, and assets in their neighborhoods. JCNI's vision is outlined below.

JCNI is an operating foundation that works in partnership with the Jacobs Family Foundation and community residents to build a stronger community through entrepreneurial projects, hands-on learning relationships, and the creative investment of resources. JCNI helps attract and leverage investment while working with residents to build the capacity of individuals, families, and their communities.

JCNI's work is rooted in the *values* of the following:

- *Relationship*—Working together in learning relationships that connect people
- *Respect*—Valuing the gifts each person brings to a community and honoring the dignity and worth of all
- *Responsibility*—Being responsible to, not for, people working on community change
- *Risk*—Being innovative and daring in our approach, regardless of the risk of failure

JCNI's *goals* are to unite residents, organizations, and funding partners to do the following:

- Build the social well-being of the neighborhoods
- Foster the creation of businesses, jobs, and community wealth
- Support the enhancement of the physical environment through neighborhood-owned assets
- Expand the avenues and opportunities for resident participation in the planning, decision-making, implementation, and ownership of community change

JCNI's work started with the redevelopment of a 20-acre abandoned aerospace factory. This work focused on economic development in the community through social-enterprise business ventures that have been described by the Jacobs Center for Neighborhood Innovation's former CEO, Jennifer Vanica, as "business ventures with a double bottom-line strategy" (Fudge, 2008). This definition expands the traditional definition of business goals to include both financial and social benefits that serve residents of the community first.

The first phases of planning began in 1997 to redevelop this 20-acre abandoned property into what is now Market Creek Plaza. This began a partnership between community residents and JCNI. The 10 acres of the Market Creek Plaza development transformed a brownfield into a commercial and cultural center that was planned, built, and now partially owned by residents. Resident ownership of the planning began with a community team that conducted over 800 needs assessment surveys in the neighborhood. Later, 79% of project construction was completed by local minority and women-owned businesses. The commercial sites were filled with a mix of national anchor businesses identified as necessary by residents (Food 4 Less Grocery Store, Wells Fargo, and Starbucks) and community-owned small businesses (a sit down restaurant, Magnolia's, and a gift shop, Where the World Meets, are two examples). Today, Market Creek Plaza has generated 251 jobs in the community, and 73% of those jobs are held by local residents.

The most unique aspect of the Plaza was the creation of a Community Development Initial Public Offering (CD-IPO) that opened physical ownership of Market Creek Plaza to 416 resident investors who live, work, or volunteer in the community. These resident investors now collectively hold a 20% share of Market Creek Partners, LLC, the company that owns Market Creek Plaza, establishing another venue for wealth to recycle back into the community. To create the broadest opportunities for ownership in the community, the cost to invest was purposefully kept low, with a minimum investment of $200. The offering began with presentations in the community, including trainings to educate residents on the benefits and process of participation in the CD-IPO. The offering was permitted by the California Department of Corporations after 6 years and three submissions. In an effort to safeguard resident investors, many of whom had never invested before, investors weren't allowed to invest more than 10% of their annual income, or 10% of their net worth, with a maximum investment of $10,000. With the CD-IPO, the Jacobs Center and residents realized their goal to create community ownership in the Diamond.

The success of Market Creek Plaza actualized residents' vision for change and renewed the economic vitality of their community. More recently, this vision of economic growth has expanded to the acres around the Plaza. In 2009, construction was completed on the Joe & Vi Jacobs Center, which houses a local cultural kitchen, conference center, and office space for many of the JCNI partner groups. Future plans for the Village at Market Creek include a connected network of affordable housing communities planned by residents, additional commercial space, and cultural venues that will offer more ownership opportunities in the future. Long-term economic investment in this community has avoided neighborhood gentrification in favor of community revitalization.

1995–2006: JCNI's Support for Youth Opportunity in the Diamond

JCNI's economic investment in the Diamond Neighborhoods of southeastern San Diego was initiated at the same time as support for community-led social initiatives including youth development, education, and health programs as part of their comprehensive community development model. JCNI's belief that economic prosperity would drive improved quality of life for residents, including increased educational opportunity, continued to guide its work.

Support for youth-led initiatives continued to be a primary goal. JCNI's trademark "listening" strategy guiding community development efforts led the current interim president, Roque Barros, to ask the residents, "What should our relationships with youth look like? What youth projects are already in existence that we can support?" Resident responses led JCNI to provide support to a neighborhood teen center and the Writerz Blok Urban Arts Park. Significant time and technical resources were also devoted to supporting the organizational development of two existing community-run educational nonprofits, the Elementary Institute of Science (EIS), a summer and afterschool science-enrichment program, and PAZ-ZAZ, a local afterschool tutoring group.

One of JCNI's earliest educational partnerships was developed with the Elementary Institute of Science. EIS was first located in a little white house that it leased from the City of San Diego for $1 per year, with the promise of fixing it up to prevent demolition. Founded by a neighborhood science teacher, Tom Watts, EIS has provided stable, high-quality, hands-on science instruction for southeastern San Diego since 1964. Since the mid-1990s, JCNI staff has provided in-depth technical assistance, guiding the nonprofit's resource development, marketing strategies, and financial management. Since 1985, EIS has been run by Doris Anderson, an active and well-known member of the Diamond Neighborhoods. As the executive director, Mrs. Anderson has led EIS to grow in popularity throughout San Diego, creating high demand for placement in its culturally relevant, hands-on, and academically challenging science afterschool and summer programs. All of the programs are taught by college students who are specialists in the specific area of the science they teach. Class sizes are capped at 10 students, and effort is made to hire culturally diverse instructors to reflect the diversity of the Diamond Neighborhoods. Throughout its growth, the organization has remained committed to the residents of southeastern San Diego, reserving spaces for neighborhood students and intentionally keeping costs for attendance low. Cost to participate in the afterschool program is capped at $140 for a 5-month session that includes four science classes a week. Weekly summer camps are also affordable, priced at $50 a week, providing four science classes a day.

EIS has filled a need for affordable, high-quality science instruction for urban students. According to Darling-Hammond and Sclan (1996), as a group, urban students have only a 50% chance of being taught by a certified math or science teacher, and Oakes (1990) found that math or science teachers in urban schools tend to rate themselves as less confident about their math or science teaching. In 2004, EIS replaced the little white house with a newly constructed 15,000-square-foot, state-of-the-art facility, complete with seven fully equipped science labs, a photography lab, a lecture theater that seats 100, a conference room, five administrative offices, and outside playing space. JCNI was instrumental in guiding EIS through the building's funding and planning as well as eventually paying off the mortgage of the new facility in 2009. Today, EIS serves over 600 students from more than 250 schools in San Diego through their high-quality summer and afterschool science programming. The success of EIS is an example of the long-term, relationship-based approach provided to organizations in the Diamond by JCNI.

An Exercise in Trust: JCNI and Schooling in the Diamond

Historically, JCNI has had limited involvement in area public schools. According to Roque Barros, JCNI's interim president, there was a lack of connection between the schools and Diamond Neighborhood residents that made initial community work difficult. Despite their physical location within the Diamond Neighborhoods, public schools were institutions outside of the Diamond community.

2007–2010: JCNI Partners Directly With Schools, the Diamond Neighborhood Learning Community, and the Opening Doors Project

In 2007, the successful completion of Market Creek Plaza brought in $42 million of economic activity to the Diamond Neighborhoods. At the same time, JCNI's work alongside residents to create the Community Development Initial Public Offering (CD-IPO) project, allowing residents to "own a piece of their block," brought additional economic stability. As the residents of the Diamond Neighborhoods began to experience sustained economic growth for the first time in decades, JCNI asked how it could further support the existing social and educational institutions in the community.

JCNI began by targeting work within local public schools. Ron Cummings, the former chief operating officer at JCNI, directed this work. Ron began with JCNI's commitment to build off of existing community assets. JCNI convened community stakeholders, including students, families, principals, and existing educational organizations. The conversation started by asking those that lived and worked in the Diamond to identify their primary challenges when educating their youth and how JCNI could support change. Then they listened. This initial conversation led to a community meeting where 12 local schools were invited to partner with JCNI. Eight schools responded, and a principals' group, named the Principals' Collaborative, was formed. They met monthly. At each subsequent meeting, JCNI reviewed the initial priorities identified by the community. Based on this list, the Principals' Collaborative began to prioritize focus areas for educational development within neighborhood schools. This group, while initially convened by JCNI, has been continued by the principals and has grown to involve teachers and other educational resource providers. With its growth the group has changed its name to the Diamond Neighborhood Learning Community.

These initial meetings identified four areas where JCNI could support existing public schools: student disengagement, family stability, teacher effectiveness, and resources. The resource topic was easiest to address, and for 2 years JCNI provided $10,000 in unrestricted funds to each school. Unfortunately, with eight schools participating, the extreme cost of this outreach, $80,000/year, prevented future contributions. However, JCNI has expressed interest in helping the schools develop a private foundation to provide additional financial resources in the future. Overarching goals for the Diamond Learning Community are as follows:

- Focus on the whole child, supporting the social, emotional, physical, moral, civic, and cognitive development of all students;
- expand the community of adults working on behalf of students and schools;
- strengthen the capacities of adults, especially families and teachers, to support children's learning more effectively; and
- focus not just on students but on strengthening the community systems that support and serve youth and their families.

The Opening Doors Project

Throughout 2008, the principals continued to meet to design a pilot named the Opening Doors Project. The goal was to create learning communities on each campus, based on much of the decentralization reform efforts of the 1990s (Comer, 1980; Darling-Hammond, 1996; Hess, 1995; Lieberman, 1995; Sizer, 1992). The Opening Doors Project was developed to address concerns with student disengagement and family stability that was identified by community stakeholders.

Program Goals

The Opening Doors Project is designed to embody the aforementioned guiding principles of the Diamond Learning Communities' (DLC) work. The goals of the Opening Doors Project are as follows:

- help *students* move from risk to resiliency and achieve academic and social success in primary and secondary schools and beyond;
- help *teachers* promote more positive behavior in the classroom and create more engaging learning environments for at-risk students; and

- help *families* create stable, structured, emotionally and physically healthy environments that contribute to the academic and social success of their children.

JCNI hired a consultant to help the group design school-wide learning communities and intervention plans. An Opening Doors team was created at each school composed of the principal, counselor, mental health case worker, parent coordinator, teachers, and support staff. These groups meet at weekly, monthly, and quarterly intervals to discuss progress toward individual student goals and school-wide programs. A handful of students in each school were identified who could benefit from additional asset-building interventions. The program identified 35 students in its initial cohort for mental health, physical health, educational, and recreational interventions across all schools. Each student was given individualized creative, academic, social, emotional and recreational resources and goals by the school's Opening Doors team. The anticipated outcomes for each stakeholder group are listed below.

Anticipated Outcomes for Students

Improved academic performance

— Better standardized test scores
— Improved grades
— Regular completion of assignments, including homework
— Increased classroom participation

Improved social/emotional competence

— Increased attendance
— Follows classroom rules
— Fewer disruptions, referrals, suspensions
— Improved emotional regulation
— Improved interactions with adults and peers
— More positive, optimistic outlook

Anticipated Outcomes for Teachers

— Greater focus on teaching, fewer distractions due to improved behavior of identified students
— Enhanced capacity to engage identified students through classroom instructional strategies
— More supported in their efforts to work with identified children in the classroom
— Greater understanding of, and links with, the families of the identified children

— Growth in shared responsibility and collaboration to meet the needs of the identified students

Anticipated Outcomes for Families

— Improved capacity to support children's physical, academic, creative, and social needs
— Greater stability through connections to services/opportunities that improve family welfare
— Increased awareness of their role in meeting a range of needs for their children
— More effective interface with the school and teachers
— Increased capacity to support children's learning at home

Today, Opening Doors is the most developed resource being provided to area schools. According to Ron Cummings, the Opening Doors Project seeks to "create a learning circle of school, family and community leaders that regularly share experiences, knowledge and resources as they work to build a support network that nurtures the unique talents of students, unleashes their unlimited potential to learn, values their diverse cultures and embraces their families" (Ron Cummngs, personal communication, July 2010).

2008–2010: Planning

In the planning stages, focus groups were conducted at each school with teachers, students, and families to identify how stakeholder groups characterized their needs, challenges, and relationships with each other. In addition, each school conducted community and school asset inventories to identify existing structures, services, and organizations within the school and the larger community that could be tapped into to address individual students' needs or needs of the school as a whole. Similarly, Chicago Public Schools also built capacity in the community as a whole by leveraging and connecting existing resources to students and families in order to build off of existing programmatic resources, reducing the need for external funding (Woestehoff & Neill, 2007).

Key findings from focus groups guided project implementation. Focus groups with teachers identified the teachers' need for input in the learning community process at their school site and to be treated with respect and as part of the team. Teachers were also interested in having more time to conduct the additional responsibilities they would be taking on as well as professional development to help them accomplish program goals. Student focus groups found that the most disengaged students reported feeling bored, unfairly treated, and unable to access help. Findings also pointed to a lack of real consequences for misbehavior and a general school climate where youth felt that doing well in school was not socially accepted by their peers. Despite this, there were some academic subjects that were exciting to all students. Student focus groups also found that more engaged students were often involved in afterschool activities. Focus groups with families found that parents wanted more consistent communication with teachers and that teachers needed greater cultural training. Parents also identified the need for more family resources at schools, such as links to counseling and services to help with discipline. All stakeholders noted the need for more afterschool activities that provided transportation.

Finally, easy-to-use evaluation and measurement tools were developed that could be administered by teachers or used by the outreach team as a whole. In addition, all participants were trained in the use of these instruments, and the learning team's responsibilities were outlined. Asset inventories were also created that identified existing community and school resources to help the learning team leverage existing capacity and build relationships within the community. A schedule of all required tasks was created for each school. Finally, a project coordinator was hired by JCNI to monitor the implementation of the program at each school site.

January 2010–June 2012: Implementation
Identifying Students at Risk

Each school identified five children and families to receive greater resources. The Diamond Learning Community defined a set of general parameters that all schools would follow when selecting students (see Figure 5.1). School principals, often in consultation with teachers and counselors, made the ultimate determination as to which students participated.

Student Attrition

A total of 35 children in six neighborhood schools have been involved in the pilot program to date. For most students, implementation began in January 2010. Three children had March 2010 start dates. They replaced children whose parents did not provide permission to participate or who had moved. Five children have left the program, where four moved to different neighborhoods and a fifth was expelled from school. Overall, the project has retained 83% of participating students.

In the pilot, 60% of the targeted children are African American, one-third are Hispanic, and 7% are Filipino. All of the children come from low-income homes. As shown in Figure 5.2, 63% of individual students identified for participation are boys. Figure 5.3 shows that 80% reside with a single parent. One child is cared for by foster parents. As shown in Table 5.1, students are evenly distributed across grade levels. Most first grade students are repeating the grade.

<u>DLC Guidelines for the Selection of Students for the Pilot Phase</u>
- Five children who will be attending the school for at least 2 years, are regularly disengaged from learning, and will benefit from intervention (children with high numbers of absences, referrals, disruptions, incomplete assignments, poor grades).
- These children do not need to be Medicaid eligible and, for the purposes of the pilot, should not already be receiving special education services.
- Parents must allow them to participate. Consider students who have siblings in the school in order to maximize impact.
- Identified students' teachers must be willing to serve on Opening Doors teams.

Figure 5.1. Student-participation selection guidelines.

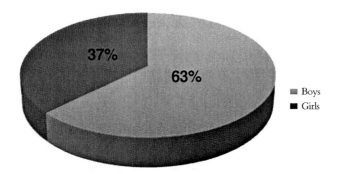

Figure 5.2. Gender.

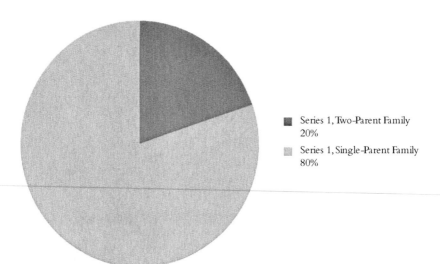

Figure 5.3. Student living situations.

Student Needs

Teachers reported that 20 of 29 students with academic performance data recorded were performing in either the bottom 20% or lowest 10% of their classes. Teacher assessments of student engagement revealed that most of the time a majority of participating students did not pay attention in class, follow directions, participate appropriately, behave respectfully, or demonstrate a positive attitude toward learning (see Table 5.3).

Services

Opening Doors specialists at each school conducted support activities including weekly one-on-one and group therapy sessions with clients, client observations, meetings with families, meetings with teachers, communication with outside

Table 5.1 Grade level of participating student

Kindergarten	First Grade	Second Grade	Third Grade	Fourth Grade	Fifth Grade
1	6	6	7	4	6

Table 5.2 Teacher assessment of academic performances
Compared with other students, the academic performance of this student is:

Lowest 10%	Bottom 20%	Middle 40%	Top 20%	Top 10%
10	10	6	3	0

Table 5.3 Teacher assessment of student engagement

In my class, this student…	VERY TRUE $\geq 75\%$ of the time	SOMEWHAT TRUE $< 75\%$ and $> 50\%$ of the time	NOT VERY TRUE $\leq 50\%$ of the time	NOT AT ALL TRUE $\leq 25\%$ of the time
seems tuned in/ pays attention	4	6	12	7
follows directions	5	9	12	3
participates appropriately	6	6	9	8
is respectful of others	5	6	12	6
has a positive attitude about learning	6	8	7	8

providers, Opening Doors team meetings, monthly JCNI meetings, quarterly DLC meetings, agency training sessions, and reporting activities.

In addition to services provided by Opening Doors specialists, students and families participated in extracurricular activities funded through the pilot. These included small-group tutoring provided by PAZZAZ, a local nonprofit; a 7-week dance/art program provided by Young Audiences; the soap box derby competition offered through PAZZAZ; and YMCA youth and family memberships. Although these opportunities were made available to all students and families, not all of the students participated. Participation was dependent upon parental permission, student interest, student need, student readiness, and logistics (see Table 5.4). In all cases, extracurricular activities were offered to both students and their siblings. In the case of the dance/arts program, students were allowed to select a peer to participate with them. These classes were also extended to other students in the school.

Opening Doors Pilot Project Preliminary Outcomes

Preliminary data compiled from the first cohort of students demonstrate small growth toward programs goals, especially in students' psychosocial development. Academic gains have been small, seen only in math, but are expected to rise as students are given more exposure to the significant assets provided by the Opening Doors Pilot Project. Other significant gains have been seen in student attendance measures and in general classroom behavior.

Student Outcomes

Student outcomes were measured through several instruments. These included surveys administered to teachers, focus groups with teachers and other Opening Doors team members, Opening Doors' specialist case notes and monitoring forms, and comparison of baseline data gathered in December 2009 with data collected in July 2010. Outcome data are organized according to the project's anticipated outcomes. It is important to note that these data do not demonstrate that specific outcomes were directly and solely the result of project activities.

Table 5.4 Student participation in outside activities

	PAZZAZ Tutoring	YMCA	PAZZAZ Soap Box	Young Audiences
# of Students	42 (includes siblings)	2	3	60 (15 Opening Doors students)
# of Student Hours	794.5	NA	NA	35

Changes in Students' Academic Performance and Attendance-Teacher Assessment Data

As seen in Figure 5.4, the numbers of Opening Doors students in the bottom 10% to 20% of their class dropped since the start of the pilot, while the numbers of students performing in the middle 40% to top 20% of their classes increased during the pilot. Figures 5.5, 5.6, 5.7, and 5.8 show that teacher observations identified that greater numbers of participating students paid attention, followed directions, participated appropriately in class, and had positive attitudes toward learning postpilot than they did prepilot.

Focus Groups With Opening Doors Team Members

In addition to survey data, project representatives conducted focus groups with teachers and other Opening Doors team members at five of the six participating schools. In general, the group felt that less progress occurred in academics than in children's emotional and social development. It is anticipated that positive changes in students' emotional regulation, engagement, attendance, and homework completion will ultimately lead to improved academic performance. A number of teachers did report seeing changes in classroom behavior that boded well for future academic success.

> Although my student did not make huge growth academically, he did make huge growth in terms of raising his hand and trying, volunteering, paying attention in the lesson, and partner talking. So he was more engaged and felt more valued inside the classroom. (Teacher)

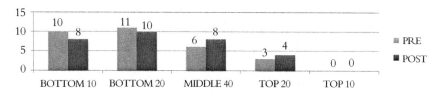

Figure 5.4. Student academic performance.

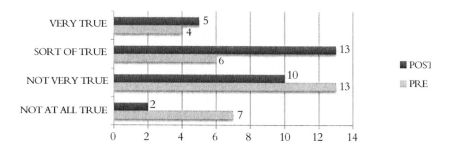

Figure 5.5. Students pay attention in class most of the time.

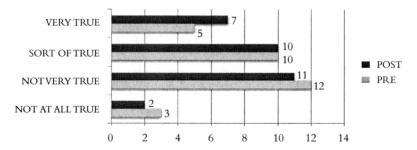

Figure 5.6. Students follow directions most of the time.

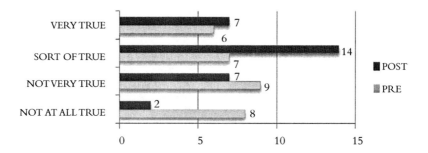

Figure 5.7. Students participate in class most of the time.

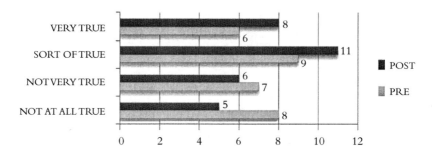

Figure 5.8. Students have a positive attitude toward learning most of the time.

Serving Families

All participating students live in difficult family situations. Most live in single-parent homes. Many are raised by grandparents, aunts, uncles, or foster parents. In addition, the adults raising these children confront problems that encompass economic challenges, homelessness, serious health issues, unemployment, and severe grief. Services administered in the project included helping families meet basic needs for food, clothing, and housing. Providers also accompanied families on doctor's visits, connected them to employment services, helped them secure bus passes, supported them in pursuing educational opportunities, developed parenting and behavioral intervention plans, and linked them to grief counselors. In many cases, the services of the Opening Doors' partner agencies identified in the project asset inventories were tapped, thereby building capacity for the families and the larger community.

One particularly beneficial partnership with Home Start provided resources for families, including counseling for two siblings of an Opening Doors student and employment assistance, résumé building, and rental support for one student's father. One child's mother received in-home parenting support for her youngest child through Home Start. All 10 families at Porter and Knox have been referred to free parenting classes at Home Start. Phone interviews with parents generated feedback regarding their experiences with the Opening Doors program. One example follows:

> [The program] has helped me a lot with [my son's] behavior—[the Opening Doors specialist] has been involved since day one. She comes for home visits and has done counseling. My son is involved in art and he is involved in tutoring. [The Opening Doors specialist] and I are working on developing different techniques for how we can discipline him. Everyone has been excellent.... Without the support of [the Opening Doors specialist] and the project, I would be completely lost.... I am so glad that this project exists. (Mother of a child at Valencia Park Elementary)

Principals were also asked how they felt the Opening Doors Project was impacting the stakeholders involved at their schools. One example is listed below.

> Opening Doors support is building capacity for the families to take on the work of appropriately supporting their struggling children. Parents are learning about interacting in the community to find activities to meet their children's interests. Parents are learning that taking your child to counseling is not a BAD reflection on them as parents, but may even be helpful to their entire family. Parents are learning that their child can succeed academically if they learn a structure to support their children (including homework, response to school reports, attending school events, understanding student academic progress through data and report cards). (Principal at Valencia Park Elementary)

Expanding to Address the Needs of Youth

While the Opening Doors pilot project was getting off the ground in area schools, other needs of youth in the Diamond were identified. The Childcare

Enhancement Center, established 8 years ago to provide high-quality child care to residents, expanded its focus to become the Family Enhancement Center. This group began strategic partnerships with the eight partner schools represented in the Diamond Learning Community and other community health organizations, creating the beginning of an integrated infant-to-high-school holistic youth development pipeline, similar to the Harlem Children's Zone model. This center grew to incorporate five pilot programs addressing social services needs identified by residents, such as mental health counseling, opportunities for physical activity, financial literacy, child social development, and child-parent interactions. By 2008, the center served over 2,300 residents in the Diamond Neighborhoods.

Roque Barros and the Community Building Department brought youth together to listen to how youth could contribute the larger JCNI community organizing efforts. JCNI developed a team of nine interns from each high school in the area, forming a group called the Youth Movement. In addition to youth, this group included nine other nonprofits that serve youth. In 2010, led by youth from Lincoln High School's Social Justice Academy, Youth Movement interns distributed needs assessment surveys in their schools. From these results, three subgroups of the Youth Movement were formed to focus on youth health, education, and youth community organizing in the larger Diamond Neighborhood. Survey results identified the need for increased safety from gang-related activity. The health subgroup took on this topic as gang activity was on the rise. The survey data led the education subgroup to focus on high school dropout prevention, and the youth organizing group prioritized developing youth leadership in the Diamond. In the summer of 2010, the Youth Movement initiated its first youth-run event, the Diamond Classic, to raise awareness around dropout prevention, and more than 900 youth attended.

Decreasing gang violence was also identified as a key area of concern for the Diamond Learning Community. In order to connect the needs of similar stakeholders in the community, the youth health group was connected to other existing groups addressing the same issue. Out of this collaboration the existing Safe Passages group was expanded into the larger Project Safe Way. Project Safe Way connects youth and adults in the Diamond to reduce gang violence in the area. Project Safe Way team members include Project Safe Way coordinators and volunteers, representatives from the San Diego Police Department, the San Diego Gang Commission, the Fourth District Council Office, local youth programs, and school staff. This group works to provide a safe passage to school for kids who are forced to walk across gang lines. Businesses along key routes have placed "Project Safe Way Partner" signs in their windows and report unsafe activity. Spurred to action by significant gang-related youth fatalities in 2008, adults in the community agreed to provide a consistent physical presence along dangerous streets. To expand the antiviolence work to schools, a youth team from Lincoln High School was sponsored by JCNI to attend a Students Against Violence Everywhere (SAVE) conference in Birmingham, Alabama, to learn how to form SAVE clubs at their schools. This antiviolence work, in addition to programs focused on the reintegration of previously incarcerated community members, youth outreach projects led by former gang members, and better relationships between police and residents have produced significantly safer neighborhoods. As a result, there has been a 57% reduction in crime in the neighborhood and no gang-related homicides in 2009.

Conclusion

While the country suffered one of the most severe recessions in history, JCNI's ability to sustain its work in the Diamond Neighborhoods was threatened. However, despite challenges, Market Creek Plaza managed to conduct $50 million in economic activity in 2008, and gross sales were up 20% from the previous year, with job counts rising. In the larger community, more than 100 new jobs were added, attracting an additional $10 million in investment. Finally, the Market Creek Plaza CD-IPO community investment strategy was profitable and paid its investors a full 10% return on investment.

In 2001 and again in 2007, JCNI administered a Quality of Life Survey in conjunction with San Diego State University's Institute of Public Health to measure resident perceptions of life in the Diamond. Despite record funding cuts in the City of San Diego's public safety services, facilities maintenance, and social services since 2003 (Haynes & Tevlin, 2008), impressive gains were seen in resident perceptions of the quality of life within the Diamond Neighborhoods. Specifically, significant improvement was seen among resident perceptions of safety. In 2007, 66% of neighborhood respondents reported "feeling safe" in their neighborhood, and 15% reported recent participation in a neighborhood watch program, which was up 4% from 2001. In addition, this report also included data from the Automated Regional Justice Information System (ARJS), which reported a 16% decrease in the crime index across the four regions surveyed between 2001 and 2007. In 2007, violent crime in the Diamond Neighborhoods was down 29%, and property crime was down 7%, after two decades of crime increases since the 1980s (Caldwell, 2004). Overall, resident perceptions around quality of life were positive, as over 50% of respondents stated that their community had changed for the better in the last 5 years. Finally, in 2007, 54% of respondents stated that they would live in the community "forever," and an additional 8% responded that they would live in the community "until retirement." Since the introduction of Project Safe Way and other neighborhood antiviolence interventions in 2008, there has been a 56% reduction in area violence. In 2008, Project Safe Way was responsible for 32 interventions that deterred gang fights or student violence, 12 incidents of illegal activity that were reported to police and resolved, as well as the correction of 55 public safety issues.

Finally, in 2008, JCNI initiated greater investment with youth in the Diamond than ever before. Youth were asked to report on their needs and take action toward satisfying them. Project Safe Way was created to respond to an eruption in gang violence, ensuring students had a safe passage to school. Eight schools in the community combined resources to form the Diamond Learning Community, which identified existing assets among all stakeholders to "build up" current educational institutions rather than start over with new programs. In addition, youth groups within the community began partnerships with the school district for the first time, and an emerging youth movement campaign rallied youth to stay in school. Overall, youth increased their involvement in community vision through the addition of 20 youth interns to ensure that youth voice is present in the organizing efforts of the Diamond. Over 40 youth working teams began contributing to community work in the Diamond. Finally, 336 youth were involved in community art projects and 3,848 youth classes, activities, and events were conducted in the Diamond, as a whole. In 2008, the educational and social needs of area residents have begun to take center stage after years of economic investment. JCNI's approach targeting root causes of poverty has begun to manifest the expected related benefits to educational and social life in the Diamond. Sustainable educational and social change is beginning, supported by a strong economic foundation.

References

Anyon, J. (1997). *Ghetto schooling: The political economy of school reform.* New York, NY: Teachers College Press.

Caldwell, R. (2004, December 12). On the street: Fighting crime in some of San Diego's toughest neighborhoods. *The San Diego Union-Tribune.* Retrieved from http://www.signonsandiego.com/uniontrib/20041212/news_mz1e12street.html

Comer, J. (1980). *School power: Implications of an intervention project.* New York, NY: Macmillan.

Darling-Hammond, L. (1996). The right to learn and the advancement of teaching: Research, policy and practice for democratic education. *Educational Researcher, 25*(6), 5–17.

Darling-Hammond, L., & Sclan, E. (1996). Who teaches and why? Dilemmas of building a profession for twenty-first century schools. In J. Sikula, T. Butter, & E. Guyton (Eds.), *Handbook of research on teacher education* (pp. 67–101). New York, NY: Macmillan.

Fossey, R. (1996, May/June). Kidding ourselves about school dropout rates. *The Harvard Education Letter,* 5–7.

Fudge, T. (2008, May 21). *These days with Tom Fudge.* KPBS. Retrieved from http://www.jcni.org/news/na/05-21-08.htm

Haynes, T., & Tevlin, A. (2008). *City of San Diego structural budget deficit* (IBA Report # 08–14). San Diego, CA: Office of the Independent Budget Analyst Report.

Hess, A. (1995). *Restructuring urban schools: A Chicago perspective.* New York, NY: Teachers College Press.

Jean-Louis, B., Shoemaker, K., & Gordon, E. (2009). The Harlem Children's Zone: An "all hands on deck" approach to transforming education and community. In H. Varenne, E. W. Gordon, & L. Lin (Eds.), *Perspectives on Comprehensive Education Series: Vol. 2. Theoretical perspectives on comprehensive education: The way forward* (pp. 161–186). Lewiston, NY: The Edwin Mellen Press.

Jehl, J., & Kirst, M. (1993). Getting ready to provide school-linked services: What schools must do. *Education and Urban Society, 25*(2), 153–165.

Lieberman, A. (1995). *The work of restructuring schools: Building from the ground up.* New York, NY: Teachers College Press.

Moran, C., Magill, A., Monteagudo, M., & Gao, H. (2007, September 2). Lincoln High School. *The San Diego Union Tribune.* Retrieved from http://www.signonsandiego.com/multimedia/utmedia/070902lincoln/index.html

Oakes, J. (1990). *Lost talent—The underparticipation of women, minorities, and disabled persons in science.* Santa Monica, CA: Rand Corporation.

Sizer, T. (1992). *Horace's school: Redesigning the American high school.* Boston, MA: Houghton Mifflin.

Tintocalis, A. (2008, July 30). New databases pinpoint San Diego Unified graduation rates. *KPBS public broadcasting.* Retrieved from http://www.kpbs.org/news/2008/jul/30/new-database-pinpoints-sd-unifieds-grad-rate/

Tintocalis, A. (2010, May 28). San Diego Unified faces more budget woes after May revise. *KPBS public broadcasting.* Retrieved from http://www.kpbs.org/news/2010/may/28/san-diego-unified-faces-more-budget-woes-after-may/

Woestehoff, J., & Neill, M. (2007). *Chicago school reform: Lessons for the nation.* Chicago, IL: Parents United for Responsible Education.

Wong, M. (1992, April). *Under siege: Children's perceptions of stress.* Paper presented at the Annual Meeting of the American Psychological Association, Washington, DC.

Programmatic and Institutional Production of Spaces of Comprehensively Conceived Education

6

RE-STORYING THE SPACES OF EDUCATION THROUGH NARRATIVE

Lalitha Vasudevan and Kristine Rodriguez Kerr

> Friends ain't even a word on this rock. You got something coming to you, and you in here, it's just a matter of time, you dig? If that decision's been made ... its only about how many times the hand on the clock goes around until it happens. You just watch TV and wait for it.
>
> C-Roc, Brazil

Introduction

The lines in the epigraph above are spoken by C-Roc, a character in the youth coauthored play *Brazil,* as he talks with a friend who has come to visit him in jail. In his words, readers and audiences are offered an invitation to consider the new realities that a young man facing the possibility of life in prison confronts while awaiting his trial. But these are more than just lines of dialogue and more than a signifier of someone's recollection or experience. The lines of a play can also be read as embodying the traces of the context in which the script was born, the imaginations through which stories were nurtured, and the relationships that coaxed scenes and characters into being. The script, the performances, and the many moments surrounding these artifacts comprise a way of enacting education that is premised upon the notion that the stories we carry with us outside the classroom and those we create together are as important as the stories we must master inside the classroom. In this chapter, we explore stories and the practices of re-storying—a concept that we discuss in more depth later—for how they shape youths' educational experiences; that is, we explore the ways they are institutionally included or excluded and, in particular, the ways that one's constantly evolving life narrative is welcomed in or excluded from educational spaces.

Many scholars who represent diverse epistemic horizons have researched and theorized about the purposes, structures, impacts, shortcomings, and possibilities of education (cf., Cremin, 1970; Dewey, 1916/1997; Greene, 1995; Ladson-Billings, 1994). These perspectives have not always tethered education to school, nor learning to education. Yet, learning and schooling remain inextricably linked in discourses about education. Too often, the business of schooling is bound up in the practices of sorting, labeling, and containing its resident actors: those marked as teachers, students, and so on. Varenne and McDermott's (1998) analysis of American schooling, in particular, delineated the ways in which a child's success or failure in school is in fact a culturally produced position. They argued that the ways that spaces such as schools are organized can afford or constrain the social positions one can inhabit. Thus, school cultures arrange "for certain types of students to take up the position of struggling [learner] by institutionalizing a set of school-related tasks on which they will be measured and found to come up short" (Alvermann, 2002, p. 196),[1] thereby perpetuating a deficit model of schooling.

However, researchers have attempted to reposition this framework by not only calling attention to and resisting these deficit perspectives—in which children and youth and their families are positioned as problems that must be fixed, remediated, or contained—but also by offering an alternative ethos of education rooted in notions of caring and knowing. Villenas (2010), for instance, argued that educators must engage in a process of "unknowing" and thereby undoing the essentializing and reductive perspectives through which they often interact with immigrant families, particularly those of the Latino diaspora. When adhering to perspectives about immigrant families that are saturated with beliefs about what they are lacking, cannot do, or as not caring about their children's education, Villenas claimed that schools serve to further dehumanize immigrant and diaspora children. She echoes the concerns of other researchers (Ferguson, 2000; Noddings, 2003; Valenzuela, 1999) who identify trends in institutional practices and policies that reflect this lack of a thoughtful knowing ethos. Particularly when young people straddle the institutions of justice and education, they are routinely subject to sustained surveillance and a culture of labeling that is embedded in institutional policies and practices, which have both immediate and lasting effects; most notably, a culture of increased surveillance and labeling largely serves to place young people at risk of being dismissed, mischaracterized, misknown, and inequitably educated (for more about the production of risk in the lives of adolescents, see Vasudevan & Campano, 2009). In response, we need new lenses through which to understand and interpret the practices and decisions of youth.

Historically, researchers and "distant others" have storied lives of court-involved youth (Smith, 2000), while the voices and perspectives of these young people, themselves, are largely absent from the research literature (for notable exceptions, see Ayers, 1998; Fisher, Purcell, & May, 2009; Sullivan; 2004). We would argue that not only must our understandings of education be located epistemologically within the experiences of these youth but we also need to make methodological adjustments in how we see and build on these new narratives. However, amid overly routinized school structures, heavy assessment demands, and increasingly few institutional spaces for any creative authoring to occur, educators are largely constrained in their abilities to cultivate emerging knowledge about the myriad forms of youths' discursive and communicative practices (c.f., Mahiri, 2005; Wissman, 2007). This growing body of research about adolescents' literacy-rich lives documents a transformative communicative landscape replete with acts of self-authoring and self-representation, much of which is largely situated outside of formal schooling. Evident within this landscape is verification of the spaces, practices, and communities of education that youth are actively seeking out and in which they are participating.

In our analysis of educational spaces that guides this chapter, we ground our understandings with the lived experiences and discursive recounting of court-involved youth for whom schooling has been an interrupted and not always "successful" experience. We explore the ways in which the youth who were mandated to attend an Alternative to Incarceration Program (ATIP), and who were involved with the Insight Theater Project, participated in this collaborative, arts-based space. We look at the ways they communicated their affiliation with and affinity for the project through their embodied practices and postures, and how they repositioned themselves within their own educational trajectories through their active shaping of the theater project. By doing so, our goal in this chapter is to compose a narrative of education about court-involved youth—who, for too long, have been the object of school failure narratives (as discussed in Duncan, 2005; Ferguson, 2000)—that interprets their actions and discursive practices as meaningful, productive, and participatory.

We include examples of reimagined educational spaces that highlight the variety of participants' experiences in the Insight Theater Project. We also intentionally weave a case study of Chris,[2] a 19-year-old Latino man and a participant from the second cycle of the project, throughout our discussion in order to more fully render the educational nature of Insight. Through his perspective, we explore the nature of participation in this space. And through Chris's interpretations of his experience within Insight, we foreground our analysis of the understandings that were shared, challenged, explored, and supported within and through engagement with Insight. Thus, unlike a traditional account of research findings, we embed data throughout in an effort to illuminate the recursive nature of the project's evolution with the participants' involvement. The context of Insight, for example, is intimately connected to the ways participants were invited into and entered that space, and subsequently to the sense they made of the evolution of their involvement. We have chosen Chris's narrative for the ways it is both representative and distinct, and we complement his case with data from several other participants as well.

In the next section, we frame our discussion of re-storying education with the theoretical perspectives of spatiality, multimodality, and narrative authoring.

While these may appear to be disparate and at times competing ideas, collectively they helped us to conceptualize the multidimensional aspects of education within the theater project we studied. Following this conceptual framing, we explore the context of the theater project in an attempt to understand the beliefs about education that were embedded in its structures and practices. Next, we provide a brief overview of youths' schooling histories that were implicitly invoked and challenged through their participation in Insight. We build on schooling histories in a following section in which we explore the theater project in more depth by illustrating the range and variation of multimodal narrative spaces that participants sought, created, and collaboratively inhabited throughout this project. Our chapter concludes with the pedagogical implications that are suggested by our study of the Insight Theater Project as a site for re-storying youths' educational narratives.

Conceptualizing Re-Storied Spaces of Education

Our analysis of re-storying education in this chapter is predicated upon three theoretical perspectives. First, we engage the lens of spatiality (Lefebvre, 1991; Sheehy & Leander, 2004; Soja, 1996), which foregrounds the dynamic nature of contexts while deemphasizing the material and physical dimensions that tend to be interpreted as static. For example, a bench in a park is not a neutral object; the meaning is found in how this material dimension of the park is ascribed with meaning. The transformation of contexts—buildings, parks, social networking sites, apartment lobbies, classrooms—into "lived spaces" (Soja, 1996) occurs through the social engagement between and among people and surrounding material contexts for a range of purposes. Thus space must be thought of as social space in which we bring with us, on our bodies, our histories of interaction, which inform not only how we interact but also how we make sense of the contexts in which we engage. A moment of dramatic improvisation, for instance, is infused with the production of social space, in which the histories of participants are present through the interaction (Leander, 2004).

We also rely on a multimodal theory of literacies to illuminate the multiple modes through which we write ourselves into the world, metaphorically and quite literally. Through the orchestration of multiple modalities of expression and communication—such as multifunction mobile phones, digital cameras, a pen, social networking platforms—individuals, and youth in particular, compose a variety of texts for a variety of purposes. The theoretical concept of multimodality provides a framework for understanding composing and, more precisely, for making sense of how multiple texts and multiple modes collectively express a multi-layered narrative (Hull & Nelson, 2005). A digital story, for example, is a text that not only brings together audio, image, written text, and narration but also one that communicates a unique message because of its multimodality; furthermore, it is an artifact of the space in which it was produced, and can be read as such. A multimodal approach to the analysis of meaning making allows educators and researchers to attend more fully to the resources involved in composing, which are especially visible in the composing of a digital story (Jewitt, 2008). In our analysis of the Insight Theater Project, we focused our attention on the everyday modalities that were engaged by participants to convey meaning, communicate with one another, and make themselves known, such as voice, the body, and a piano in the rehearsal area.

To our understandings of Insight as a multimodal, social space, we bring the perspective of narrative authoring. Beyond merely the verbal telling of tales, we author ourselves through the engagement of cultural artifacts, both objects and symbols, which have been collectively ascribed with meaning (Holland, Lachiotte, Skinner, & Cain, 1998). Thus, we identified the ways in which youth authored themselves across space and time and through the engagement of various artifacts, modes, and modalities of expression (Rowsell & Pahl, 2007). Among the authoring moments we observed were the ways youth interacted with objects in rehearsal studios and each other; the varied or consistent postures the same young man or young woman assumed in response to varied stimuli; and the impact of audience on the stories the youth shared.

For Chris and his fellow Insight participants, education was at once a carefully crafted and improvised experience of which they were not only the architects but also the beneficiaries. The perspectives previously introduced help us to ground our discussion of re-storying, which we define as the reimagining of possibilities through lived and embodied performances. Whereas written narratives and verbal storytelling were the hallmark of Insight, we also attended to the nonverbal and performative nature of this space. While working collaboratively to compose a script for performance, participants were rewriting their own stories and themselves in meaningful ways.

Consider the significance of the piano in the following scene. Before, between, and after rehearsals, the piano, which had seemingly been forgotten in the corner of the practice room, became the center of interplay between the actors, texts, and practices in this composition space. Often sharing the bench seat, one participant played while others gathered around the piano to sing, climbed on stage to dance, or linked arms to sway with the beat. In one video clip, recorded during one instance of spontaneous piano play, participants move in and out of the camera view, changing location within the room while remaining part of the activity. Starting one verse and abruptly moving to a new song, the group transitioned through the hits of artists popular in the 1980s and 1990s. The change between songs was equally prompted by either lyrics sung out in the space between songs or by piano chords tentatively struck as the player became more confident in the match between the sounds in the air and the song in his or her head. Developing organically from the group, the spontaneous performances around the piano became an important part of rehearsal, particularly for Chris, as his vocal ability was revealed and his identity as someone who could and liked to sing was positively reinforced. As we will see through the unfolding of Chris's case, these spontaneous performances became one of many ways for Chris to playfully experiment with the many facets of his role as performer while crafting an expectation of group participation within Insight project space.

Our focus on re-storying education, therefore, addresses the ways in which the young people involved with Insight, many of whom described having highly interrupted schooling experiences prior to their arrival at ATIP, contributed to the creation of new educational geographies in the ways they participated in and helped to constitute the theater project. We explore how they lived, performed, and re-storied education across space and modalities.

Contextualizing Insight

The Insight Theater Project was born out of a collaborative desire between two teachers, Dave and Norman, to provide a venue for the stories of court-involved youth to find diverse and interested audiences, and for the youth to engage in storytelling and dramatic performance in the process of making their stories accessible. In order for the reader to more fully appreciate the context of the Insight Project, we provide a description of ATIP, the institutional context within which Insight was born and facilitated.

ATIP is one of several incarceration alternatives available for court-involved youth in New York City, ages 17 to 23, and has a legacy of youth advocacy and innovation reaching back over 40 years. The youth population at ATIP mimics the trends of "minority"[3] youth overrepresentation found in jails and detention facilities around the country. Approximately 55% of the youth are identified as African American, 40% are identified as Latino, and the remaining 5% are identified as having other ethnic and racial backgrounds. The program uses a case-management approach to facilitate a customized implementation of the wide range of services available for youth. These services included an employment and internship program, academically focused GED and college preparatory classes, drug and alcohol treatment, counseling, and other arts and media electives—of which Insight was one. The latter is a program strand that has enjoyed an organizational presence in a variety of ways throughout ATIP's history in the form of dramatic performances and painting and mixed-media classes. With financial support garnered from an external grant and internal institutional funds, two teachers piloted their theater initiative in the spring of 2008.

Between 2008 and 2009, three cycles of the Insight Theater Project were facilitated, out of which two plays were produced and three sets of performances were held. The three cycles also included the participation of 33 young men and women, of whom 11 completed both phases of a full cycle. Each cycle concluded with participants performing their coauthored plays on stage for three nights of packed audiences. Following each performance, the actors engaged with the audience in the form of question and answer talkbacks. While at first blush this statistic—a 33% completion rate—might raise concern, as we will see from Chris's case, completing all phases of the project was not the only marker of "success" or meaningful participation in this project. Performance was a significant indicator of participation and engagement within this project and, as Gustavson (2007) notes, "performance does not only happen at the end of the process" (p. 4). Throughout the different phases of the Insight Project, participants engaged in intrinsically aesthetic and artistic crafting that enabled what Lefebvre (1991) has defined as work, as that which is distinct from product. He notes, "Whereas a work has something irreplaceable and unique about it, a product can be reproduced exactly, and is in fact the result of repetitive acts and gestures" (p. 70). This creative work entailed many forms of learning, some of which are noted here and others that emerge throughout the rest of the chapter. For instance, the young men and women of Insight learned basic acting techniques, such as short and long-form improvisation, and performed several skits using these techniques. They listened to one another's stories and had audiences for their narratives, which they shared orally and sometimes in performance. In rehearsals leading up to the final performance, participants collaborated with each other, their teachers, and a playwright to compose full-length scripts that evolved out of improvised skits. As one student who did not finish the full cycle recalled, "One day we did that and the next day—it was always something new. That's what made it fun and interesting. I looked forward to coming here" (Rashaad, interview). For youth like Rashaad, whose previous schooling did not always provide a reason for attendance, the realization that institutionally sanctioned activities could be generative and afford opportunities for participation was significant.[4]

During postproduction interviews, some participants, who did not finish a full project cycle, communicated a sense of accomplishment and pride in discussing their involvement, echoing the findings of Hull, Kenney, Marple, and Forsman-Schneider (2006), who analyzed the multilayered understandings of success that circulated among adolescent males involved in a digital storytelling project. As Jamaal noted, "[It] [f]eels like I accomplished something. I had to make up my mind and say you know what? I'm going to try it. And I'm glad I did. Like, now I have like hard evidence, hard proof that I, you know, that I did it. And I tried to go all the way through, but you know. It was fun. And I had a ball ... I would do another one in a heartbeat." In some cases, feelings of accomplishment were mixed with regret for personal decisions that caused the end of their participation, while others commented on the bad luck of an illness the week before the final performance. For those who were not able to perform in the final production, they maintained ownership over the specific scenes and characters they had helped craft, despite a replacement actor filling in. Education as a lived experience was embodied in each phase of this project.[5] Youth felt that they could participate and be a part of this project and that their presence and input was valued. Even when they were no longer physically able to participate, traces of their participation—via the stories they had told, the characters they had created, and the scenarios they had improvised—remained. When asked to reflect on their experiences with Insight, participants expressed a heightened awareness of how education was alive in this space. Additionally, as we show in the next section, this recognition also presented participants with an opportunity to reflect critically on their past schooling experiences through the prism of this "successful" experience.

Participants became involved with the program on the recommendation of someone at ATIP—a case manager, a teacher, or another participant—who recognized they might be interested and urged them to audition for the project. Chris, like many of his fellow participants who had never previously performed, was reluctant to audition. He reflected on this anxiety during an interview following his involvement with the second cycle of Insight. "Yeah, I didn't want to go, I didn't want to ... I told 'em I wasn't interested. I didn't want to do it. But then it was just like, I was nervous, I had stage fright" (Chris interview, January 29, 2009). Encouraged by his case manager to audition, Chris seemed both surprised and proud of himself for trying out. When he recalled the director's (Dave) reaction to his audition, Chris stated, "They liked me, so I guess, that's how I got in." Over the course of the Insight Project, Chris, whose hair was often cut close both on his head and on his face, developed into a confident performer who was able to channel his quiet, contemplative nature into an authentic creation and powerful portrayal of his character, C-Roc. As Chris and the other participants took on varied roles, so, too, did Dave, their director and one of the project facilitators.

Dave's position was unique as a teacher. With more freedom than in the Pre-GED classes he taught, Dave was able to embrace a sense of the unexpected within the pedagogical identity he performed in the context of Insight. He brought in talented teaching artists like Todd,[6] the group's writer in residence, and Mel, a professional actor who spent time with the group at various stages of play development, rehearsal, and even performance. Dave was not only the facilitator and project director, but he also shared stories, performed improvs with the participants, and took acting and narrative risks similar to those he asked of the youth. As a teacher, Dave modeled deep listening, and the participants followed his example. In this site, the broader landscape of adolescents' emerging literacies (e.g., texting, social networking, video and photo sharing) was organically integrated into the larger context of these new geographies as teachers placed primacy on knowing their students in order to teach them (Vasudevan, 2009).

The data we include in this chapter were collected during the three cycles of the Insight project between 2008 and 2009, as part of a documentation project that is a part of a larger ethnography of the education, digitally mediated lives, and literacy practices of court-involved youth at ATIP. These data include participant observation field notes, multiple audio-recorded interviews with project participants, participant surveys, audience surveys, audio recordings of the talkbacks, and a variety of artifacts. The latter consisted of data that were spontaneously created within the project space, such as video of unscripted moments of group singing and audio recordings of group dinner conversations, as well as data that were produced specifically to meet project needs, such as head shots of the participants that lined the entrance to their public performances, programs that were distributed to the audience members, and masks, some of which were incorporated into the performances. Interviews and performance talkbacks were transcribed and analyzed for emergent themes. Field notes and surveys were also coded for emergent themes, and the project team—including researchers and project facilitators—met together regularly to reflect on the process and discuss emergent themes as well. Collectively, these data tell multiple stories of how the spaces of education were reimagined, performed, and embodied by Insight participants, many of whom had experienced schooling as an interrupted and highly charged space.

Participants' Schooling Histories

When asked to reflect on their Insight experiences, participants often drew direct comparisons to their schooling histories and educational opportunities. While all participants spoke about interrupted schooling and being labeled at young ages, the stories surrounding when and why their trouble with school began were different. In this section we briefly look at how they articulated understandings of their past school participation, including the role of teachers. We offer these interview excerpts as a canvas against which to render a contrasting image of education beyond the walls and outside the trappings of schooling culture that the Insight Theater Project engendered. In saying so, it is not our intent to portray Insight as a utopian space, but rather as one in which authoring risks could be taken, roles were not fixed, and expectations were collectively negotiated.

Some participants remembered being well behaved in elementary school, while others remembered fighting and getting into trouble at the same age. As Chris recalls, "Um, and then it started showing when I was in like the fourth grade, fifth grade. I started running out the class. Acting like a knucklehead. Running around. Chasing all the girls." Common themes shared by participants as explanations of their behavior and/or decision to stop attending school included concerns about peers, distractions regarding the opposite sex, and boredom. Jesse suggests another reason for a slow separation from school when he states that he "didn't want to go to school anymore [because] [i]t got boring." Changing schools, either because they moved from one school district to another or because they graduated to a new building, also contributed to participants' continued frustrations. And as Rashaad notes, regardless of the disruptions, his experience of education in schools often boiled down to a simple reality: "Different building, same things. Got in trouble."

In trying to make sense of their patterns of past behavior, participants also shared frustrations with not feeling known or understood at school. One young man stated "[I was] smart. I was challenging. No one gets me. No one got me. Never get me. I wasn't fully understood." While some participants shared stories of positive experiences with teachers and learning, others shared contrasting accounts. For instance, another young man made the following claim: "I can't learn with a teacher that's just that just comes to do her job and not really put an effort into it." He echoed other participants who also reported feeling misunderstood by teachers; their responses only served to underscore the increasingly rigid constraints that are placed on teachers today—particularly with increases in standardized testing, mandatory curricular requirements, and increased surveillance in schools—that make it difficult to exercise the pedagogical flexibility that Dave employed. He was responsive through his pedagogy to the voiced and unspoken needs of the participants, which was crucial in cultivating an overall ethos of trust that came from a shared commitment to listening and understanding. For the project to be meaningful, participants needed to be comfortable and willing to share, listen, value, and work within each other's personal stories. These were characteristics of an educational space that stood in stark contrast to the spaces with which they had been familiar previously.

Re-Storying School by Storying Education

Elsewhere we have described in further detail the many ways in which authoring occurred within Insight across six dimensions: improvisation, focused storytelling sessions, composing scripts, rehearsals, performances, and talkbacks (Vasudevan et al., 2010). As a result of the direct storytelling and listening that were characteristic in each of these dimensions, participants cultivated an ethos of trust within the group. While there was a mutual vulnerability in sharing personal stories and emotions, there was also a sense of experimentation that made sharing possible. In an interview discussing the creative process, one participant, Jamaal, explained his willingness to experiment with storytelling, noting "it's not nothing that you can really criticize me for cause I didn't have no time to work on this or anything. This is just something that I'm doing off my head, so." Freed from the pressure of uninformed critique, participants authored and inhabited multiple roles within the space of Insight, illustrating that there was more than one way to "be" a participant. There were several ways the Insight Theater Project supported participants to re-story educational spaces through their involvement in and engagement of this narrative space. We explore two of these affordances next. First, we discuss how the participants were able to perform multiple selves—not only the roles they played but also the social and cultural identities they revealed—using a variety of discursive modes. And the second that we explore here was the ways in which the participants' stories—their histories, lived experiences, and sense making about the worlds in which they live—were recognized, appreciated, and integral to the narrative process.

Performing Multiple Selves Through Multiple Discursive Modes

The many contours of Chris's voice could be heard across myriad spontaneous performances within Insight in forms that sharply contrasted with his description of his behavior during his "most successful" time in traditional school settings. In an interview about school history, Chris described himself during his elementary school years as "basically, always quiet, real quiet, real, real quiet. Never talked to anybody. Um, even though I was still having issues at home, I never said nothing. I was just cool. I stayed to myself." Despite admitting to having "issues at home," about which it may have been helpful to seek out an adult to talk to, successful participation in school meant being quiet and staying to himself. While Chris continued to have a soft-spoken quality, Insight became a place for Chris to make himself known (and to claim a voice in multimodal ways).

Often captured in photographs with a downward gaze, Chris's participation in Insight seems to directly contrast with his soft-spoken nature, small stature, tightly fitting clothing, and closely cropped hair (all features that would seemingly allow him to remain invisible or at least to fade into the background). In spite of his history of quiet participation in school, Chris became an engaged and committed participant of Insight. Both serious in his performance and spontaneously playful, Chris was undeniably an active member of this group. Both on and off the stage, Chris participated "loudly," by which we mean that his presence was felt and heard; he often joined his peers during spontaneous piano performances and contributed when others were sharing stories or other narrative moments, some of which we illustrate later in this chapter as we discuss participants' various enactments of education throughout the narrative spaces of Insight.

In addition to the role of a vocal performer off stage, Chris took on the identity of talented actor—an identity which he not only embraced but which was also mirrored back to him through other Insight participants. Kalil, another participant, said in an interview about Chris: "He was a good actor. He knew how to say lines. Like he made you really believe, like, that he was the character." In this way, Chris became known through his embodied actions—for example, as an active, consistent participant—and the way he accessed and used the space to author and perform multiple selves.

Other participants described the experience of changing and "trying on" new characters almost as an escape—a way of avoiding individual concerns for a few hours. Jamal explains this feeling of escape:

> What it really did for me was it took me, like as soon as I walked into this building, I was away from the world. Like I stepped into a new world. I knew that I wasn't Jamal no more. I came in [as] T. Like, I came in like 'oh how can I say this line or which way can I do this and how can I perform,' you know so it took me out of my own, all my troubles. I just left everything behind and I just became a new person, you know. (Interview)

Echoing Jamal's reflections, we see Insight as a space of possibility, where participants were able to play with multiple identities. Characters and characterizations afforded participants' occasional respite from daily routines. This theme of escape is also echoed in the overarching theme of the play *Brazil* in which one of the characters delivers a monologue about the desire to hide away on a beach in Brazil, the country. Escape did not, however, represent a false reality. Rather, in these moments when scenes were being depicted, Dave pushed participants to imagine more fully the histories, motivations, communities, priorities, and choices of the characters they were portraying.

While the participants' depictions of their prior schooling experiences paint a picture largely rooted in regimentation and routine, it was also clear that their educational geographies were not quashed beyond repair. Through their participation in this theater project, each of these young men and women were actively engaged in meaningful and "deliberative" (Varenne, 2007) interactions throughout their daily lives. In the ways they interacted with the different dimensions of the project, these young people were involved in acquiring, exchanging, producing, critiquing, and disseminating knowledge about a range of concepts, including their own lives.

Creating Spaces of and for Youths' Stories

Within the spaces of education, the arts can foreground creativity and cultivate a more complex understanding of relationships between learners and their environments than is currently evident in schools and even in afterschool programs (Gadsden, 2008). Dramatic interpretation and engagement with the stories of youth catalyzed these new understandings within Insight, often through the creation and consideration of new characters. Chris describes the experience of taking on unfamiliar characters in this way: "Like, it's cool like, I like, I don't know like, it's just cool like, acting like another person. Putting, really putting your whole self, like getting out of your body and jumping into that body. It's just, it's cool." This embodying of new characters was reflective of an ongoing narrative of feeling heard and having one's stories validated. In describing the collaborative process of working with Todd, the playwright who rehearsed with participants throughout the process, Chris recalls, "he was taking notes and whatever we told him, the words, like what really goes on in life, like we telling him like, this is how you say it. These are the words we've got to use. And he really put that in the play and the actual scripts." Like Chris, nearly every interviewed participant mentioned the collaborative work with Todd as unique to the Insight experience. Perhaps in response, participants began listening to each other—becoming more aware of the word choices they used and heard in real-world conversation as they questioned, challenged, and worked to develop a valid script. Reworking scenes with Todd allowed the participant–actors to assume authority over the scripting process.

Coupled with the opportunity to embody, however temporarily, the realities of a scripted character came the chance to become familiar with new physical surroundings. Jamal's reflection about entering "the building" refers to the professional theater space, which housed the rehearsal studios and performance stages in which the Insight plays were performed. Community spaces—the dance studio, museums, galleries, and, in our case, the professional theater—hold great significance for cultivating art and "artists' work in their own setting" (Heath, 2001, p. 15). Thus, the multilayered storytelling structure that was grounded in the youths' lived experiences was further animated by the theater context. The space and the stories came to have mutually constitutive effects on the other, wherein participants would take up postures of comfort and community: leaning against the piano while another played; walking around the studio rehearsal space to "get into character"; sitting in a corner with their backs to the room and to engage in close reading of scenes and the whole script. Laughter, music, and familiar tones of call and response filled the air in this space where stories were shared and personal histories intermingled with collective future possibilities.

By swapping characters, situations, goals, and personalities, theater projects in particular "provided real life contexts for learning as the outcome of diverse struggles rather than as the passive reception of information" (Giroux, 2000, p. 127). In discussing his character's interaction with another during the play, Chris explains,

> Well, like, basically he talks to [my character] about just decisions I make in life, in general. Um, he talked about like, how his son is doing, which is my friends—we all grew up together. That's how we had that close bond. Um, he tells me, he's giving me advice because I'm facing 25 to life. Gives me advice on how to handle it. And how, I can fight it in court and stuff like that, so, that was ... and I tell him about um, his son and all that. You know, things like that. I was giving him advice. We's basically feeding each other with that. (Interview)

Along with the dialogue that develops out of an educational engagement with the arts, the dialogues that develop between and about characters "[help] these young playwrights consider the multiple voices and perspectives of the people in the stories they share" (Fisher, 2008, p. 97). The collaborative nature of the Insight theater project allows the participants as well as the characters they developed to "feed each other with advice" and to enter into new relationships, support and challenge existing power dynamics, and explore new spaces of identity formation (Fisher, 2008; Leard & Lashua, 2006).

Our discussion of education resonates with the work of some anthropologists (Bartlett, 2007; Varenne, 2007) who seek to broaden discussions of education beyond schooling and the classroom and outside of institutionally sedimented roles of teacher and student. Such an ethos is evident in youth media and arts organizations, where adults and youth engage in a collective and "collegial" (Soep & Chavez, 2005) pedagogy in a way that builds on the strengths of a community toward the accomplishment of collectively established goals. We conclude, then, on a note of possibility that renewed social arrangements, grounded in the meaningful work of stories, can bring about for reimagining educational spaces.

Pedagogical Considerations of Re-Storying Education

Much of the agency that we saw youth in Insight asserting was grounded in a narrative authority that we have described here, through the experiences of Chris, as re-storying. We strongly advocate for the design of educational spaces that attend to lived and embodied performances of education that youth carry with them as they move through the walls of various institutions. Institutions, such as schools and youth-development organizations, must build on the knowledge gained from arts-based programs in which youth are more likely to assume authority over their educational experiences. One approach to realizing this goal includes creating opportunities for the narratives of youth to inform and shape educational contexts.

We agree with Gustavson (2007), who argues that "if we are to create, support, and sustain schools that are meaningful and rigorous learning spaces for youth, we—teachers, administrators, and parents—need to cultivate genuine interests in the ways youth work and learn in their everyday lives" (p. 7). Both youth participants and adults who bore the designation of "teacher" functioned as educators in the Insight Theater Project in which members of this community learned with and from each other. Storytelling can offers a way for youth to participate in and also shape classrooms, schools, and other institutional spaces.

Reflecting on his involvement with Insight and his growth from reluctant to active participant, Chris offers the following advice: "Don't be afraid to try new things. I mean, you never know what'll be the outcome. What is likely, if you try something new it will always be a positive outcome. Even if you don't like it, it will still come out with a positive outcome." Chris followed his own advice when he accompanied us as a copresenter at an academic conference in 2009. Quiet Chris, who never shed his quiet gestures but whose presence was undeniably pronounced, developed into a confident performer on as well as off stage. A narrative space, which need not be limited to theater projects, provided the rich context for Chris and his peers to craft terrain in which they felt welcome, had their stories heard and engaged, and were invited to participate in meaningful and myriad ways. These young people re-storied the spaces of education through their actions, relationships, participation, and literacy practices, and it is in their embodied performances that we can find educative possibilities.

Notes

1. Alvermann (2002) uses the word *reader* in the original quote; however, within her broader discussion of Varenne and McDermott's "culture as disability" critique, in which this articulation of struggling reader is embedded, Alvermann underscores the power of ascribed reading identities to shape children's and adolescents' overall schooling experiences. Thus we invoke the term *learner* here to signify that implicit connection.
2. All names are pseudonyms.
3. We recognize that the term *minority* is problematic in the way that it adheres fixity to the meaning of one's physical and social characteristics, even as we know and believe in the fluidity and complexity of one's identity. However, we use *minority* in this instance

to echo the language used in reports of criminal-justice statistics and to underscore the overrepresentation of Black and Latino males, ages 18 to 25, who are under some form of correctional control.

4. There were a variety of circumstances that prevented students from completing the full process, from audition through to public performance, which included mandatory participation in a 28-day alcohol-treatment program, illness during the week of final performance, and conflicting financial obligations, among others; we offer these reasons not as excuses for why participants did not "complete" the cycle but rather to highlight the conditions and pressures that youth at the intersection of multiple social institutions are subject to by virtue of their age and status.

5. For a more complete discussion of the Insight process and six dimensions of authoring, see Vasudevan, Stageman, Rodriguez, Fernandez, and Dattatreyan (2010).

6. Actual first names of the teaching artists have been used at their request.

References

Alvermann, D. E. (2002). Effective literacy instruction for adolescents. *Journal of Literacy Research, 34*(2), 189–208.

Ayers, W. (1998). *A kind and just parent: The children of juvenile court.* Boston, MA: Beacon Press.

Bartlett, L. (2007) Human capital or human connections? The cultural meanings of education in Brazil. *Teachers College Record 109*(7), 1613–1636.

Cremin, L. A. (1970). *American education: The colonial experience 1607–1783.* New York, NY: Harper & Row.

Dewey, J. (1997). The democratic conception in education. In *Democracy and education* (pp. 81–99). New York, NY: Free Press. (Original work published 1916)

Duncan, G. (2005). Critical race ethnography in education: Narrative, inequality, and the problem of epistemology. *Race, Ethnicity and Education, 8*(1), 95–116.

Ferguson, A. A. (2000). *Bad boys: Public schools in the making of black masculinity.* Ann Arbor: University of Michigan Press.

Fisher, M. T. (2008). Catching butterflies. *English Education, 40*(2), 94–100.

Fisher, M. T., Purcell, S. S., & May, R. (2009). Process, product, and playmaking. *English Education, 41*(4), 337–355.

Gadsden, V. L. (2008). The arts and education: Knowledge generation, pedagogy, and the discourse of learning. *Review of Research in Education, 32*(1), 29–61.

Giroux, H. A. (2000). *Stealing innocence: Youth, corporate power, and the politics of culture.* New York, NY: Palgrave.

Greene, M. (1995). *Releasing the imagination: Essays on education, the arts, and social change.* San Francisco, CA: Jossey-Bass.

Gustavson, L. (2007). *Youth learning on their own terms: Creative practices and classroom teaching.* New York, NY: Routledge.

Heath, S. B. (2001). Three's not a crowd: Plans, roles, and focus in the arts. *Educational Researcher, 30*(7), 10–17.

Holland, D. C., Lachiotte, W., Jr., Skinner, D., & Cain, C. (1998). *Identity and agency in cultural worlds.* Cambridge, MA: Harvard University Press.

Hull, G., & Nelson, M. E. (2005). Locating the semiotic power of multimodality. *Written Communication, 22*(2), 224–261.

Hull, G., Kenney, N. L., Marple, S., & Forsman-Schneider, A. (2006). *Many versions of masculine: An exploration of boys' identity formation through digital storytelling in an after-school program.* Afterschool Matters Occasional Paper Series. New York, NY: Robert F. Browne Foundation.

Jewitt, C. (2008). Multimodality and literacy in school classrooms. *Review of Research in Education, 32*(1), 241–267.

Ladson-Billings, G. (1994). *The dreamkeepers: Successful teachers of African American children.* San Francisco, CA: Jossey-Bass.

Leander, K. M. (2004). A spatial history of a classroom literacy event. In K. Leander & M. Sheehy (Eds.), *Spatializing literacy research and practice* (pp. 115–142). New York, NY: Peter Lang.

Leard, D. W., & Lashua, B. (2006). Popular media, critical pedagogy, and inner city youth. *Canadian Journal of Education, 29*(1), 244–264.

LeFebvre, H. (1991). *The production of space.* Oxford, England: Wiley-Blackwell.

Mahiri, J. (2005). Street scripts: African American youth writing about crime and violence. In J. Mahiri (Ed.), *What they don't learn in school: Literacy in the lives of urban youth* (pp. 19–42). New York, NY: Peter Lang.

Noddings, N. (2003). *Caring: A feminine approach to ethics and moral education* (2nd ed.). Berkeley: University of California Press.

Rowsell, J., & Pahl, K. (2007). Sedimented identities in texts: Instances of practice. *Reading Research Quarterly, 42*(3), 388–404.

Sheehy, M., & Leander, K. M. (2004). Introduction. In K. Leander & M. Sheehy (Eds.), Spatializing literacy research and practice (pp. 1–14). New York, NY: Peter Lang.

Smith, B. J. (2000). Marginalized youth, delinquency, and education: The need for critical-interpretive research. *The Urban Review, 32*(3), 293–312.

Soep, E., & Chavez, V. (2005). Youth radio and the pedagogy of collegiality. *Harvard Educational Review, 75*(4), 409–434.

Soja, E. (1996). *Thirdspace: Journeys to Los Angeles and other real-and-imagined places.* Oxford, England: Blackwell Publisher Ltd.

Sullivan, M. L. (2004). Youth perspectives on the experience of reentry. *Youth Violence and Juvenile Justice, 2*(1), 56–71.

Valenzuela, A. (1999). *Subtractive schooling: U.S.–Mexican youth and the politics of caring.* Albany: State University of New York Press.

Varenne, H. (2007). Difficult collective deliberations: Anthropological notes toward a theory of education. *Teachers College Record, 109*(7), 1559–1588.

Varenne, H., & McDermott, R. (1998). *Successful failure.* Boulder, CO: Westview Press.

Vasudevan, L. (2009). Performing new geographies of teaching and learning. *English Education, 41*(4), 356–374.

Vasudevan, L., & Campano, G. (2009). The social production of adolescent risk and the promise of adolescent literacies. *Review of Research in Education, 33*(1), 310–353.

Vasudevan, L., Stageman, D., Rodriguez, K., Fernandez, E., & Dattatreyan, G. (2010). Authoring new narratives with youth at the intersection of the arts and justice. *Perspectives on Urban Education, 7*(1), 54–65.

Villenas, S. (2010). Thinking Latina/o education with and from Latina/Chicana feminist cultural studies: Emerging pathways, decolonial possibilities. In Z. Leonardo (Ed.), *Handbook of cultural politics and education* (pp. 451–476). Rotterdam, Netherlands: Sense Publishers.

Wissman, K. K. (2007). "Making a way": Young women using literacy and language to resist the politics of silencing. *Journal of Adolescent and Adult Literacy, 51,* 34–349.

7

THE DRUM IN THE DOJO

Re-Sounding Embodied Experience in Taiko Drumming

Kimberly Powell

In proposing alternative anthropological perspectives on education, Hervé Varenne stated that "Many suggest that schools—as organized almost anywhere around the world—are not particularly good at educating—especially about what is most important in a person's life, whether it be religion, political ideology, artistic identity, and all that makes the particular character of a person's outlook on life" (Varenne, 2007, p. 1539). The arts have long provided critical places through which those involved respond, explore, and express complex social issues. A number of community- and ethnically based performance ensembles use music, dance, theater, and visual forms to address such issues as identity, racial and ethnic marginality, and community empowerment. Perhaps because of their relationship to heightened and orchestrated somatic modes of attention, the arts and artistic venues are often studied and cited for offering alternative ways of knowing that highlight the role of the body and the senses (e.g., Bresler, 2004).

In this chapter, I discuss *taiko* drumming as an educational and cultural practice that orchestrates embodied and, specifically, sonic forms of knowing. North American taiko drumming is a distinctive practice situated in a history of Japanese drumming practices, Japanese American experiences of immigration and internment, Eastern philosophies of mind and spirituality, and world music influences. I first discuss the history of taiko, highlighting its aesthetic conventions of sound and movement, and then focus specifically on one particular influential taiko ensemble, San Jose Taiko, an arts organization that runs a conservatory and a professional performance ensemble in San Jose Japantown, California. I frame San Jose Taiko as an educational institution through a discussion of its pedagogical framework, philosophy, and specific teaching and learning practices. Through a specific focus on critical somatic and sonic aspects of the educational environment, I address multimodal ways of composing not only musical practices but also identities-in-practice that emerge through sound and embodied experiences with learning taiko. Such experimentation will be addressed in terms of the recomposition of Asian American identity, as practiced through the balance between prescriptive forms of sound and movement with the musical agency of San Jose Taiko's members.

Three Founding Contemporary Taiko Organizations in North America

As a means of contextualizing San Jose Taiko as a cultural institution that enables and facilitates the larger cultural practice of Asian American identity, I discuss some key influences on their musical, curricular, and pedagogical approaches to taiko. Taiko scholars generally agree that the first ensembles of taiko, in which different drums played different parts of a whole piece when played together, generally referred to as *kumidaiko* (harmony drum), were established in the 1950s in Japan (Uyechi, 1995). Kumidaiko is the practice of playing several different drum sizes and styles together in relation to each other, so that one type of drum might carry a supporting rhythm; another carries a melody, or main theme; and yet another carries supporting, complementary rhythms. There is also a soloistic style that is incorporated by one player carrying a melody or improvised rhythm over a steady rhythm maintained by the other players. At the Tokyo Olympics of 1964, *Osuwa-Daiko* performed as part of a festival of the arts. Osuwa-Daiko was one of the first ensembles of this new style of drumming in 1951, in which rhythmic patterns were distributed across several different drums incorporating both traditional Japanese (e.g., the steady *ji,* or base beat) as well as jazz rhythms (Takata, 1998). This style is what dominates the musical style of North American taiko, most likely due to the widespread teaching of Osuwa-Daiko founder Daihachi Oguchi (Takata, 1998).

Oedo Sukeroku Taiko, another Japanese taiko ensemble has also directly influenced North American ensembles. Oedo Sukeroku Taiko, started in 1959 at Yushima Tenjin Shrine in Tokyo, aimed to preserve the heritage of traditional Japanese drumming and to create a new contemporary style (Oedo Sukeroku Taiko, 2002). Prior to their formation, ensemble drumming was mostly found at festivals, such as summer *Obon.* Members were mainly Obon drummers but also studied taiko patterns from Japanese classical music in addition to drumming styles from different Japanese prefectures. Unlike many other festival drumming styles, which involve little body movement, the Sukeroku style, as it has come to be known, is characterized by identifiable movements that correspond with a slanted drum configuration in which the drum and the drummer's stance are aligned on a diagonal plane, a style that has been adopted by many North American ensembles.

Historical events in the United States have also shaped the art form and imbued it with meaning related to the internment of Japanese Americans. As one player formerly with San Jose Taiko commented, "If you can understand the World War II concentration camp experience of Japanese people and the effects that that has had in real, human terms on the Nikkei community to this day, then you can understand the great significance of the upsurge of the American taiko movement" (Hayase, 1985, p. 47). The development of taiko in Canada has dealt with similar concerns in terms of using the art form as a cultural rebirth in the wake of tough U.S. and Canadian immigration policies, helping to support the diaspora of not only Japanese Canadians but also other Asian Canadians (Kobayashi, 1994). North American taiko ensembles often support a mission to connect Japanese Americans with Japanese heritage as well as with contemporary cultural and artistic expression for and of Japanese American identity politics (Hayase, 1985; Hirabayashi, 1988; Uyechi, 1995).

Taiko has arguably become an international Asian diaspora based on an identifiable sound (Kobayashi, 1994).[1] Within North America, there are currently over 150 taiko ensembles (Rolling Thunder, 2011), catering to all age levels (e.g., children and adults) and expertise (recreational, amateur, and professional). The sound of North American Taiko borrows from such musical forms as jazz, Native American drumming, and salsa and typically involves the kumidaiko (ensemble drumming style) that includes a variety of drum types as well as bells, cymbals, shakers (gourds), conch shell, and Japanese flutes. Sometimes the hybridity of styles is as specific as taking on actual rhythms associated with another cultural style, such as Afro-Cuban rhythms (Sano, personal communication, 1998). The most noticeable appropriation is the American jazz idiom of improvisation. Many North American ensembles alter segments of precomposed segments with soloistic episodes in which individuals improvise within the rhythmic style of the song.

In addition to instruments, contemporary taiko ensembles use *kata* (form and movement) from classical Japanese dance, martial arts, and other stylized movements, sometimes invented by the players or appropriated from other cultural styles of dance or drumming. These movements are highly coordinated and synchronized, many of which correspond to the type of drum or instrument being used. The effect is an integrated performance involving both movement and music. Its visual impact is as important as its aural impact and is an integral aspect of sound production (e.g., stylized arm movements are associated with particular dynamics and drum tones). Fusing content to form via the body, kata, it has been argued, is an approach within Eastern artistic practices that stands in sharp contrast to the dualism of content and form that attends much of Western philosophy and practices (Yano, 2003). Rather, it is content that attends to form (Matsunobu, 2007). Like the music itself, kata is a hybridized form created through classical Japanese form, martial arts, and the players' own backgrounds and expertise with movement (e.g., modern dance, hip-hop).

There are many groups with particularly notable styles, but three are credited with significantly influencing the majority of North American ensembles and therefore have been important educational and cultural institutions within the taiko landscape. San Francisco Taiko Dojo is the first established North American taiko ensemble, founded in 1968 by Sensei Seiichi Tanaka, credited with bringing taiko, and specifically the ensemble style of kumidaiko (multiple drums playing as an ensemble), to the United States. The ensemble is composed of approximately 200 students, ranging in age from 4 to 60, and performs a combination of "traditional and contemporary rhythms, dance, and martial arts" (San Francisco Taiko Dojo, 2011). A key aspect of San Francisco Taiko Dojo is that it is a school, not just a performance organization, in which there is a focus on spiritual and martial arts. For them, "the Dojo teaches not only the skillful playing of percussion instruments, but also the discipline of mind and body in the spirit of complete respect and unity among the drummers" (San Francisco Taiko Dojo, 2011). In addition to drumming in the kumidaiko style, a noticeable stylistic quality of the ensemble also consists of solo improvisation. San Francisco Taiko Dojo has performed for and/or appeared in popular films such as *Apocalypse Now, Return of the Jedi, The Right Stuff,* and *Rising Sun,* playing one of their signature pieces, *Tsunami,* in one of the film's crucial scenes.

Another founding taiko ensemble in the United States is Kinnara Taiko, established by Reverend Masao Kodani and George Abe in 1969 at the Senshin Buddhist Temple in Los Angeles, California, as a form of Japanese American Buddhist expression. As a Buddhist taiko group, Kinnara introduced concepts of Buddhist drumming that were located in a uniquely Japanese American style. Commenting on the Kinnara style, early member Johnny Mori was quoted as saying, "this particular taiko, this Japanese-American Taiko, had no roots whatsoever in Japan, nothing at all" (Fromartz & Greenfield, 1998). It was a style that was improvised and situated within the group's knowledge base, expertise, and proclivities that blended with traditional Japanese rhythms such as *kizami,* (straight, steady base rhythm), and *oroshi,* a slow succession of beats that accelerate to a drum roll, as well as the concept of *ma,* or the space between sounds that is increased or decreased that gives expression to sound in terms of tension or release (Kodani, 2000). Kinnara also pioneered the use of oak wine barrels for the body of the large *chu-daiko,* one of the main drums (and drum shapes) used in ensemble taiko drumming. Traditionally carved from a single piece of wood by master Japanese drum makers, this Japanese American appropriation allowed many groups to fashion their own drums and start their own ensembles, revolutionizing taiko as it became more accessible to a larger audience (Kim, 2010).

A third founding taiko group in the United States is San Jose Taiko, founded in 1973 by Roy and P. J. Hirabayashi. Inspired and shaped by the teachings and ideas of San Francisco Taiko Dojo and Kinnara Taiko, San Jose Taiko shares many similar characteristics with these previously mentioned ensembles while also maintaining and creating their own unique aesthetic and pedagogical practices. My aim with this brief historical account of taiko was to set the context for understanding taiko as a cultural practice in which music and identity politics are deeply entangled, engaged in aesthetic explorations of sounds, rhythms, and movement.

The account in this chapter is taken from my ethnography of San Jose Taiko, conducted over 18 months and informed by ongoing contact with the group members. As part of this ethnography, I engaged in their apprenticeship program in order to more closely study and, indeed, fully embody, their teaching and learning practices. I first discuss their history, situated in San Jose Japantown, California, their pedagogical framework and practices, focusing in particular on the use of the body and the development of *sound* knowing, learning and mastery focused on musical understandings of, deliberations with, and experimentations in sound. While the examples relate specifically to San Jose Taiko, their qualities, embedded in a lineage of taiko playing in Japan and North America, reflect the larger, shared practices of taiko, underscoring taiko as a cultural project engaged in an education of Japanese American—and more broadly, Asian American—identity defined through sound and embodied practices and performances.

San Jose Japantown and the North American Taiko Movement

San Jose Taiko is located in San Jose, home to one of three Japantowns in the United States, the other two of which are located in San Francisco and Los Angeles. The city has an active Japanese American community, hosting an annual *Obon* festival, spring festivals, and events sponsored by the Buddhist temple located in Japantown. Japantown is located near downtown San Jose, roughly between 1st and 7th Streets. Perhaps the most significant historical event that would alter and affect the Japanese American community of San Jose Japantown was the internment of thousands of Japanese Americans that was facilitated by President Franklin Roosevelt's Executive Order 9066, on February 19, 1942. According to Japantown San Jose's official website (2011), most of Santa Clara's 3,000 Japanese American residents were interned at Heart Mountain, Wyoming, forcing the closure of Japantown's 53 businesses during internment. In December of 1944 the Japanese internment policy was revoked, and by 1947, 40 businesses and 100 families had reestablished themselves in San Jose's Japantown. According to a 2003 demographics report, 26% of San Jose's approximately 643,000 residents were Japanese American, with approximately 15% of Asian Americans residing within a 1-mile radius of Japantown.

The cofounders of San Jose Taiko, Roy and P. J. Hirabayashi (managing director and creative director, respectively, who are also married to each other), have developed their approach to taiko into a forum for social action, community development, cultural preservation, and Asian American identity, characteristics that mark many North American taiko ensembles (Hayase, 1985; Hirabayashi, 1988; Uyechi, 1995). San Jose Taiko has established a conservatory, "the first of its kind in the United States, to serve as a national resource for this vibrant Asian American art form" (San Jose Taiko, 2011). Through the Taiko Conservatory, they continue to provide professional development opportunities, technical assistance, and a "comprehensive array of support and information about North American Taiko to individuals and organizations around the world" (San Jose Taiko, 2011). As part of the conservatory, they host tour residencies and the Junior Taiko program for youth ages 8 to 18, with a current enrollment of about 70 students (San

Jose Taiko, 2011). They also conduct public workshops for local youth and adults, schools visits, and other public outreach initiatives and participate regularly in the community events of Japantown.

Additionally, there is the professional adult performing ensemble, the principle focus of my 18-month ethnography and brief apprenticeship. There were approximately 14 performing members (including the two directors) during the time of my study (2000–2002), defined as those individuals who engage in regular practices and performances of taiko, ranging from ages 18 to 50. Nine of the 14 performing members were of Japanese American descent, many of whom are Sansei or Yonsei (third and fourth generation). Two other members were of other Asian American descent (Chinese American and Filipino American), and three were White, non-Asian Americans. Seven of the 14 members were women, an issue that several members commented upon in relation to the importance of positive female gender identity within Asian American identity politics (Powell, 2008). In addition, I also studied participants involved in a 2-year apprenticeship program known as the Audition Process (typically referred to as AP). At the onset of my AP, there were 13 participants; towards the end of the first year, two women had been accepted into the second year of the apprenticeship and had moved into becoming performing members of the ensemble. As of 2011, there are 18 members (San Jose Taiko, 2011b) that reflect Japanese American membership in addition to other Asian American and Caucasian (White) members.

The diversity of intergenerational, multiracial, and gendered membership afforded opportunities for discussions about various social positions and their meanings in relation to taiko, such as when one auditioning member discussed her reasons for wanting to join taiko as related to seeing physically strong, Asian American female role models that countered the stereotypes of Asian and Asian American women. Stylistically, there was a diversity of musical and movement arts informing their taiko playing, as people integrated their expertise with multiethnic art forms and instruments (e.g., hula, karate, Afro-Cuban drumming, didgeridoo) and contemporary popular music (e.g., funk, pop, jazz). The process of such integration was held in dynamic tension with what were considered to be traditional Japanese philosophical and pedagogical practices regarding the body and sound. The following sections depict San Jose Taiko's pedagogical framework and the ways in which members learn to create, inhabit, and push the boundaries of a culturally authentic sound and style.

San Jose Taiko's Pedagogical Framework: A Mind-Body Philosophy

San Jose Taiko (SJT) configures a pedagogical and philosophical approach to taiko around four elements: attitude; musical technique; kata (physical form); and *ki* (spiritual energy). Each of these elements is explicitly taught to both performing and apprenticing members. To understand San Jose Taiko's pedagogical framework,

I refer to a larger context of Eastern philosophy and the ways in which it is tied to mind-body practice as well as contemporary Western approaches to teaching and learning that have influenced the group. Philosopher Yuasa Yasuo (Yasuo, Shigenori, & Kasulis, 1987) posited that the Eastern view of the body was incommensurate with Western philosophical categories in that Asian traditions do not treat the mind and body as ontologically distinct; rather, truth is a way of *being* in the world rather than thinking about the world. Moreover, mind-body unity in Eastern philosophy is an achievement through disciplined practice and mastery. Disciplined artistic pursuits are central to achieving mind-body unity, and, as such, position aesthetics as a central focus of and for study. In contrast, Yasuo argued that in Western philosophical approaches such as phenomenology, psychoanalysis, and neurophysiology, mind-body unity is viewed as constant rather than developed, universal rather than variable across individuals, and does not consider "exceptional achievements," a "theoretical possibility rather than a state that is actualized through religious or artistic masters" (Yasuo et al., 1987, p. 2).

In descriptions of Japanese teaching and learning environments, there is a generally held observation that explicit verbal direction and conceptual understanding are intentionally avoided, as they may distract from a whole-body grasp of artistry that is gained only through experience (Hare, 1998, cited in Matsunobu, 2007; Sato, 2004; Yasuo et al., 1987). Yet, when interviewed about their practice, Roy and P. J. Hirabayashi (founders and directors) both stated their explicit attempt to develop a pedagogical style that reflected both Japanese traditions of the *dojo* (place of learning) and Western teaching. For San Jose Taiko's founding members, P. J. and Roy Hirabayashi, their own learning experiences in taiko instilled in them a desire for making their practices explicit, in order to "standardize" the art form so that they knew what they wanted from their players and from the music itself. P. J. explained:

> In the old days [of learning taiko], you don't go through this one-on-one, you don't have a "grading system" … And what we're trying to kind of cut through is, "well, just tell me what I need to do!" [laughs] You know? And that way we feel it's more the western approach. What are you doing well at? And what can you improve at? So that you can improve more readily instead of second-guessing. What are *you* looking for? What are *we* looking for? (Hirabayashi, cited in Powell, 2006, pp. 53–54)

The process of getting clear and articulating what they had learned through their own taiko training has developed over the years into a curriculum that includes structured activities and forums for self-evaluation and group evaluation, explicit membership guidelines and performance standards, and opportunities for the professional development of members within the ensemble. Assessment occurs throughout the rehearsal and training process in both informal and formal ways. For example, an essential part of the Audition Process (AP) included videotaped and private evaluations, which determined not only a participant's progress, but also whether or not a participant would continue with the apprenticeship and eventually become part of the performing ensemble. Videotaped evaluations were a tool that San Jose Taiko used so that participants can watch and evaluate their own progress, developing, in the process, a "critical eye." These videotaped evaluations were held midway through each of the three phases, in which apprentices would perform songs they had learned so far, watch their performance on tape, and discuss in evaluative terms what they observed about themselves and others. An important follow-up practice after the evaluation of videotaped performances was the implementation of these comments. P. J. periodically would tell us to remember our feedback in order to implement these comments in further practice. For example, after watching and evaluating each member's performance of *Oedo Bayashi* patterns, the group then practiced it again. P. J. and Yumi took up their positions of observing each of them and working with them individually.

With the design of this framework, which centers around the four previously named aspects—kata, ki, attitude, and musical technique—they also sought to connect the philosophical elements of kata or ki, for example, with artistic expression, a voice for Asian American experience (Hirabayashi, 2000). As a result, their teaching practices include not only extensive practice sessions for apprenticing and performing members but also tours of the local Japantown, reading materials that situate their work within the larger taiko project as well as theoretical writings about Asian American experience, and performing in local festivals such as Oban. The pedagogical framework is further discussed in the following sections.

Kata

One of the ways in which the Japanese arts have been preserved and transmitted is through kata (form), through which practitioners learn and assume the form of an art but also patterns of artistic and social behaviors, and moral and ethical values in accordance with prescribed movements, postures, and training (Matsunobu, 2007; Yasuo et al., 1987). Training is a "discipline for shaping one's body into a form. Art is embodied through cumulative training; one comes to learn an art through one's body" (Yasuo et al., 1987, p. 105). Discipline and training are meant to harmonize the mind and body so that the mind's movements accord with the body's (Yasuo et al., 1987). This is a practical rather than conceptual understanding, brought about through direct experience with disciplined practice.

For San Jose Taiko, kata is a means through which members can achieve "oneness" with the taiko—kata literally links the body with the drum (San Jose Taiko, 2001a). Training involved the practice and mastery of a coordinated set of movements involving a low, strong, wide-legged stance that helps to center the body and optimize arm and other physical movements required of drumming. Some of these stances derive from martial arts, such as the lowered pelvic stance used for

stabilizing the body. Choreographed movements often correspond with particular drum strikes, deriving from Japanese traditions of drumming. Individuals and the group as a whole also developed their own signature movements. Indeed, in my interviews, many of the group's members described San Jose Taiko's performance style as being very fluid, rhythmic, dance-like, and "happy." Often, this style is exerted during the improvisational sections of a standard song, in which members created their own rhythms and movements that were attuned with the stylistic conventions of a song yet also demonstrated creativity and individual flair. One member, for example, added a signature twirl to the end of her arm extensions, in which the *bachi* (cylindrical drum sticks about 16 inches long) would noticeably twirl in quick circles.

During my ethnographic study and apprenticeship, a significant part of practice was spent learning and practicing kata. Working extensively with the Eastern philosophical concept of the *hara* (the center of the body, located in the lower abdomen), movements were practiced through the pedagogical tools of metaphor, guided imagery, slow-motion movement, repetition, and imitation. More generally, we worked on developing a heightened awareness of the body and the habitation of space. In the first few classes, and periodically throughout the apprenticeship, we were guided through imagery of sites and planes beyond the body (Powell, 2004, 2006) in order to understand the body in relation to space, to drums, and to others. This understanding was critical to successful performance, for members are physically integrated, coordinating not only arm movements (and their corresponding rhythms) but also movements that involved rotating around drums and other players, coordinating drum hits between two drums, and jumping or spinning between and around drums and other players.

Repetition, mimesis, and slow-motion movements are techniques found in many Japanese artistic practices, such as the Suzuki method of music teaching (Peak, 1998), the popular music genre of Enka (Yano, 2003), *Noh* drama (Yasuo et al., 1987), pottery (Singleton, 1998) and in meditative practices (Shusterman, 2008; Yasuo et al., 1987). These are concerted pedagogical efforts to fuse form to body. Indeed, several members of the performing ensemble, including the directors, cited the importance of repetition for building a muscle memory that would lead to mastery of techniques as well as the release of consciousness that led to "playing with more abandon" (M. Lehner, personal communication, May 1, 2000).

Musical Technique

As kata is often the visual expression of sound, kata and musical technique are intricately bound together. Similar to the teaching and learning of kata, repetition, imitation, and slowing down rhythms were key aspects of practice. Rhythmic drills were an important and regular component of rehearsals in both the apprenticeship classes and in the rehearsals of the performance ensemble. Drills often consisted of repetition of some aspect of rhythm, movement, and/or technique,

with the idea being that repetition built muscle memory. The slowing down of movements aided in the breaking down of complicated patterns or focusing on the nuances of muscular technique required for the development of dynamics (volume) and speed. Weekly practices, especially those with apprenticing beginners, would often include at least an hour of repetitive movements to develop a sense of muscle memory and strength. Members also practiced drills to strengthen and train fingers, hands, and arms in order to produce consistent tone quality and also to increase coordination for complicated rhythmic patterns.

Taiko rhythms are taught through a series of syllables called *kuchishoka,* a phonetic system of syllables in which each beat to the drum and its corresponding kata are represented by a syllable. Along with telling a player how to hit the drum, the different syllables also signify the timing and rhythm of each drumbeat. These syllables are sung (spoken), usually before members play the actual rhythms. Once they have mastered the syllables, the kuchishoka and the corresponding movements are then transferred to the drums. As P. J. expressed, "If you can say it, you can play it." While taiko is an oral tradition, many pieces are written down in kuchishoka notation along with corresponding beats and handedness (right or left).

An obvious aspect of musical technique included learning the ensemble's repertoire. I have previously discussed the origins of taiko drumming and the musical influences on sound. During interviews, both P. J. and Roy expressed a desire to develop a musical style unique to their own musical experiences and expertise as well as those of their members. It was very important, stated P. J., that "our music be a reflection of who we are. So it was an instrument to be our expression, our voice.... So we regarded ourselves as never, ever from the very beginning becoming copycat taiko from Japan" (Hirabayashi, quoted in Powell, 2005, p. 59). Similarly, Roy stressed the need for a musical identity. "Soul and jazz were derived from the Black experience, but nothing on the popular market could be referred to as the 'Asian American experience.' ... We were Japanese Americans who found taiko as a connection to our ethnic identity" (Hirabayashi, quoted in Powell, 2005, p. 278). On their website, San Jose Taiko (2011a) states their musical style as follows:

> SJT has broadened this historical art form into a style that joins the traditional rhythms of Japanese drumming with other world rhythms, including African, Balinese, Brazilian, Latin, and jazz, bridging many styles, while still resonating with the Asian soul in America. Company members study both traditional and contemporary dance with leading choreographers, producing performances that are theatrical extravaganzas of movement and music.

All compositions performed by SJT are written or arranged by the ensemble's members, and they exhibit a range of influences. *RumbaKo,* written in 1993 by Janet Koike and Toni Yagami, fuses traditional rhythms from both Japan and Cuba. *Currents,* written by Jose Alarcon in 1976, combines a series of musical influences

that occur in sequence, including a Muslim song, traditional Japanese rhythms, and jazz and Latin rhythms. *Currents* also employed the traditional conch shell that is blown during Buddhist rituals and some community festivals. *Gendai Ni Ikiru* (Living in the Present), written by Gary Tsujimoto in 1978, was often referred to as the signature piece of San Jose Taiko by Roy, P. J., and other members, integrating traditional taiko and modern jazz rhythms. *Ei Ja Nai Ka?* (Isn't it good?), written by P. J. in 1994, incorporates dances from folk festivals of Japan, in which the group engages in a choreographed, synchronized pattern of steps performed to a few instruments. Each of these songs requires different numbers of people, instruments, and levels of skill.

As discussed earlier, most of these compositions reflect a jazz format of precomposed rhythmic sections alternating with improvised ones, often referred to as "solos." In effect, improvisation is composition in process. Learning to compose is a process, beginning with exercises in musical improvisations. During my apprenticeship, we learned to improvise slowly and within the first few months of our training. The first exercise was a "call and response" drill, in which members repeat the rhythm they have just heard the teacher (or another member) play. Another exercise involved "passing" around a rhythm, in which we had to incorporate some of the rhythms that the previous player had just created. As P. J. explained, this was a means for unifying the individual solos into a whole by integrating common patterns. Other exercises included mixing up sequences of patterns in a song (e.g., playing the second "line," or four measures, before the first four measures of rhythm), which allowed us to hear new possibilities in previously established forms by recontextualizing them in new relationships.

Knowledge of sound was crucial for understanding the ways in which a soloist's musical ideas fit within a particular song's performance conventions. One particular exercise used with my apprenticing group was to perform a melodic (rhythmic line) that we had learned but to improvise the last several beats or measures. Apprentices were also called upon to prepare a solo ahead of time, which, while seemingly paradoxical, was a means of practicing and internalizing a particular song's style. Improvisation was a highly coordinated event among all players, as the members who aren't soloing at the moment are required to maintain the beat, basic rhythms, and physical kata of the song. Soloing is thus a highly interdependent, ensemble art that is coordinated with multiple players (Powell, 2005).

While San Jose Taiko referred to kata as a distinct aspect of their training that links movement to form, it is conceptually possible to frame *all* of their training and practice routines within/as kata. In his discussion of Enka, a Japanese popular song style, Yano (2003) discussed three types of kata: textual, musical, and bodily. Musical kata refers to the different musical styles, including meter and form. Yano refers to two types of musical kata: compositional, the written musical score, and performative, the improvised embellished style of vocal expression found in these songs. In relation to bodily kata, there are similarities to be found in taiko's musical kata of compositional and performative kata, in that the performative kata allows individuals to work with the musical form while also extending it. The pedagogical practices of San Jose Taiko that I have discussed so far reveal the ways in which mind-body unity is taught through physical and musical kata, undergirding the principle of disciplined teaching for the purpose of mastery over and through the form.

The compositional kata of the group is a continual process of negotiation. In order to ensure a consistency of style, San Jose Taiko started a process of evaluating new composition, in which a member wishing to compose a piece fills out a form stating the intention of the piece, proposed titles, number of composers (sometimes there are multiple composers), estimated number of personnel (players), suggested personnel, instruments used, song ideas/description, and drum arrangement. Ultimately, Roy stated, each member, and the group as a whole, considers the question, what makes taiko *taiko*?

Performing members, rather than apprenticing ones, were allowed to compose a piece, suggesting that original compositions are encouraged only after there has been demonstrated mastery of the form. Similar to the performative kata of improvisation, the compositional kata of taiko also has a performative element to it in that a member precomposes sound and movement in ways that both stay within and extend the genre. Once a piece was accepted, the composer was responsible for teaching the rest of the group that song. The original composition was often recomposed as members practiced, making suggestions for how to tweak the sound or physical kata. Again, this process requires a complex acoustic knowledge of musical conventions of taiko and those of the particular group, an understanding of the ways in which one might compose and bring in new sound elements that fit within the musical sound and style of taiko yet also allow for distinctive sound elements that might be from other musical influences.

Attitude and Ki

While different in many ways, the third and fourth principles, attitude and ki, share a disposition towards taiko that indicates a holistic approach to creating music. "Attitude" concerns a respect for self, others, and the drums, positivity, patience, focus, and discipline. The training of attitude manifested itself in a disciplined athletic regime of physical calisthenics, timed runs, drum maintenance, studio cleaning, and building maintenance. It was also encouraged in our musical and kata training as well; in my apprenticeship, we were explicitly taught to make eye contact with one another, to smile, to sensitize ourselves to other players' concerns, including mistakes that we might rectify as a "mis-take" (Klemp et al., 2008), a way of recontextualing an error through our own playing so that the mistake did not sound like one.

Ki (or *chi,* in Chinese) is based in Eastern spiritual and philosophical thought and practice. Ki is often translated as spirit or energy flow. For San Jose Taiko, ki was defined as "the spiritual unity of the mind and body" (San Jose Taiko, 2001). Ki is an essential principle of martial arts and a basic element of kata. In Eastern thought, the *tanden,* located in the center of the hara (abdomen) is the place from which spiritual energy emanates (Reed, 1992). Ki contrasts with the Western concept of the body's center as located in the heart or the mind. Kata and *kiai* (shouted syllables) are means through which ki is developed. Through ki, SJT believed that oneness with the taiko, with other members, and even with the audience can be achieved through sound and energy, what they call a physical communication. Ki expresses the spirit of taiko, and yet is perhaps the most elusive because it is based on a concept of spiritual energy and unity. Kata and kiai are perhaps the most visible signs of creating and maintaining ki.

The embodiment of ki concerned a grasping of the holistic relationship that exists among the discrete elements involved in taiko playing. This involved attending to others' playing, knowing how to support someone's solo, coordinating and synchronism rhythms, maintaining energetic playing, and using kiai (conventional shouted syllables of taiko playing and martial arts), often in relation to the former elements as a means of keeping tempo, signaling to others, and keeping up the energy required for playing. Because kiai involves producing sound, the focus of teaching and learning kiai, as part of ki training, was on the quality of sound as it was produced and felt in the body. So, for example, apprenticing members practiced "passing" sound back and forth between people. Sounds that were explicitly taught in this manner included "Yoh" and its response, "Hoh." Other aspects of ki that were explicitly taught included locating one's hara and connecting that feeling of centeredness through the kata of a low and wide stance often found in many martial arts practices. We also practiced relaxing our body and mind while focusing on our hara, pairing up and pushing on each other as tests of strength and focus.

In terms of spiritual aspects of ki, musical technique included learning how to hold and respect the bachi, a significant aspect of taiko drumming. P. J. situated its significance in Buddhist practice: "The *bachi* is considered the sacred link between the spirit world and the earth, connecting the body to the sky" (Hirabayashi, cited in Powell, 2004, p. 190). The taiko drum body, the hide, and the large metal tacks that are used to affix hides to drums all carry cultural significance in Buddhism. While San Jose Taiko is not a Buddhist taiko group, P. J. and other members of the group were cognizant of these origins and refer to each of the drum elements as comprising the spirit of taiko.

Ki, like the other three principles, underscores a holistic pedagogical approach to musical practice and performance taken by San Jose Taiko—and indeed many other taiko groups—reflecting an Eastern mind-body philosophy that is situated alongside Western and other cultural influences on sound and kata. "Composing, choreographing, designing and producing costumes, and handcrafting of the drums are part of the holistic process in which all members participate," wrote San

Jose Taiko (2011), on their web site. "Through this singleness of mind and spirit, harmony is achieved and the music rings with unity and clarity."

Somatic Identity

The practices of San Jose Taiko, as well as many other taiko ensembles, reveal an embodied pedagogy that carries significance for taiko as a cultural project. Kata, the visible form of taiko and a principle means through which Japanese arts and mind-body practices are taught and preserved, serves also to establish patterns of behavior and ethical values. Kata somaticizes identity that is simultaneously artistic, gendered, racialized, and nationalized (Yano, 2003). While kata is a disciplined, choreographed training that shapes the body into a prescribed form, its practice in taiko is simultaneously performative in that musical improvisation (which encompasses physical form) and individual compositions encourage unique expressions, creativity, and innovations (Powell, 2008). In describing the Japanese popular music of enka, Yano (2003) stated that "true mastery *of* kata means mastery *over* kata" (p. 123). Kata has been argued as empowering and transformative in its ability to confront and recreate gendered and (de)colonized identities (Kato, 2002; Mayuzumi, 2006). With taiko drumming, the performance of the body is a show of strength, stamina, fluidity, and extension that, coupled with the loudness of the drums, constructs a resounding body of undeniable presence that juxtaposes against racial stereotypes of Asians and Asian Americans, such as passive, compliant, and quiet (Oren, 2005); for some of the women in the group, the strong bodies they witnessed on stage presented a critical show of female strength (Powell, 2008), suggesting that taiko might be a venue through which the countering of racist and sexist narratives of Asian and Asian American women could be achieved (Wong, 2000).

The musical kata (composed pieces as well as improvised solos) also opens spaces for moving with and through prescribed forms. San Jose Taiko's focus on the question of what makes taiko *taiko* showed a willingness to create and recreate a taiko identity with musical forms, sounds, and practices. These experiments with composition also constitute a recomposing of Asian American identity through self-conscious attention to hybridization that holds in a sensitive balance prescriptive form and performative possibilities that reinscribe form.

The reinscription of form is evident not only in the music and kata of taiko; it is also seen in the juxtaposition of the larger Eastern and Western pedagogical practices in which taiko and kata are situated. The unique offering of taiko as an educational practice lies in its foregrounding of mind-body unity as facilitated through bodily practices and sound practices. The fusing of Eastern mind-body philosophy with Western notions of assessment, for example, compels questions about the necessity of hybridity as culturally based groups attempt to configure a sense of cultural authenticity (Wong, 2004) while also contesting the very assumptions upon which the notion of "authenticity" rests. This renders a complex picture of identity politics that is continually (re)configured through artistic practice, a process of continual becoming(s).

Thinking Comprehensively About Taiko Drumming as Educational Practice

I began this chapter by framing San Jose Taiko as an educational institution in which music and identity politics are entangled, a setting in which engaged aesthetic explorations of sounds, rhythms, and movement in members compose not only musical practices but also identity practices in relation to a larger Asian American landscape. I have underscored the hybrid practices embedded in Eastern and Western philosophies of mind-body unity and between prescriptive forms of sound and movement with the musical agency of San Jose Taiko's members.

By thinking comprehensively and relationally about education (e.g., Cremin, 1975/2007), I consider taiko organizations and ensembles such as San Jose Taiko as places of learning in society that engage multimodal forms of knowing (e.g., sound), aesthetic practices (e.g., improvisation, kata), and cultural practices for larger purposes of social change. Taiko is an engagement with skills, values, conventions, and practices across global contexts that are continually recomposed by those who participate. My discussion of somatic identities and hybridity of cultural practices suggests a comprehensive view of music education as more than teaching and learning notes or rhythms. The continually threatened position of music and the arts in schools (and our larger society) has led to restricted learning opportunities in arts classrooms as time allotment and opportunities have dwindled, and the performance-oriented curricula of many school music programs (e.g., concerts and football halftime) limit our understandings and experiences of music. I do not suggest that schools, or other sites of music education, adopt the apprenticeship model or pedagogical framework depicted here. Instead, I am suggesting that taiko as a cultural practice manifested in specific institutions like San Jose Taiko supplements school-based music practices—and popularly held conceptions of what counts as music—and creates a more comprehensive picture of music education. Music does not merely reflect society; a sense of identity grows out of the processes whereby people are connected through and with music. Particular instruments, rhythms, and voices communicate a symbolic sense of place. As music literally travels around the world, cultural theorists have argued that *affective* alliances between people can be used to promote social change (Negus, 1996).

Relationally, taiko evokes the call for a pedagogy of multiliteracies (New London Group, 1996) and multimodal literacies (e.g., Jewitt, 2008) within language and literacy education that have recognized the multiplicity, complexity, and interrelationship of different modes of meaning in which people engage: audio, gestural, spatial, visual, and multimodal (the latter of which recognizes the dynamic relations among the former modes). Framed within the field of literacy, these modes, called *metalanguages,* draw attention to the intertextuality of literacy events as well as to the importance of appropriate pedagogy for cultural and linguistic diversity. Recognizing this significant contribution to the legitimization of multiple modes of representation and communication and to the expansion of what counts as literacy, my discussion in this chapter extends beyond the idea of audio meaning as a grammatical language. Indeed, multimodal pedagogy is a situated response to school-based notions of literacy and accountability that privilege certain definitions of literacy. The multimodality described in this chapter is of a different sort: it is to consider sound as a "dimension of experience in and of itself" (Stoller, 1984, p. 567), an organizing presence that connects the material (drums, bachi, bodies) with the nonmaterial (mind-body unity, sound), giving form to abstract concepts such as identity within a culturally artistic practice. We might attend to the question raised by the directors of San Jose Taiko: What is taiko? When is taiko *not* taiko? Translating those questions more generally, they might read as the following: What does it mean to be Asian American or Japanese American in the 21st century? In what ways do we compose and remodulate community, race, and/or culture through sound? How does a cultural project based on the agency and transformation of individuals also maintain its mission of cultural preservation? What is music? When is music *not* music? Paraphrasing Gutiérrez and Dixon-Román (2011), how can thinking about education comprehensively help us reenvision music education as a means of critical participation in a more just society? These questions, like taiko practice itself, resist closure and instead invite our sensing bodies to tune in to the ways in which somatic and sonic knowledge are central modalities of participation in and with the world.

Note

1. For further details of this assessment process, including my own experience with being assessed, please see Powell (2006).

References

Bresler, L. (Ed.). (2004). *Knowing bodies, moving minds: Embodied knowledge in education.* Dordrecht, The Netherlands: Klewar Press.

Cremin, L. (2007). Public education and the education of the public. *Teachers College Record, 109*(7), 1545–1558. (Original work published 1975)

Fromartz, S., & Greenfield, L. (1998). Anything but quiet: Japanese Americans reinvent taiko drumming. *Natural History, 107*(2), 44–50.

Gutiérrez, R., & Dixon-Román, E. (2011). Beyond gap gazing: How can thinking about education comprehensively help us (re)envision mathematics education? In B. Atweh, M. Graven, W. Secada, & P. Valero (Eds.), *Mapping equity and quality in mathematics education* (pp. 21–34). Springer.

Hare, T. (1998). Try, try again: Training in Noh drama. In T. P. Rohlen & G. K. LeTendre (Eds.), *Teaching and learning in Japan* (pp. 323–344). New York, NY: Cambridge University Press.

Hayase, S. (1985, Winter/Spring). Taiko. *East Wind,* 46–47.

Hirabayashi, R. (1988). *Odaiko newsletter.* San Jose, CA: San Jose Taiko.

Japantown San Jose. (2011). *History and walking tour.* Retrieved from http://www.japan townsanjose.org/

Jewitt, C. (2008). Multimodality and literacy in school classrooms. *Review of Research in Education, 32*(1), 241–267.

Kato, E. (2002). The sword behind the chrysanthemum: Modern Japanese tea ceremony practitioner's self-empowerment through explicit and implicit motifs. *Semiotica* (141), 111–144.

Kim, S. (2010). *All in the drum: Building taiko in America.* Retrieved from http://www.janm. org/exhibits/bigdrum/exhibition/article.php

Klemp, N., McDermott, R., Raley, J., Thibeault, M., Powell, K., & Levitin, D. (2008). Plans, takes and mis-takes. *Outlines: Critical Social Studies* (1), 4–21.

Kobayashi, T. (1994). Heartbeat in the diaspora: Taiko and community. *Fuse, 12*(5/6), 24–26.

Kodani, M. (2000). *Gagaku.* Unpublished manuscript. Los Angeles, CA: Kinnara Taiko.

Matsunobu, K. (2007). Japanese perspectives and research on the body. In L. Bresler (Ed.), *International handbook of research in arts education* (pp. 1107–1108). Amsterdam, The Netherlands: Springer.

Mayuzumi, K. (2006). Tea ceremony as a decolonizing epistemology: Healing and Japanese women. *Journal of Transformative Education, 4*(1), 8–26.

Negus, K. (1996). *Popular music in theory.* Hanover, NH: Wesleyan University Press.

New London Group. (1996). A pedagogy of multiliteracies: Designing social futures. *Harvard Educational Review, 66*(1), 60–93.

Oedo Sukeroku Taiko. (2002). "Oedo sukeroku taiko official home page." Retrieved from http://www.oedosukerokutaiko.com/english-1.html

Oren, T. (2005). Secret Asian man: Angry Asians and the politics of cultural visibility. In S. Dave, L. Nishime, & T. Oren (Eds.), *East main street* (pp. 337–360). New York, NY: New York University Press.

Peak, L. (1998). The Suzuki method of music instruction. In T. P. Rohlen & G. K. LeTendre (Eds.), *Teaching and learning in Japan* (pp. 345–368). New York, NY: Cambridge University Press.

Powell, K. (2004). The apprenticeship of embodied knowledge in a taiko drumming ensemble. In L. Bresler (Ed.), *Knowing bodies, moving minds: Embodied knowledge in education* (pp. 183–195). Dordrecht, The Netherlands: Klewar Press.

Powell, K. (2005). The ensemble art of the solo. *Arts and Learning Research Journal, 21*(1), 273–295.

Powell, K. (2006). Inside-out and outside-in: Participant observation in taiko drumming. In G. Spindler & L. Hammond (Eds.), *Innovations in educational ethnography: Theory, methods and results* (pp. 33–64). Mahwah, NJ: Erlbaum.

Powell, K. (2008). Drumming against the quiet: The sound of Asian American identity politics in an amorphous landscape. *Qualitative Inquiry, 14*(6), 901–925.

Reed, W. (1992). *A road that anyone can walk: Ki.* Tokyo: Japan Publications.

Rolling Thunder: Your Taiko Resource. (2011). Retrieved from http://www.taiko.com/index.php?option=com_wrapper&Itemid=35

San Francisco Taiko Dojo. (2011). *San Francisco Taiko Dojo.* Retrieved from http://www.sftaiko.com/about_sftd.html

San Jose Taiko. (2011a). *History.* Retrieved from http://www.taiko.org/history-traditional-japanese-drumming-rhythm-world-beats/

San Jose Taiko. (2011b). *Performers.* Retrieved from http://www.taiko.org/members-taiko-administrative-artistic-apprentice/

Sato, N. E. (2004). *Inside Japanese classrooms: The heart of education.* New York, NY: Routledge Falmer.

Shusterman, R. (2008). *Body consciousness: A philosophy of mindfulness and somaesthetics.* Cambridge, England: Cambridge University Press.

Singleton, J. (Ed.). (1998). Craft and art education in Mashiko pottery workshops. In J. Singleton (Ed.) *Learning in likely places: Varieties of apprenticeship in Japan* (pp. 122–133). Cambridge, England: Cambridge University Press.

Stoller, Sound in Songhay cultural experience. *American Ethnologist, 11*(3), 559–570.

Takata, T. (1998, January). The thundering world of the taiko. *Look Japan, 43*(502).

Uyechi, L. (1995). *University taiko: Roots and evolution.* Manuscript presented at Symposium on North American Taiko, Stanford University Invitational.

Varenne, H. (2007). Difficult collective deliberations: Anthropological notes toward a theory of education. *Teachers College Record, 109*(7), 1559–1588.

Wong, D. (2000). Taiko and the Asian/American body: Drums, rising sun, and the question of gender. *The World of Music, 42*(3), 67–78.

Wong, D. (2004). *Speak it louder: Asian Americans making music.* New York, NY: Routledge.

Yano, C. R. (2003). *Tears of longing: Nostalgia and the nation in Japanese popular song.* Harvard University Asia Center.

Yasuo, Y., Shigenori, N., & Kasulis, T. (1987). Theories of artistry. In *The body: Toward an eastern mind-body theory* (pp. 99–110). Albany, NY: Suny Press.

Nondominant Everyday-Spatial Practices of Comprehensively Conceived Education

8

THE CULTURAL MODELING OF COMPREHENSIVELY CONCEIVED EDUCATION

Carol Lee

Education fulfills many roles for the individual, communities, and the nation and takes place in many spaces: in homes, neighborhood institutions, churches, schools, and informal activities that are often peer directed. Social science research has tended to focus on learning within particular spaces rather than looking comprehensively at learning *across* spaces. Educational outcomes for youth have typically focused on formal schooling with regard to school completion and scores on high-stakes accountability measures (Perle, Moran, Lutkas, & Tirre, 2005). Since the 1960s, such outcome data on African American, Hispanic, Native American, and Asian/Asian Pacific Islanders and youth from low-income communities has documented persistent disparities in both educational achievement and opportunity to learn (Ramani, Gilbertson, & Fox, 2007). The dominant orientation to these disparities has addressed presumed deficits; risks rather than resilience, assumptions about dysfunctional families and neighborhoods, unmotivated students, or the structure of and resource allocation to formal schooling (Lee, 2009; Spencer et al., 2006).

In this chapter I take a more comprehensive view of learning as an outgrowth of the relations among the varied spaces in which youth participate, all of which provide opportunities for learning, some of which are complementary and others of which are in tension (Bronfenbrenner & Morris, 1998; Spencer, Cole, Jones, & Swanson, 1997; Weisner, 2002). This orientation reflects an ecological perspective on learning and development, which I argue must also encompass a cultural perspective (Lee, 2008). An ecological perspective encompasses people's movement within and across spaces (e.g., home, school, church, formal and informal neighborhood/community activities). A cultural perspective addresses the systems of beliefs, knowledge, and practices that people learn, perpetuate, and transform over time as a consequence of their routine participation in particular practices (Cole,

1996; Rogoff, 2003; Slaughter-Defoe, Nakagawa, Takanishi, & Johnson, 1990). These two orientations—the ecological and the cultural—are necessarily intertwined. Together, they offer a comprehensive lens through which to understand what and how, in this case, youth learn within and across spaces (Lee, 2010).

In order to understand more fully how and what youth learn within and across the varied routine practices in which they engage, we must understand also how such practices are organized and how the organization helps to shape what is learned. Practices that affect positive outcomes are responsive to the kinds of risks that youth face broadly speaking, and in relation to the particular domains of competence to be developed, and recruit resources that youth bring with them as well as provide additional resources that are needed to increase the likelihood of successful learning. Complementary aims for youth development across the routine practices of their lives (e.g., family, church, organized peer activities, community organizations, school) are more often empowering, whereas conflicting aims for youth development across routine practices are more challenging, as youth must learn how to navigate and make sense of conflicting messages and goals (Spencer, 1985). The latter is more often the case in many low-income communities. Among ethnic minority youth, there are also challenges of navigating across societal level negative stereotypes compounded by more restricted access to robust learning environments in schools and neighborhood-based youth institutions. There is comprehensive research indicating that positive racial socialization can serve to buffer the impact of negative racial stereotyping among ethnic minority youth, particularly amongst African Americans. Such socialization provides youth with psychological resources and relationships so as to make sense of negative stereotyping and discrimination and to resist them (Bowman & Howard, 1985; Boykin & Toms, 1985; Mandara, 2006). These are youth who are more likely to be in schools with less per-pupil funding, fewer highly qualified teachers, punitive discipline policies, more restrictive curriculum, less technology, and underresourced libraries (Darling-Hammond, 2004). Gordon, Bridgall, and Meroe's (2005) call for broad supplementary education is in part a response to the risks that schools in such communities often pose to youth.

Institutions, formal and informal, need knowledge of what makes learning environments robust as well as the capacity to bring such features into action, adapting them to the differences in specific goals for development and the local contexts of youths' lives (Nasir, Rosebery, Warren, & Lee, 2006). Robust learning environments take into account the following attitudes, beliefs, and strategies:

- Position the learner as competent
- Anticipate sources of vulnerability
- Examine and scaffold resources that the learner brings
- Make public the social good and utility
- Make problem solving explicit and public
- Provide supports as learners are engaged in complex problem solving

- Provide expansive opportunities for learning within and outside of school
- Remain adaptive and dynamic

We can find these features in both formal and informal learning spaces. Interestingly, there has been a large body of research showing many informal learning spaces, especially in low-income neighborhoods, as highly effective in supporting the holistic development of young people whereas schools in the same neighborhoods are not (Fisher, 2003; Heath, 2004; McLaughlin, 1993). The attributes of a robust learning environment are important in part because they can be warranted from research in cognition (Anderson, 1993; Bransford, Brown, & Cocking, 1999; Tomasello, 1999), human development (Bell, 2010; Kunda, 1999; Spencer, 2006), and some fields of the cognitive, cultural, and social neurosciences (Chiao et al., 2010; Meltzoff & Decety, 2003; Miller & Rodgers, 2001; Nadel, Lane, & Ahern, 2000; Whitehead, 2010). These warrants suggest that the needs addressed by such features are rooted jointly in our biology as humans as well as our participation in human cultural practices (Wilson, 1998). The jointly biological and cultural need for a sense of competence, efficacy, and psychological and physical well-being fulfills fundamental roles in the success of our evolution as a species. The socially organized ways that humans adapt to and transform their environments include the ways that different cultural communities address common needs for human development. The documentary film *Babies* illustrates poignantly how basic needs of infants (e.g., learning to coordinate their body movements, including walking; communicating with others in the absence of competence in formal language; manipulating objects for personal goals, etc.) are supported in very different ways and instantiated in different goals across different cultural communities (Super & Harkness, 1986; Weisner, 1984). For example, the baby from Namibia learns to walk by balancing an object on his head and learns hand-eye coordination by pounding a mortar and pestle. These are tasks that are part of the social life of the rural Namibian community that he must learn to master. In contrast, the infants in rural Mongolia and urban San Francisco learn these tasks of walking and hand-eye coordination in completely different ways and because of different social goals (e.g., learning to pick up different kinds of objects that serve different social goals).

We know that social relationships with other people matter greatly for human development. From birth, infants pay more attention to human faces than to objects (Johnson & Morton, 1991). A newborn learns that getting his or her needs met requires understanding the internal states of others and finding ways to communicate his or her needs. Positive social relationships are a source of motivation, particularly when the tasks to be accomplished are risky (Bugental & Goodnow, 1998). This is why, for example, group cohesion—what the Marines call *semper fi* (short for semper fidelis, meaning "always faithful")—a sense of belonging is a central principle of military training. We also know that perceptions matter, particularly perceptions of risk, for our willingness to participate, for the effort we put forth, for the goals we set. Perceptions are a consequence of the meaning we impose on prior experiences that are encoded in neural networks and sparked by the release of particular chemicals in the brain (McEwen, 1998). Such chemical responses are often an outgrowth of a perception associated with a strong emotional valence—positive or negative.

From our evolutionary past, humans are predisposed to desire a sense of efficacy, an ability to impact our environments (Quartz & Sejnowski, 2002). Our emotional responses to experiences are associated with our perceptions of those experiences. From what I already know and feel, is this experience one that makes me feel safe, competent, and capable of achieving some goal that is personally meaningful (Maslow, 1954)? It should be noted that even personal meaningfulness is an outgrowth of the individual in a social and cultural context. For example, in what Markus and Kitayama (1991) identify as cultural communities (often defined by ethnicity, within and sometimes across national borders—e.g., Asian cultures) oriented toward an interdependent view of the self, individual personal goals will be influenced by individual traits and life experiences but also likely will be directed toward interdependent social goals influenced by family and societal expectations and norms (e.g., pursuing personal goals that facilitate incorporation into the family, fulfilling the expectations of one's parents). The question, then, for educators (i.e., parents, teachers, coaches, pastors, etc.) is how to structure learning environments (i.e., the practices within family life, within schooling, in sports, in arts organizations, in churches, etc.) that accomplish these basic human needs in ways that are responsive to differences in local contexts.

In this chapter, I propose Cultural Modeling (Lee, 2007) as one framework for thinking about how to design learning that is (a) ecologically broad, (b) culturally responsive, and (c) addresses basic human needs for a sense of efficacy, belonging, and resilience. I situate the discussion of Cultural Modeling in the context of formal schooling for several reasons. First, the empirical work in Cultural Modeling has been in schools, addressing learning in particular academic domains. Second, designing learning that addresses these broad principles has been most challenging in formal schooling. Third, among the fundamental principles of Cultural Modeling is to connect learning in informal settings with learning in schools, and thus inherently include an ecological dimension.

The Cultural Modeling Framework

Cultural Modeling is a framework for the design of robust learning environments that draws on the knowledge that youth develop in routine, everyday practices to scaffold learning in academic domains (Lee, 1993, 1995a). Everyday knowledge includes knowledge of content, epistemological orientations and dispositions, and particular practices. Often, such knowledge is tacit, having been learned by intent observation through participation with the support of more expert persons (Rogoff, Paradise, Mejía-Arauz, Correa-Chávez, & Angelillo, 2003). A goal of Cultural Modeling is for people designing learning environments to identify and articulate potential points of convergence between the content knowledge, problem-solving strategies, and epistemological orientations and dispositions of everyday practices with those required for complex problem solving in a target academic domain. This requires equally focused and detailed analyses of everyday practices as well as the problem-solving practices of particular academic domains.

Once points of synergy have been identified, the facilitator or teacher's task is to identify what I call *cultural data sets.* This may be done by examining relevant research literatures and artifacts of popular culture as well as engaging with students directly. These are texts broadly defined and/or tasks in the everyday domain that require the same kind of reasoning, epistemological orientations, and dispositions as the target academic domain. Cultural data sets must be ones to which students bring significant prior knowledge. Often the target knowledge in the academic domain is tacit, meaning that students carry out complex tasks without knowing how they do it. In the first phase of instruction, the foci on problem solving with the cultural data sets are to make public and explicit knowledge that is tacit.

A second core task in Cultural Modeling is to design problems in the target academic domain that require generative knowledge (e.g., knowledge that facilitates tackling a wide range of problems essential to the domain) (Perkins, 1992). Sequencing such problems can be challenging. The first series of problems should be ones for which the learner brings some significant prior knowledge and interest. This is similar to the idea of "near transfer" tasks in cognition (Schwartz & Nasir, 2004; Singley & Anderson, 1989). In the study of literature, the principles of sequencing would include tackling an interpretive problem, such as understanding how symbolism functions (e.g., generative because it is applicable across many different kinds of literary texts), to works of literature in which the social world of the text is closer to the life experiences of students, while later texts would still include complex presentations of symbolism, but the social world of the texts is further removed from students' everyday lives. This kind of sequencing serves a primarily cognitive function, although it also addresses students' needs to feel competent, efficacious, and safe to take intellectual risks. However, when we consider the broader cultural and ecological challenge I have raised, another design opportunity becomes prominent, namely the content focus of instruction.

A central concern of Cultural Modeling, indeed a broader aim of this chapter and this volume, is to address the comprehensive and holistic development of youth, particularly youth who face persistent intergenerational risks due to race, ethnicity, and poverty (Lee, 2009). For these youth in particular, comprehensive education—that is, what and how they learn within and across the routine spaces of their lives—should be coordinated in ways that help them to be resilient in the face of the societally inscribed risks. This means not only resilience as individuals, but ultimately the resilience of families and communities. Thus, I argue, to the extent that learning tasks embedded in the various routine practices of their lives, including the work of formal schooling, can focus on community-based problem solving, the greater the opportunities for transformation at multiple levels of contexts. I will illustrate an example of such a content decision in Cultural Modeling in the next section. From my perspective, comprehensive education is not only about the education of individuals but about the development of self-sustaining communities as well.

Another important feature of Cultural Modeling is the design of environments in which modes of communication engage the fullest set of resources that learners have available. In Cultural Modeling, our term for the discourse around problem solving with cultural data sets is metacognitive instructional conversation. The goal of metacognitive instructional conversation is to make problem solving explicit for students. This kind of conversation accomplishes another important goal of helping students feel competent and prepared to engage in the kind of problem solving needed for the next phase of instruction, where students will apply their emerging understandings to new tasks that are further removed from their everyday experiences—two of the features of robust learning environments. In addition, the metacognitive instructional conversations around cultural data sets assume that students are knowledgeable peers with their teachers at the beginning of instruction because, typically, students should know as much or more about cultural data sets as do teachers. However, there is an important qualitative difference between what students and highly competent teachers understand. Teachers understand how to map what students' intuitive abilities are onto the target domain, including understanding the emergent and incomplete aspects of students' knowledge that needs to be further developed.

Metacognitive instructional conversations continue as instruction transitions into the formal inquiry of the academic discipline. The overarching point is to direct students' attention toward how they are making sense of the phenomenon in question. Such conversations include the use of students' everyday languages. This may be speaking or providing resources in Spanish or a hybrid mixing of Spanish and English, for example, for students who are most competent in the Spanish language. For speakers of African American English, this has meant the incorporation of African American English as a medium of communication. In either case, the teacher's role is to create an environment for learning in which youth are able to bring the full breadth of intellective resources (prior content knowledge, linguistic resources, epistemological orientation and dispositions) available to them.

Because Cultural Modeling seeks to bridge everyday intuitive and domain-specific academic knowledge, the transition from the informal to the formal entails a developmental trajectory of expertise. In the early phases of instruction, students' representations of their understanding will be incomplete, otherwise noted as "intermediary representations" (Penner, 2000). Intermediary representations include some but not all aspects of the problem-solving processes that are formal to the target academic domain. Over time, the goal is to help students expand their understanding of the formal representations of the academic discipline, including its structures of argumentation (i.e., what counts as most powerful kinds of questions, as evidence, and as warrants). This transition from novice to more expert-like representations involves problems of translation. In the cycles of instruction, Cultural Modeling distinguishes between how students represent their emergent understanding and problems of translation into the formal discourses and forms of argumentation of the target academic discipline. Translations into formal discourses may include both oral and written communication. In oral communication, it means moving from nonstandardized dialects or another national language to Standard Academic English. In written communication, it means appropriate academic uses of grammatical forms, rhetorical structures, and making explicit the disciplinary principles to which the student is appealing when making arguments. In the context of formal schooling, negative assumptions and stereotypes about nondominant uses of languages (in the case of English Language Learners and speakers of dialects such as African American English or Appalachian English) restrict the range of resources available to students to think deeply (Ball, 2002). Confusions about the form of how students represent their understanding and their ability to translate those understandings into formal registers (oral and written) can often interrupt learning. Teachers must have a comprehensive understanding of trajectories of expertise in the target academic domain in order to guide students through problems of representation to problems of translation.

Together, these principles of Cultural Modeling support bridging learning across contexts, in this case, the everyday and the academic. I argue that such bridging contributes to the comprehensive development of young people across spaces. Cultural Modeling seeks to help students develop knowledge transfer, to expand their knowledge and linguistic repertoires, and to expand their psychosocial resources for achieving a sense of competence, relevance, efficacy and well-being. Because Cultural Modeling connects the everyday and the academic, helping youth construct continuities across the multiple spaces in which they routinely participate, it facilitates comprehensive development rather than simple narrow goals of development.

Cultural Modeling in Action

I will illustrate the principles of Cultural Modeling in action in two academic domains. The first is from my own empirical work in response to teaching literature. The other example was not developed as an explicit instantiation of Cultural Modeling but reflects the principles of the framework: in mathematics, the algebra project developed by Robert Moses. The literature and mathematics work take place largely in schools serving low-income African American students. The focus of instruction in both programs explicitly involves scaffolding intuitive knowledge in the everyday lives of students to support discipline-specific academic learning, including explicit attention to the everyday language practices of youth in these communities. Finally, each program is comprehensive in the sense of helping students use academic learning in the specific domains to address social and political identity issues that are central to their development as members of particular communities. In each of these dimensions—connecting everyday and disciplinary knowledge, incorporating everyday linguistic resources, developing students' sense of competence and efficacy by making problem solving explicit, and using the development of academic disciplinary problem solving to address issues beyond the bounds of the classroom—these instantiations of Cultural Modeling are comprehensive in their scope.

Applying Cultural Modeling to Teaching Literature

Cultural Modeling always requires a careful analysis of problem solving in the target domain. That means articulating the kinds of knowledge, epistemological beliefs, and dispositions that are required to do complex thinking in the domain, including identifying the kinds of problems that are most generative. In response to literature, we have identified big interpretive problems that readers of canonical texts must tackle, no matter the genre or national tradition. These interpretive problems include symbolism, irony, satire, and problems of narration, including unreliable narrators. Drawing on other empirical work in the fields of literary response as well as critical theories of literary interpretation (Booth, 1974, 1983; Rabinowitz, 1987; Smith, 1989; Smith & Hillocks, 1988), we have been able to identify specific strategies that good readers use to detect such problems and to reconstruct what are nonliteral interpretations. In addition to discipline-specific strategies, literary reasoning also entails particular dispositions toward language. Comprehending and interpreting complex literary works requires attention to and appreciation of the rhetorical tools, ways of using language used by writers to bring readers into the subjunctive worlds of the author's imagination (Vipond & Hunt, 1984). It requires an appreciation of language play as an aesthetic end in itself, beyond just the content of texts—the "how" as well as the "what" of a text.

Speakers of African American English routinely participate in a genre of talk called *signifying* (Smitherman, 1977). Signifying involves ritual insult (e.g., ("Yo mama so skinny she can do the Hoola Hoop in a Cheerio). Signifying requires careful attention to language play. The intuitive strategies speakers use to comprehend and produce signifying involve figuration that includes symbolism, irony, satire, and unreliable narration (Lee, 1995b). In addition to African American English linguistic resources, these students are also active participants in youth culture, including listening to rap music. Rap lyrics routinely involve the use of similar interpretive problems and figurative language (i.e., symbolism, irony, satire, and problems of narration) as well as aesthetic uses of word play (Rose, 1994). As with signifying, those listening to rap lyrics intuitively comprehend figuration and language play.

The exemplary unit I will describe was taught to high school seniors and addressed interpreting symbolism in literary texts and wrestling with the question of resilience in the face of horrendous life challenges. I was teaching in an urban high school in a Midwest city serving a predominantly low-income

African American community. The school and the students had histories of low academic achievement in reading, as measured by standardized test scores. The cultural data sets that I applied included signifying dialogues as well as popular rap lyrics. I chose the canonical novel *Beloved*, by Toni Morrison, followed by such texts as William Faulkner's "A Rose for Emily," chapters from Amy Tan's novel *Joy Luck Club*, and poems such as Emily Dickinson's "Because I Could Not Stop for Death" and Dylan Thomas's "Do Not Go Gentle Into That Good Night."

I selected a rap song called "The Mask" by the Fugees as a cultural data set. It is a complex text involving multiple narrators, shifts in settings, political critique, and complex symbolism. The chorus repeats the line as to how everybody wears the mask, and questions how long this will last. The idea of wearing a mask to disguise one's identity reflects an observation of the great African American intellectual and social–political analyst W.E.B. DuBois. DuBois (1903/1968) talked about what he called the "double consciousness" of the African American, "this sense of always looking at one's self through the eyes of others, of measuring one's soul by the tape of a world that looks on in amused contempt and pity" (p. 3). Cultural navigation, especially in the face of societal stereotypes, remains a crucial and difficult life task of people of African descent in the United States. Thus, the efforts of students to make public how they understood the social critique of the Fugees was intended to serve a broader goal than simply understanding symbolism. The themes invited by both the cultural data sets and the canonical texts were aimed at a more comprehensive set of goals for development, goals rooted in the needs and challenges of the students as members of particular communities.

Beloved, by Toni Morrison (1987), was selected as the anchoring canonical novel for equally comprehensive goals for the students' development. For African American youth, understanding the legacy of the enslavement of their ancestors remains necessary for understanding both the explicit as well as subtle ways that racism continues to manifest itself in their lives. I and many others argue there are important lessons for current generations of African Americans in understanding how prior generations, especially those who lived under the African Holocaust, were able to be resilient in the face of horrors we cannot even imagine (Boykin, 1986; Hilliard, 1995, 1998). Those lessons in resilience must have some meaning, even in today's world. *Beloved* is the story of Sethe, a woman who escapes from slavery but then kills her baby to prevent her child from being taken back into enslavement. It is the story of the consequences of that unimaginable act for Sethe and her children. It narrates the trauma of enslavement on those who endured its monstrous daily indignities and terror and how they learned to survive, to assert their humanity and to be resilient so that new generations were possible. Considering the levels of intracommunity violence today in too many low-income African American communities, the lessons of *Beloved* may be all the more poignant today.

I offer two examples of students' response to the instruction, one involving the analysis of a cultural data set and the second an analysis of *Beloved*. In each example we find students with previous histories of low academic achievement displaying skilled strategies in literary analysis, deep engagement with difficult texts, and appreciation of complex language play.

In the first example, Jonetha responds to a stanza from "The Mask," in which the narrator describes how he once worked at Burger King. During this employment, he explains that his manager complimented him on his good work and offered him a 25-cent raise to work the register. However, the manager also said that he would have to spy on who is stealing French fries or getting high at work. The narrator vehemently rejects the offer and states, why should I spy for you when you have been spying on me?

Jonetha responds,

> I'm saying I think he had a mask on when he was fighting, when he beat him up, because in order for him to have the mask on, he was spying on that person. He was spying on somebody. I don't know who he was spying on. But in order for him to realize that the man was spying on him, he had to take off his mask. In order to realize that the man was saying ... I don't know. Shoot!

Jonetha is willing to hypothesize when she is not certain. This willingness to engage in uncertainty is an important prerequisite for complex problem solving. Schools in low-income communities oftentimes have restrictive curricula that focus on right and wrong answers as opposed to critical thinking. After many years of learning within these parameters, many students come to view uncertainty as an indicator of weakness and failure. In addition, Jonetha is focusing on parallels in the text (i.e., the *king* taking on a task to hide his identity in working at Burger King and taking off his mask in order to understand that the manager is trying to use him; the functions of the mask for the worker and the manager) as well as ironies (i.e., the reference of oneself as a king while still taking orders). Such attention to rhetorical details is a necessary component of complex literary analysis. It is not surprising that Jonetha and the other students understood the symbolic meaning of the mask as an image, but it is significant that she and others are able to analyze rhetorically how the symbolism is structured.

The students hit the ground running in their analysis of *Beloved*. They were able to understand the subtle inverted chronologies found throughout the text. They were able not only to target key symbols in the text in isolation but to follow the buildup of a complex network of associations as images were repeated across the text.

One chapter begins, "A fully dressed woman walked out of the water. She barely gained the dry bank of the stream before she sat down and leaned against a mulberry tree. All day and all night she sat there, her head resting on the trunk in a position abandoned enough to crack the brim in her straw hat" (p. 50). Morrison does not tell us who the woman is. However, the students in this class immediately asserted that the woman was the ghost of the baby that Sethe had killed, back from the dead as a full-grown woman. They supported this claim with detailed evidence from this and prior chapters (e.g., she couldn't be Baby Suggs [Sethe's now dead mother-in-law] because this woman's dress had tiny buttons and Baby Suggs hated buttons; she must be the baby because of telling descriptive details: she's very sleepy, thirsty, pees a lot, has flawless skin). In the midst of this heated discussion, Taquisha, emboldened, asserts,

> Now wouldn't you want to know? You know! The questions—hair all straight like a baby, you know and stuff, drinking all this water? Okay! You know she said she ran away and stuff. You got some *brand new* shoes on yo' feet. You *too* clean to run away. Yo feet ain't swole. You ain't gonna expect nothing? You ain't gonna ask her *no* questions?

Taquisha's claim is significant in several ways. First, she is emotionally emphatic with her word choice; use of bold typeface indicates that she is deeply engaged. She uses African American English rhetorical prosody to exhibit how deeply she feels about the conundrum she raises. Consistent with what Samuel Taylor Coleridge (2005) in 1817 called "the willing suspension of disbelief," Taquisha has entered the subjunctive world of the text and addresses her fellow students as if they were all there observing credulously the sudden appearance of this woman at Sethe's doorstep. She has attended closely to the details of the text by pulling together the examples of the ghost of Sethe's baby Beloved as extremely dangerous. And equally important, Taquisha has invoked, albeit not consciously, the question of authorial intent. She wants to know why the author, Toni Morrison, has not had Sethe and Paul D recognize that this woman, baby ghost returned, is dangerous. There are all the signs, Taquisha argues, that this woman is not who she says she is.

While these examples come from one class that I taught, the intervention took place in the entire school, and this unit was taught to all seniors. Assessments developed by the project, based on a hierarchy of question types for comprehending fiction by Hillock and Ludlow (1984), showed students able to comprehend the most challenging tasks in the hierarchy (Lee, 2007).

While I do not argue that the skills and dispositions that these students learned in this Cultural Modeling intervention were sufficiently robust to transfer to many other contexts of their lives, I do argue that if schools, community organizations, and, indeed, families were coordinated in supporting the kind of intellectual risk taking, deep engagement with text analysis, attention to foundational questions about these youth's developmental tasks (as African American adolescents living in low-income neighborhoods), the impact could be multiplicative, and thus comprehensive; comprehensive not only because such complementary development took place in several settings but also because its goals for development were not merely cognitive. An equally important challenge to this intervention was the lack of intellective cohesion across departments within the high school, and the inability to sustain the intervention, even in the English department, across time. The intervention was very successful while we were at the high school, but when our research team left and a new principal came in, all that had been accomplished, both with our program and others in the school, was dismantled.

In terms of the idea and goal of comprehensive education, as Gordon et al. (2005) describe it, the inability to sustain our work at this high school is all the more devastating because of tragic events that would follow more than a decade later. In 2010, a young man from this same high school was brutally killed, literally beaten to death on the streets by a mob of his peers. It is certainly highly speculative to consider the possibility that examining literary works that wrestle with the meaning of life and death, with the consequences of taking a life, may have made any difference in the consciousness of Derrion Albert's peers. But it is certainly an interesting question.

Mathematics and the Algebra Project

The second example is in the domain of mathematics and involves the algebra project (AP), developed by mathematician and civil rights activist Dr. Robert Moses (Moses, Kamii, Swap, & Howard, 1989; Silva, Moses, Rivers, & Johnson, 1990). The AP does not claim itself as an example of Cultural Modeling. However, its design principles map nicely onto the Cultural Modeling framework, and so I offer it as an example of how to conceive math education within a similar structure.

Like our work in Cultural Modeling, the AP seeks to scaffold youth's intuitive knowledge derived from everyday practice to teach generative skills in an academic domain, in this case, algebra. Moses (1994) argued that a central challenge in the movement from arithmetic to algebra is understanding positive and negative numbers. In arithmetic, students focus on numbers as quantities (i.e., what he calls the "how many" question). However, rational numbers include the attributes not only of quantity but also of directionality (what he calls the "which way" question). Thus, on a number line with positive numbers to the right of zero and negative numbers to the left of zero, these integers take on a directional position with regard to a point of origin. Moses argued that comprehending the number line was analogous to how students who routinely travel on an urban transit system understand how to get from one station to another (e.g., the outbound vs. the inbound train).

What Cultural Modeling would refer to as a cultural data set is the foundational activity in AP of taking urban youth in an algebra class on the mass transit and asking them to create problems of how to get from Station A to Station B. Early scaffolding in the AP focuses directly on translating intuitive representations (i.e., drawings of moving from Station A as a point of origin to Station K by moving so many stations in a particular direction) to formal algebraic representations.

The AP also takes seriously the ways in which students' home language serves as a linguistic resource; that is, students may talk about their mathematical representations and reasoning in African American English, in Hmong, in Spanish, and so forth. Moses referred to the use of everyday language as "people talk." In the appendix of the book, Moses (Moses & Cobb, 2001) wrote about the intellectual and political foundations of the AP, and he discussed in detail the sequence of everyday situations in which students develop intuitive and emergent conceptions of mathematical ideas about linear equations. The AP then has students engage in reasoning about these everyday models as a scaffold to formal mathematical explanations. For example, students create diagrams that "illustrate (in people talk) that the *Park Street* Station is 3 stops inbound from *Central Square* ... and that *Harvard Square* is 4 stops outbound from *Park Street*" (Moses & Cobb, 2001, p. 200). What in Cultural Modeling is called "metacognitive instructional conversations," the AP calls "how to do that" questions or "feature talk." As Moses noted, "we take students' people talk' (their writings, pictures, verbal exchanges, etc.) and identify the relevant mathematical features, develop symbols for these, and construct questions (if we can) that will elicit '*feature talk.*' This is the hard conceptual work without which the abstract mathematical symbols fly away from all but a small percentage of students" (p. 201).

The AP also takes a holistic view on the education of youth in its programs around the country. Consistent with the argument that robust learning environments are organized to help learners feel competent, safe, and efficacious, the AP curriculum makes problem solving explicit and provides supports as learners are engaged in mathematical reasoning. In addition, the AP addresses the comprehensive view of learning I have described within a cultural and ecological framework. As with Cultural Modeling, the AP attempts to use domain-specific academic learning as a springboard for the development of both the individual learner and his or her community. Moses, a veteran of the civil rights movement and one of the founders of the Student Nonviolent Coordinating Committee, asserts that mathematical literacy is one of the major civil rights of the 21st century. Competence in algebra, he claims, is the doorway to the study of higher mathematics, which in turn is the gatekeeper for entry into the technical professions. Thus, not only does the AP address the development of competence in algebra through modeling from knowledge constructed from everyday practice, but it also designs the tasks students tackle to be situated in terms of applications of mathematics to civic and community-based issues.

In addition, the AP has developed the Young People's Project as a formal part of its program, where young people use mathematics to address community-based issues as well as promoting mathematical literacy among their peers. Paulos (1995) illustrated how mathematics is used in newspapers and other popular media to argue political points of view but that the mathematics used is not accurate. Here, both Moses and Paulos argued that mathematical competence serves an important civic function. When youth from disempowered communities can see mathematics as a tool for both personal and community development through practices within and across the multiple settings of their lives, an important resource for community transformation can certainly take place.

Conclusion

I have attempted to argue in this chapter for the essential role that complementary robust opportunities for learning can play in both individual and community resilience within and across the multiple spaces where young people spend their time, especially young people from racial- and ethnic-minority and low-income communities. I believe this is the view of comprehensive learning that has been articulated by our esteemed elder scholar, Dr. Edmund Gordon. I have argued that the features of robust learning environments remain relatively constant across contexts and that these features are robust, in part, because they can be warranted from research documenting the joint influences of human biology and human culture on our development. The cultural nature of human development helps us understand the range of variation that contributes to adaptation, the myriad ways that human communities organize themselves to accomplish the basic tasks of growth over the life course.

I have further attempted to illustrate how such a comprehensive view of learning, one contributing jointly to personal as well as community development, can be accomplished, at least in part, through the organization of learning in formal school environments. I offer Cultural Modeling as a framework for the design of learning that scaffolds informal learning in everyday contexts to domain-specific academic learning in schools in such a way that academic problem solving can both serve as a resource for the intellective development of youth and help youth utilize their academic learning for the positive development of their families and communities. The connection to community, family, and individual identity highlighted through Cultural Modeling can contribute to a comprehensive education of youth, in terms of their intellectual, psychosocial, emotional, and civic development.

References

Anderson, J. (1993). *Rules of the mind.* Hillsdale, NJ: Erlbaum.

Ball, A. (2002). Three decades of research on classroom life: Illuminating the classroom communicative lives of America's at-risk students. In W. Secada (Ed.), *Review of research in education* (Vol. 26, pp. 71–112). Washington, DC: American Educational Research Association.

Bell, D. C. (2010). *The dynamics of connection: How evolution and biology create caregiving and attachment.* Lanham, MD: Lexington.

Booth, W. (1974). *A rhetoric of irony.* Chicago, IL: University of Chicago Press.

Booth, W. (1983). *A rhetoric of fiction.* Chicago, IL: University of Chicago Press.

Bowman, P., & Howard, C. (1985). Race related socialization, motivation and academic achievement: A study of black youths in three generation families. *Journal of American Academy of Child Psychiatry, 24,* 134–141.

Boykin, A. W. (1986). The triple quandary and the schooling of Afro-American children. In U. Neisser (Ed.), *The school achievement of minority children* (pp. 57–92). Hillsdale, NJ: Lawrence Erlbaum.

Boykin, A. W., & Toms, F. D. (1985). Black child socialization: A conceptual framework. In H. P. McAdoo & J. L. McAdoo (Eds.), *Black children: Social, educational, and parental environments* (pp. 33–52). Newbury Park, CA: Sage.

Bransford, J., Brown, A., & Cocking, R. (1999). *How people learn: Brain, mind, experience and school.* Washington, DC: National Academy Press.

Bronfenbrenner, U., & Morris, P. A. (1998). The ecology of developmental processes. In W. Damon & R. M. Lerner (Eds.), *Handbook of child psychology: Theoretical models of human development* (5th ed., Vol. 1, pp. 993–1028). New York, NY: Wiley & Sons.

Bugental, D. B., & Goodnow, J. J. (1998). Socialization processes. In W. Damon (Ed.), *Handbook of child psychology* (Social, emotional and personality development ed., Vol. 3, pp. 389–462). New York, NY: John Wiley & Sons.

Chiao, J., Hariri, A., Harada, T., Mano, Y., Sadato, N., Parrish, T., & Iidaka, T. (2010). Tools of the trade: Theory and methods in cultural neuroscience. *Social Cognitive and Affective Neuroscience, 5,* 356–361.

Cole, M. (1996). *Cultural psychology, a once and future discipline.* Cambridge, MA: The Belknap Press of Harvard University Press.

Coleridge, S. T. (2005). *Biographia literaria.* Whitefish, MT: Kessinger.

Darling-Hammond, L. (2004). The color line in American education: Race, resources, and student achievement. *Du Bois Review, 1*(2), 213–246.

DuBois, W.E.B. (1968). *The souls of black folks: Essays and sketches.* Greenwich, CT: Fawcett. (Original work published 1903)

Fisher, M. T. (2003). Open mics and open minds: Spoken word poetry in African diaspora participatory literacy communities. *Harvard Education Review, 73*(3), 362–389.

Gordon, E. W., Bridgall, B. L., & Meroe, A. S. (2005). *Supplementary education: The hidden curriculum of high academic achievement.* Lanham, MD: Rowman & Littlefield.

Heath, S. B. (2004). Risks, rules, and roles: Youth perspectives on the work of learning for community development. In A. N. Perret-Clemont, C. Pontecorvo, L. B. Resnick, T. Zittoun, & B. Burge (Eds.), *Joining society: Social interaction and learning in adolescence and youth* (pp. 41–70). New York, NY: Cambridge University Press.

Hilliard, A. G. (1995). *The maroon within us: Selected essays on African American community socialization.* Baltimore, MD: Black Classic Press.

Hilliard, A. G. (1998). *SBA: The reawakening of the African mind.* Gainesville, FL: Makare.

Hillocks, G., & Ludlow, L. (1984). A taxonomy of skills in reading and interpreting fiction. *American Educational Research Journal, 21,* 7–24.

Johnson, M. H., & Morton, J. (1991). *Biology and cognitive development: The case of face recognition.* Cambridge, MA: Blackwell.

Kunda, Z. (1999). *Social cognition: Making sense of people.* Cambridge, MA: MIT Press.

Lee, C. D. (1993). *Signifying as a scaffold for literary interpretation: The pedagogical implications of an African American discourse genre.* Urbana, IL: National Council of Teachers of English.

Lee, C. D. (1995a). A culturally based cognitive apprenticeship: Teaching African American high school students' skills in literary interpretation. *Reading Research Quarterly, 30*(4), 608–631.

Lee, C. D. (1995b). Signifying as a scaffold for literary interpretation. *Journal of Black Psychology, 21*(4), 357–381.

Lee, C. D. (2007). *Culture, literacy and learning: Taking bloom in the midst of the whirlwind.* New York, NY: Teachers College Press.

Lee, C. D. (2008). The centrality of culture to the scientific study of learning and development: How an ecological framework in educational research facilitates civic responsibility. *Educational Researcher, 37*(5), 267–279.

Lee, C. D. (2009). Historical evolution of risk and equity: Interdisciplinary issues and critiques. *Review of Research in Education, 33,* 63–100.

Lee, C. D. (2010). Soaring above the clouds, delving the ocean's depths: Understanding the ecologies of human learning and the challenge for education science. *Educational Researcher, 39*(9), 643–655.

Mandara, J. (2006). The impact of family functioning on African American males' academic achievement: A review and clarification of the empirical literature. *Teachers College Record, 108*(2), 206–223.

Markus, H., & Kitayama, S. (1991). Culture and the self: Implications for cognition, emotion, and motivation. *Psychological Review, 98,* 224–253.

Maslow, A. H. (1954). *Motivation and personality.* New York, NY: Harper.

McEwen, B. S. (1998). Stress, adaptation, and disease: Allostasis and allostatic load. *Annals of the New York Academy of Sciences, 840,* 33–44.

McLaughlin, M. W. (1993). Embedded identities: Enabling balance in urban contexts. In S. B. Heath & M. W. McLaughlin (Eds.), *Identity and inner-city youth: Beyond ethnicity and gender* (pp. 36–68). New York, NY: Teachers College Press.

Meltzoff, A. N., & Decety, J. (2003). What imitation tells us about social cognition: A rapprochement between developmental psychology and cognitive neuroscience. *Philosophical Transactions of the Royal Society of London, Biological Sciences, 358,* 491–500.

Miller, W. B., & Rodgers, J. L. (2001). *The ontogeny of human bonding sytems: Evolutionary origins, neural bases, and psychological manifestations.* New York, NY: Springer.

Morrison, T. (1987). *Beloved.* New York, NY: Alfred A. Knopf.

Moses, R. P. (1994). The struggle for citizenship and math/sciences literacy. *Journal of Mathematical Behavior, 13,* 107–111.

Moses, R. P., & Cobb, C. E. (2001). *Radical equations: Math literacy and civil rights.* Boston, MA: Beacon Press.

Moses, R. P., Kamii, M., Swap, S. M., & Howard, J. (1989). The Algebra Project: Organizing in the spirit of Ella. *Harvard Educational Review, 59*(4), 423–443.

Nadel, L., Lane, R., & Ahern, G. L. (Eds.). (2000). *The cognitive neuroscience of emotion.* New York, NY: Oxford University Press.

Nasir, N., Rosebery, A. S., Warren, B., & Lee, C. D. (2006). Learning as a cultural process: Achieving equity through diversity. In K. Sawyer (Ed.), *Handbook of the learning sciences.* New York, NY: Cambridge University Press.

Paulos, J. A. (1995). *A mathematician reads the newspaper.* New York, NY: Doubleday.

Penner, D. (2000). Cognition, computers, and synthetic science: Building knowledge and meaning through modeling. *Review of Research in Education, 25,* 1–35.

Perkins, D. (1992). *Smart schools: Better thinking and learning for every child.* New York, NY: The Free Press.

Perle, M., Moran, R., Lutkas, A., & Tirre, W. (2005). *NAEP 2004 trends in academic progress: Three decades of student performance in reading and mathematics.* Washington, DC: National Center for Education Statistics, U.S. Department of Education, Institute of Education Sciences.

Quartz, S. R., & Sejnowski, T. J. (2002). *Liars, lovers, and heroes: What the new brain science reveals about how we become who we are.* New York, NY: William Morrow.

Rabinowitz, P. (1987). *Before reading: Narrative conventions and the politics of interpretation.* Ithaca, NY: Cornell University Press.

Ramani, A. K., Gilbertson, L., & Fox, M. A. (2007). *Status and trends in the education of racial and ethnic minorities.* Washington, DC: Institute of Education Sciences National Center for Education Statistics.

Rogoff, B. (2003). *The cultural nature of human development.* New York, NY: Oxford University Press.

Rogoff, B., Paradise, R., Mejía-Arauz, R., Correa-Chávez, M., & Angelillo, C. (2003). Firsthand learning through intent participation. *Annual Review of Psychology, 54,* 175–204.

Rose, T. (1994). *Black noise: Rap music and black culture in contemporary America.* Hanover, NH: Wesleyan University Press.

Schwartz, D., & Nasir, N. (2004). Transfer of learning. *Encyclopedia of Education 4,* 1449–1452.

Silva, C. M., Moses, R. P., Rivers, J., & Johnson, P. (1990). The algebra project: Making middle school mathematics count. *Journal of Negro Education, 59*(3), 375–392.

Singley, K., & Anderson, J. R. (1989). *The transfer of cognitive skill.* Cambridge, MA: Harvard University Press.

Slaughter-Defoe, D., Nakagawa, K., Takanishi, R., & Johnson, D. J. (1990). Toward cultural/ecological perspectives on schooling and achievement in African- and Asian-American children. *Child Development, 61*(2), 363–383.

Smith, M. (1989). Teaching the interpretation of irony in poetry. *Research in the Teaching of English, 23,* 254–272.

Smith, M., & Hillocks, G. (1988, October). Sensible sequencing: Developing knowledge about literature text by text. *English Journal,* 44–49.

Smitherman, G. (1977). *Talkin and testifyin: The language of black America.* Boston, MA: Houghton Mifflin.

Spencer, M. B. (1985). Cultural cognition and social cognition as identity factors in black children's personal-social growth. In M. Spencer, G. K. Brookins, & W. Allen (Eds.), *Beginnings: The social and affective development of black children* (pp. 59–72). Hillsdale, NJ: Erlbaum.

Spencer, M. B. (2006). Phenomenology and ecological systems theory: Development of diverse groups. In W. Damon & R. M. Lerner (Eds.), *Handbook of child psychology* (6th ed., Vol. 1, pp. 829–893). New York, NY: Wiley.

Spencer, M. B., Cole, S. P., Jones, S., & Swanson, D. P. (1997). Neighborhood and family influences on young urban adolescents' behavior problems: A multisample multisite analysis. In J. Brooks-Gunn, G. Duncan, & J. L. Aber (Eds.), *Neighborhood poverty: Context and consequences for children* (Vol. 1, pp. 200–218). New York, NY: Russell Sage Foundation Press.

Spencer, M. B., Harpalani, V., Cassidy, E., Jacobs, C., Donde, S., & Goss, T. N. (2006). Understanding vulnerability and resilience from a normative development perspective: Implications for racially and ethnically diverse youth. In D. Chicchetti & E. Cohen (Eds.), *Handbook of developmental psychopathology* (Vol. 1). Hoboken, NJ: Wiley.

Super, C., & Harkness, S. (1986). The developmental niche: A conceptualization at the interface of child and culture. *International Journal of Behavioral Development, 9,* 545–569.

Tomasello, M. (1999). *The cultural origins of human cognition.* Cambridge, MA: Harvard University Press.

Vipond, D., & Hunt, R. (1984). Point-driven understanding: Pragmatic and cognitive dimensions of literary reading. *Poetics, 13,* 261–277.

Weisner, T. S. (1984). Ecocultural niches of middle childhood: A cross-cultural perspective. In W. A. Collins (Ed.), *Development during middle childhood: The years from six to twelve* (pp. 335–369). Washington, DC: National Academy of Sciences Press.

Weisner, T. S. (2002). Ecocultural understanding of children's developmental pathways. *Human Development, 174,* 275–281.

Whitehead, C. (2010). The culture ready brain. *Social Cognitive and Affective Neuroscience, 5,* 168–179.

Wilson, E. O. (1998). *Consilience: The unity of knowledge.* New York, NY: Knopf.

9

THEORETICAL ANALYSIS OF RESILIENCE AND IDENTITY

An African American Engineer's Life Story

Ebony McGee and Margaret Beale Spencer

> I never had a Black engineering professor, so I don't know what people are saying about Black professors because I have never had one. Not a [Black] math professor either. Actually I only had one Black professor in my entire college career, and he taught African American Studies.
>
> Tinesha, 27-year-old female, high-achieving Black bioengineering master's degree student

The above excerpt comes from an interview obtained by the first author in a research study designed to explore the voices and experiences of academically successful Black college students majoring in mathematics and engineering (McGee, 2009). At the time of the initial interviews, Tinesha was a master's student in bioengineering. Twenty-seven at the time of the study, she provided a reflective and thoughtful self- and societal analysis. Her narrative emphasized interdependence and interconnectedness and reflected a complex view of her world.

Tinesha's quote and the experiences of the successful Black mathematics and engineering students in the larger study indicate that some Black students must negotiate a delicate balance in their lives. As suggested in the earlier study, human vulnerability gives rise to levels of risk and protective factors associated with the style and character of reactive coping. Black students' lives frequently appear burdened by disproportionately high levels of risk or inadequate accessibility to protective factors, resulting in higher vulnerability (e.g., fewer models with whom to identify; see Spencer, 2006, 2008b; Spencer et al., 2006). Thus, understanding where and how they access and obtain supports through their use of protective factors appears critical. The above excerpt suggests the salience of Tinesha's engineering narrative context and raises considerations regarding mathematics and engineering learning and academic engagement among Blacks. Most salient is that such considerations are infrequently raised in current math and engineering education research on Black students. Also represented in Tinesha's narrative was her negotiation of socially constructed gender boundaries in society, boundaries more pronounced in fields like engineering. Unlike the statistics demonstrating that Black women generally outpace Black men in the college pipeline, in engineering Black men are more commonplace than Black women, and disproportionately so in comparison to Whites and Asians (Carlone & Johnson, 2007). For example, Tinesha remarked that she has never had a female professor for any course in her academic career. Rarely do we hear about successful students like Tinesha who talk about and frame their experiences as Blacks in the contexts of mathematics and engineering.

Human Vulnerability and Resilience

The authors' approach to unpacking Tinesha's life represents a particular perspective on human vulnerability and resilience. Although erroneously portrayed as synonymous with the term *risk,* human vulnerability has a unique meaning (see Anthony, 1974). As used by Anthony, the term *vulnerability* suggests that humans are burdened by levels of risk and that their growth and development are facilitated by a variety of protective factors. As recently described for the population more generally (see Spencer, Swanson, & Edwards, 2010), life-changing events as context for youth development are recurrent for all humans.

As aspects of normal everyday experience, life transitions and traditional developmental tasks are challenges and are coped with on a daily basis. Thus, the need for adaptive coping processes continues unabated and is experienced by all youth (i.e., independent of unique protective factor accessibility or the availability of supports). One's adaptive responses (i.e., as opposed to maladaptive reactions to challenge) become internalized with positive outcomes for youth, which support subsequent protective outcomes as expressions of resilience. Importantly, and as supported by recent theorizing from a recursive perspective (see Spencer 2006, 2008b), positive processes, outcomes, and demonstrations of resiliency decrease one's subsequent levels of vulnerability. Specifically, the prior successes and demonstrations of resiliency are internalized as protective factors. Thus, the process of decreasing vulnerability is accompanied by an increased level of protective factor presence or a reduction of risk.

Unfortunately, Black students pursuing science, technology, engineering, and mathematics (STEM) career paths and parallel academic trajectories have been exposed to generally underexamined challenges and potential sources of support. In addition to tasks as challenges faced by all young people, Black students in general and mathematics/engineering students specifically have an unusual confluence of challenges in their academic contexts. These challenges are unique and worthy of exploration.

It is critical to acknowledge that because of structurally determined barriers and, thus, significant risks, marginalized individuals may require the use of what have been traditionally viewed as maladaptive coping responses. However, it is our view that short-term or "expedient shortcuts" are not necessarily maladaptive and, in fact, may suggest necessary and strategic responses for attending to frequently unacknowledged, structurally organized barriers and systemic challenges. These responses are strategic and, in fact, helpful, so long as they do not serve to undermine future efforts, are sought after productive outcomes, and are forms of patterned coping that do not result in harm to others or the self (McGee & Martin, 2011).

As suggested, although generally underacknowledged and infrequently analyzed as such, positive young-adulthood transitions may be influenced and determined by the identification of and access to culturally specific and strategic supports (e.g., sources of assistance that recognize and respect the diversity of human traditions and group identifications). Risk factors are experienced by youth as diverse challenges. They include the need to address normal human developmental tasks, such as achieving an identity, as well as engaging in experimentation with a variety of roles without significant risk or life-changing consequences, for example, work roles, nontraditional career paths, social roles, and personal roles (e.g., provider of support to others, such as civic engagement). However, the normative becomes extraordinary when challenging contexts or conditions are in place or traditional supports are unavailable, unidentifiable, or inaccessible.

The degree to which societal supports, such as quality schooling opportunities, show cultural consonance (i.e., continuity as opposed to discontinuities and feelings of dissonance), respectfulness, and connectedness with valued traditions improves the relevant outcomes (e.g., academic success). That is, context features of intended youth supports and their cultural fit, given early socialization traditions, are important. During adolescent transitions, the features of intended support can influence the salience of early- and middle-childhood protective factors, supports, and cultural capital investments. Such supports include sensitive teachers, positive models, and culturally relevant sources of identification, which provide a belief that "I can, as well." The latter are associated with family, community, and societal investments and supports. At the same time, if dissonance-producing conditions prevail (e.g., inadequate schooling) but the consequent challenges are acknowledged, responsibility for change owned, and their structured character candidly unpacked and confronted, *resiliency is possible* (i.e., good outcomes can be obtained in the face of challenging conditions). Without a doubt, the period of adolescence provides great opportunities for the scaffolding of a healthy adulthood and myriad demonstrations of resiliency.

Blacks in America have a history characterized by oppression, discrimination, resilience, and resistance, which has contributed to a unique "raced" identity. The role of racial identity—that is, the extent to which societal and personal meanings of race influence a person's self-concept and consequent behavior (Cross, 1991; Helms, 1990, 1995, 1996; Sellers, Smith, Shelton, Rowley, & Chavous, 1998)—in the lives of Black students is a complex phenomenon. Extant theoretical and empirical work in psychology, sociology, and social psychology has demonstrated links between racial identity and positive psychosocial adaptation (Banks & Banks, 1993; Cross, 1991; DuBois, 1973; Sellers et al., 1998; Steele, 1997, 1999).

Racial identity is also based on one's perception that an individual shares a common racial heritage with a particular racial group (Cross, 1991; Helms, 1990; Sellers et al., 1998). The literature on racial identity development among Black students also suggests that realistic beliefs about race play a protective role in their lives. Students who identify strongly with their racial group are better able to negotiate potentially negative environments, deal with discrimination and prejudice, and have high self-esteem (Bowman & Howard, 1985; Grantham & Ford, 2003; Rowley & Moore, 2002; Sanders, 1997).

Allowing for linkages between a student's experiences and "race-based epistemologies" (i.e., Black racial identity) has provided a more holistic approach for illuminating how Tinesha made meaning of racialized experiences and interpreted what it means for her to "be Black" in her academic context.

Positionality and Researcher Subjectivity

In formulating the perspectives in this chapter, we juxtaposed our scholarly backgrounds and our experiences as advocates for African American students. Studying high-achieving African American learners requires that we acknowledge and discuss our own positionality and subjectivity. We both self-identify as Black women and agree that the phenomenological variant of ecological systems theory (PVEST) framework is a critical tool for understanding globally shared human vulnerability and for exposing the particular risks and protective factors of the nation's most marginalized and stereotyped students. There are many similarities and shared experiences between us, as well as in common with the marginalized students and individuals we research and teach. As individuals who have endured the challenges associated with being Black and being female, we are sensitive to the struggles that encompass broad sectors of African American experience. As advocates for African American children—we are also mothers of African American adult and adolescent children—we believe that our shared cultural frames of reference allow us to generate relevant and useful knowledge about these students.

In terms of our individual trajectories, the first author has academic backgrounds and high-level training in mathematics, engineering, educational psychology, and mathematics education. The second author is a national authority on child and developmental psychology, whose long-standing adolescent-focused research addresses the resiliency, identity, and competence formation processes of African American, Hispanic, Asian American, and European American youth. Moreover, the second author has foundational undergraduate training in the basic sciences (bachelor's degree earned in pharmacy) as well as longstanding research and programming application experiences addressing youths' emerging capacity for healthy outcomes and constructive coping methods while developing under generally unacknowledged and highly stressful conditions. We come together in this chapter to attempt to characterize learning and participation for a high-achieving Black female college student that draws on identity, sociohistorical knowledge not only about mathematics and engineering but also about issues of race, African American identity, and struggle.

Research Questions

This study sought to better understand, through first-person account, how one specific African American engineering college student maintains, interprets, and frames high academic achievement and success within an educational arena in which African American presence is scarce. In addition, this study validates the myriad sociohistorical and structural forces of racism, classism, and other forms of oppression characteristic of Black experience. The larger questions guiding this study include those listed below. Although each of these questions is quite complex and worthy of study on its own, their interconnectedness and the likelihood of the participant addressing them led to a rich analysis and powerful results that serve as data for ongoing research:

- How does a successful student give meaning to and negotiate what it means to "be African American" in the context of doing mathematics and engineering?
- If the early experiences of an African American student included resilience-promoting behaviors, what meaning(s) do they provide in relation to earlier resilience-promoting behaviors and subsequent success in college mathematics and engineering?
- To what extent does an academically successful African American college student characterize and respond to learning and participation in mathematics and engineering as racialized forms of experience?

Unlike the vast majority of existing research on mathematics and engineering education among African American students, this research focused on important themes relating to (a) resilience, and how resilience is developed and framed by students; (b) perceptions of opportunities and constraints in various mathematical and engineering-based contexts; (c) strategies used by students to negotiate successful participation in mathematics and engineering; and (d) the salience of racism in the lives and the mathematical and engineering experiences of students, including the ways in which this student interprets and responds to the socially constructed meanings for race (Gutierrez, 2000; Martin, 2000, 2006a, 2006b; McGee, 2009; Spencer, 2006; Stinson, 2006).

Methods

Tinesha is a participant from a larger study on 23 high-achieving mathematics and engineering juniors and seniors in bioengineering, with a 3.4 grade point average (on a 4.0 scale). The academic criteria for inclusion in the study (at least a 3.0 out of 4.0 grade point average) emphasized conventional, quantitative measures of academic achievement and persistence outcomes (U.S. Department of Education, 2002). However, the analysis of first-person data suggests a number of other psychosocial factors that expand the notion of success and resilience for African American students in these disciplines.

Accordingly, to better understand how race and resiliency factors shape the educational and social experiences of these participants, a narrative-based approach was used. This required speaking with students in depth about their lives. The narratives were obtained through the integration of counter-storytelling and life-stories methodologies.

Delgado and Stefanic (2001) defined counter-storytelling as the telling of stories of and by people whose experiences are not often told, such as African American and Latino students in city schools. Counter-storytelling can serve as a tool for exposing, analyzing, and challenging the stories of those in power, which are often a part of dominant discourse. Counter-storytelling is not only a tool for telling the experiences of marginalized individuals but also challenges the dominant stories of those in power whose stories are regarded as normative (Delgado, 1995, 2000; Solórzano & Yosso, 2001, 2002).

The current study's approach to counter-storytelling has incorporated a condensed form of life-story methodology to better understand the construction of African American students' life experiences. McAdams (2001) defines *life story* as "an individual's internalized narrative rendering of his or her life in time, entailing the reconstructed past, perceived present, and anticipated future" (p. 475). McAdams (2008a, 2008b) asserts that people provide their lives with unity and purpose by constructing internalized and evolving narratives of the self. Life stories function to establish identities, which assist individuals who are trying to make sense of their lives at a particular moment. McAdams contends that the story is the best available structure that persons have for integrating and making sense of their lives in time and space, and it functions to establish identity as opposed to establishing traits, motives, values, and so forth (McAdams, 2001, 2008a, 2008b; McAdams, Josselson, & Lieblich, 2006). Individually and collectively, the stories told by Tinesha in this study help in developing a better understanding of the meaning she gives to her experiences in engineering.

Researchers who employ interview, counter-storytelling, and life-story methods understand that there exists a complex relationship between what really happens in a person's life and how the person chooses to remember and understand his or her experiences (McAdams, Reynolds, Lewis, Patten, & Bowman, 2001). Life-story interviews do not necessarily look for objective facts but rather inquire about one's perceptions, values, personal motivations, and so on. Therefore, the life story includes a subjective, value-oriented interpretation by the storyteller. This strategy mirrors PVEST, formulated as a synthesis perspective by the second author, which accounts for the life-story process as a person's "meaning making process." It emphasizes one's unavoidable requirement to reactively cope with challenges as well as to benefit from supports, and accounts for identifications and identity outcomes (see Spencer, 1995, 2006, 2008b). In sum, conceptually parallel with the identity-focused cultural and ecological PVEST framework, the life story is a means of fashioning identity, and therefore assists in efforts to understand the multiple identities of African American mathematics and engineering college students, including their racialized experiences in these contexts.

Coding and Analysis of Interview Data

The interview data were central to this study (Chenail, 1994) and called for a coding and categorizing of the data. During the coding process, Tinesha's transcription cited not only experiences of racism but also the strategies she employed to maintain or develop success in engineering as well as other statements that spoke to resiliency in the face of academic and life obstacles. Analysis of the interview data incorporated an iterative coding scheme. This process of sorting and resorting, coding and recoding of data led to emergent categories of meaning. In analyzing the data, themes were identified that emerged in the transcript of the counter-story.

Once the interview was coded, data were initially categorized by theme, after which data were scanned "for categories of phenomena and relationships among the categories" (Goetz & LeCompte, 1981, p. 57). After numerous revisions, categories and subcategories revealed different strategies that led to success for Tinesha. Coding proceeded as follows: Codes were identified, and quotes that reflected the codes in the interviews were connected. For example, one code that recurred throughout the interview was the presence of racial experiences in the academic/engineering setting.

Tinesha's story presented the following themes: introduction, childhood experiences, racial identity, racialized mathematics experiences, college experiences, and future aspirations.

Tinesha's Life Story

At the time of the first interview, Tinesha was just months shy of graduating with her master's in bioengineering from Medium University. She was also employed part time at a progressive youth program that was founded on the mathematics teachings of the civil rights movement (Moses & Cobb, 2001). Although Tinesha was suffering with a bad cold during the first meeting, her warm disposition and calm demeanor were immediately evident; and due to her interest in pursuing a PhD in mathematics education, as the first author obtained, she was just as interested in the mutual exchange. Before Tinesha agreed to participate in this study, two phone conversations were initiated that resulted in a sharing of history between her life and that of the first author, which revealed that each had been victims of stereotypes about women engineers (the first author received her BS and MS in engineering). In fact, when revisited for the current publication, Tinesha and both authors had all experienced gender bias in their respective training in male-dominated undergraduate schooling experiences (i.e., engineering for Tinesha and the first author and undergraduate pharmacy training for the second author). Tinesha expressed the necessity for developing survival skills to navigate among her mostly male peers and faculty. She learned and in part developed adaptive coping strategies to successfully incorporate the engineering norms and culture by observing and imitating those who were successful, but never losing track of the fact that she is a Black woman. Tinesha later revealed that the first author's gender, race, and educational background as an African American female mathematics/engineering professional played a pivotal role in Tinesha's desire to participate in this study.

Tinesha's story, like those of so many other successful Black mathematics and engineering students, is one of resiliency in the face of life and educational obstacles. Tinesha and her five siblings were raised by their mother in a Midwestern city where over 80% of families live below the federal poverty line. Although her family experienced significant difficulty, Tinesha found a wealth of fulfillment in their love, support, and strength. In contrast to the standard perceptions of the hardships associated with an upbringing like hers, Tinesha's journey demonstrates the protective factors associated with being raised in an extremely poor, predominately Black city—that is, the "good in the 'hood": she managed to escape the blatant forms of racism she might have endured without the shelter that being surrounded by her own offered.

Tinesha's Childhood Experiences

Tinesha grew up in an "all-Black community (except for the gas stations' and convenient stores' owners)" that she describes as a "Blackout." The city was once home to one the largest concentrations of industrial production in the United States; however, most of the companies that formed the nucleus of this industry had deserted the city long ago. Yet for Tinesha, living in the public housing projects of this city had its advantages and offered unique forms of protection. Although her early childhood was riddled with economic despair, during her K–12 years, Tinesha was buffered from the overt forms of racism that often plague Blacks who live in racially mixed or predominately White neighborhoods. Tinesha's life as a female growing up in the city projects offered her another unique form of protection. Tinesha did not feel pressure to engage in risk-taking behaviors such as violent or delinquent activities that validate masculinity (Cunningham, Swanson, Spencer, & Dupree, 2003).

Tinesha's mother found work cleaning a "White lady's house" during most of her childhood; she described harsh memories of the family's financial struggles.

As a result of the challenges that financial poverty often brings (e.g., house robberies, early exposure to drug-addicted people, sexual abuse), she endured multiple forms of risk perpetuated by her low socioeconomic, historically Black, urban environment. Tinesha developed early feelings of anxiety and fears of being ill-treated. Tinesha's family was "constantly moving" within the city limits, although never relocating into neighborhoods where her mother could say, "Oh, great, just go outside and play."

> I can remember, like, being awoken in the middle of the night and just some random crackhead banging on the door, like, trying to come in, you know? We were always getting robbed. I can remember living in a house where the basement—you could see all the way down from the top floor into the basement 'cause there was a huge hole in the floor.

These experiences added to Tinesha's net stress as some traumatic situations in her childhood challenged her sense of well-being. Tinesha's mother spent most of her life working several jobs at a time in her attempt to provide a better life for herself and her five children; Tinesha refers to her mother as the "strongest person I know, period." A salient, protective factor emphasized was the ever-present influence of the family as the biggest source of support. Using an identity-focused, cultural-ecological perspective exposed that Tinesha's risk contributors were offset by specific protective factors, which contributed to her overall life and academic resilience.

The entire maternal side of Tinesha's family lived within a 3-mile radius of her household; she describes her family as "close-knit and emotionally strong." During Tinesha's childhood, her grandmother's home was the one house that remained constant and served not only as the place for all family gatherings but also as a source of strength and endurance. Tinesha's early dependence on a family support system served as a protective factor and supplied adult role models that helped her cope with environmental, context-driven risk. Tinesha's older brother was an engineering major as well; thus, early in her educational career she benefited from having encouragement to pursue engineering and an out-of-school support system. Tinesha said what she benefited from most was knowing what engineering was and its many possibilities. With her brother's informal teaching and modeling, engineering become less abstract, more real, and more tangible in her life and her academic goals (i.e., additional significant sources of protective factors and support). Her early exposure to engineering helped to establish an academic context for incorporating engineering into Tinesha's developing identity.

Constant relocations due to her mother's unstable employment situation were a particularly difficult aspect of her childhood. She attended six different schools during her elementary years; until the sixth grade Tinesha was always "the new kid in class," and she discovered that "fighting the new girl" was a disturbingly common recess pastime. Tinesha remembers second and third grades as the best time for her during her elementary years, because she attended the same school continuously—the longest time she was in one school. Despite the difficulty, the turmoil in Tinesha's life did not appear to negatively impact her educational outcomes.

Although American adolescents face tremendous risks, African American adolescents are especially vulnerable. Tinesha's demographic factors and low socio-economic status placed her at risk for less than optimal development and exposed her to multiple risk factors. However, Tinesha's positive family interactions and social support factors had a positive impact on her achievement outcomes and her sense of self-worth. However, Tinesha's upbringing impacted her developmental process and offered both challenges and sources of support. For example, living in a predominately Black city, Tinesha has not been able to develop adaptive coping processes to deal with the "new" forms of racism she was exposed to as a result of attending a historically White university.

Tinesha's Racial Identity

One source of stress for Black youth transitioning into adulthood is the perception that society devalues their racial group. A critical aspect of self-worth is the establishment of a racial identity that strongly identifies with one's racial group (Chavous et al., 2003). Tinesha possesses a high degree of Black self-worth, consciousness, and awareness, as indicated through her interview statements. Tinesha suggested that her racial pride is also tied to her resilience and, thus, is a protective factor against racial discrimination (e.g., particularly, racialized incidents experienced by other Black college students).

Tinesha proudly invokes her Black centrality in her style of dress, natural hairstyle, club affiliations, and social activities. Being Black is fundamental in how she views the world and in determining her future goals. Tinesha shared vivid descriptions of her Black pride and unconditional love for the African American community. Tinesha has also developed very personal notions regarding the potential for social change and has gained a greater sense of her power to control her own destiny and impact the destinies of her racial group:

> And they're [her younger cousins] always call[ing] me a "Black activist," which, I mean, I can't help it. I figure if I'm gonna do something, and I like to help people, and it should be Black people. And not that other people are less important at this particular point in time, but Black people are the ones [in] need of help; so now if the paradigm changes, and Black people are all good, and, you know, we're doing all well, then maybe I'll focus my attention on someone else and other people. But until then I'm gonna be fighting for Black people.

Her racial identity certainly demonstrates the links between racial identity beliefs and youths' political attitudes (see Spencer, 2008a).

Tinesha's Racialized Engineering Experiences

Being placed in the lowest level mathematics class available at Medium University shocked Tinesha into realizing just how ill-prepared she was in mathematics. Having come from the highest mathematics class in her high school, Tinesha took issue with the differences in opportunities to learn mathematics between the schools in her community. Stark educational discrepancies are often dependent on the economic and social resources available to students. This became "very, very physical"—that is, exceedingly evident—to Tinesha as she progressed from the lower level mathematics classes, which contained mostly Black and Latino students, to her higher level mathematics classes, where she was frequently the only Black student.

In her advanced classes, Tinesha felt the burdened of being labeled an "affirmative action student," and realized just how much of a stigma of perceived inferiority is associated with Blacks pursuing engineering and mathematics degrees (Martin, 2009). When Tinesha walks into a classroom, she often reports feelings and inferences that she is perceived as a less qualified student who got into college based on her race. She believes her predominately White and Asian classmates may feel that she took a slot away from a more deserving White or Asian student. As a Black student in a field with very few Blacks, Tinesha perceived judgment of her status as a member of an ill-regarded minority group rather than as an individual. Tinesha has felt the responsibility to "be on point" (i.e., to perform at a consistently high level) academically to combat others' perceptions, not only of her but also of "the next Black person in the class."

> By the time I was in my upper-level classes, I was, like, unstoppable. Folk would say, "Let's do a study group," and I was like, "Okay, I gotcha on that." And it felt so good. I guess partially because I don't care, but also I don't want these people to think bad of me and, like, 'cause if they do think bad of me, then I'm the person coming to their class, so I, like, really, really made sure that I was not at the bottom. [If] I answered one question wrong, I knew they would say, "Look at this girl. Affirmative action: I know that's how she got here." And so the fact that people asked me for help was like, was like the icing on the cake, and I was like, "*Yes!* I'm the only Black person in this class, and I got the highest scores on exams. So *boo-yah!* I knew that I could do it."

As Tinesha employs various coping strategies, her identity as a high-achieving female engineering student is further fostered through her continued academic success, and, as a result, these strategies produce desirable outcomes for her ego and her sense of self-worth. These adaptive strategies have been used over time and have become part of her emergent identity (Spencer, 2006).

Tinesha related an episode from one math class that left little ambiguity regarding the low expectations some professors hold for their Black students:

> This was Math #—calc, calculus—so he's [the professor is] throwing out questions, and kids are answering. And this [Black] guy, Prince, he answers one of the questions, and the professor literally stops class and says, "Wow, that was right." He was, like, really shocked that this guy got it. And so that kind of, like, threw me for a loop, and I came to realize, like, these people don't expect too much of me in this class. And so I've always had the idea that if you tell me that I can't do something, then I want to prove to you that I can. And so, for the rest of the time in all my upper-level classes, that was my goal. I want these people in this class [to know that] I might be the only Black person here, but I'm certainly not the dumbest.

Tinesha not only is challenged by the racial stigma of being a Black women in higher education but has to further contend with the fact that her field (bioengineering) has a severe underrepresentation of Blacks. She reports that there are even fewer Blacks in that field than in other engineering disciplines, such as mechanical or electrical engineering. When Tinesha received her graduate degree in 2007, she and another Black master's degree recipient were the only two Black graduates in the bioengineering field out of approximately 100 for that year.

Tinesha's College Experiences

College offered Tinesha a host of new racialized experiences, both inside and outside the classroom. During her first few months at ethnically and racially diverse Medium University, meeting and connecting with people outside of her race were surprising delights. However, Tinesha soon realized that the level of racial diversity on campus went hand in hand with perceptions of racial isolation. Although there were many ethnic cultures represented at Medium, students from the same racial groups mostly stuck together and rarely interacted with students from other racial backgrounds. Studies have cited the consistent likelihood of self-segregation of ethnically similar students on college campuses, even when the demographic makeup of the campus is diverse (Antonio, 2001; Villalpando & Solórzano, 2005). Although some scholars theorize this segregation as voluntary (Buttny, 1999), others have framed their analysis around institutional racism and reveal how and why marginalized college students benefit from associating with their same-race peer groups by creating a community sense of support for their cultural resources, to better navigate the racialized barriers erected by universities (Villalpando & Solórzano, 2005).

Tinesha's interactions with some African students, whose very countries she had studied as a source of racial pride in high school, to her disbelief, left her dismayed. She despaired at experiencing Black-on-Black prejudice from American college students of African descent, some of whom had grown up in countries other than the United States.

> The one thing that was eye-opening when I came to Medium was I had never been, like, around Black people who didn't like Black people. Black people who were like, "I don't mess with Black people like that." And, you know, I think that was, that for me was like, "Wow! These [Black] people were like, 'I don't hang out with Black people; I don't date Black people; I don't do anything that have to do with Black people.'" I was like coming from [a predominately Black city] where it's just Black people. And it was like … and it started to really take a toll on me. So I took a step back, and I observed for a minute, and then I started, like, reentering the Black community. But for a minute I couldn't handle it.

These experiences left Tinesha "not feelin' good" about herself. This new racial experience created an emotionally stressful time for Tinesha, but also created the potential for innovation in ways of thinking about racism as a system of oppression that impacts all racial groups, including Blacks throughout the African diaspora. She experienced great disappointment given emergent perceptions and inferred conclusions that some Black students devalued their group membership or skin tone.

Initially, Tinesha was truly troubled by these students who purposely avoided most Black people, and who dissociated from all extracurricular activities on campus involving Blacks. After a few weeks of reflection, Tinesha immersed herself in the pro-Black part of the Black community at Medium. Black poetry sets and the Black Student Union became safe havens and were, in Tinesha's words, a "saving grace." It is important to note that Tinesha took the initiative to analyze how this society is structured and how institutions and the people associated with them are organized and behave. Tinesha learned how to manage by change rather than simply by reaction. Tinesha's adaptation to her new experiences of racism suggests that she can adapt to some uncertainty and surprise.

Tinesha's Future Aspirations

During her interview, Tinesha discussed the vulnerability of Blacks in math and engineering professions as forms of both risk and protection. Tinesha was troubled by the view that her outstanding academic progress and engineering pursuits were not guarantees of secure employment opportunities in the face of discriminatory hiring practices. The anticipation of her master's degree in bioengineering would offer no real protection from racialized employment situations. Tinesha also discussed the challenges she expects to face as a professor: "When I become a Black female engineering professor, people's preconceived notions are always going to be there. That's not something we can change." Tinesha believes that her racial group membership will always be a risk factor and that her degree will be undervalued in comparison with other nonracial minorities in her field.

Tinesha's story offers a powerful rebuttal to the conclusions that have dominated the of mathematics/engineering-relevant fields over the past 25 years. Conventional research predicts that a student like Tinesha will underachieve in engineering or drop out of the field entirely. But Tinesha has achieved and done so without "acting White" (see Spencer, Noll, Stoltzfus, & Harpalani, 2001) and has done so while thriving within a "Black cultural frame of reference." She has developed a strong Black identity and has come to recognize social inequalities and the existence of differential rewards and opportunities. Tinesha's personal encounters with racial discrimination and social class inequalities have heightened her recognition of racial and class barriers.

Tinesha's future plans are directly related to the interplay between the centrality of her commitment to her race and the love she has for herself as a Black person, and the realities of the racism and racial discrimination Black people endure. Her keen awareness of structural constraints that exist for aspiring Black mathematics students comes from her own experience and the continued struggle she witnesses in teaching mathematics to Black and Latino youth; obviously her purpose, commitments, and nascent perspectives have evolved from her emergent political attitudes, which have been underanalyzed and explored as sources of risk for some and protective factors for others (see Spencer, 2008a). She plans to enroll in a mathematics education doctoral program and become a mathematics education professor to challenge the ways in which Blacks are taught mathematics, as well as the norms and expectations of schooling, which privilege White and individual identities over Black and collective identities. Her level of Black self-consciousness empowers Tinesha to believe she can affect the academic and mathematics self-efficacy beliefs of Black students.

However, Tinesha's dream job, which reflects her concerns and perspective, is quite unique:

> I would own a business. A company specifically that designs orthopedic devices specifically to integrate into human bodies. And then I would have those [proceeds] from the company, um, go to—some of the money that I make go to building a school for Black youth to become successful without ignoring their own culture. So, say I am successful; ideally, I mean, I'm the number one in the country. Hopefully, all-Black engineers—just to kind of put the idea out there, you know … 'cause I think, like, Black engineers, you know, are shoved under the carpet sometimes.

The proceeds from her business would go into caring for her family and starting a culturally affirming, engineering- and mathematics-based school. The school, which would teach not only Black students but all students, would draw on culturally relevant pedagogy and would be staffed by Black engineers. Tinesha strongly believes that all students could benefit from an academic environment like the one she envisions. Tinesha's resiliency has evolved out of her observations, experiences, and feedback between the social system and social dynamics, which has balanced protective factors and risk factors and ultimately has allowed her to maintain academic and life success.

Summary and Implications

Identity and race-related theoretical perspectives (i.e., PVEST, resiliency, racial identity) have made it possible to better understand the major factors potentially influencing Tinesha's development in several interacting dimensions. The first is that the inclusion of significant others, such as parents, siblings, and educators, aided in her interactions and meaning making of those experiences. Also exposed were contextual factors, such as cultures, ideologies, and the presence of racialized experiences. What is often overlooked is that a retrospective account of some of Tinesha's normative processes of development permitted a better understanding of variables that changed over time. How she understood and thought about events and circumstances is critically important in determining their impact. Current and future studies focused on academic achievement of underrepresented students could benefit from the dimensions of analysis presented in this study.

Tinesha achieved, academically and socially, while maintaining her collective Black identity; however, she used her knowledge of the dominant cultural capital in co-construction of her own Black cultural capital (Carter, 2003) to create a better teaching environment for the next generation of Black mathematicians and engineers. Her Black cultural knowledge has proven useful within her academic navigation strategies, despite society's failure to recognize its value, particularly in promoting academic success. Her awareness of racism and prejudice has become a reason for her both to excel as well as prepare in the fight against these evils (Sanders, 1997). Tinesha's narrative illustrated that there is no one best way to achieve in these fields; however, racism and racialized experiences have strong implications for how these students navigate the educational terrain.

Tinesha's story reminded us as researchers that the lives of students like her and the world they live in are not one-dimensional. There is no one metastory that defines Black students in mathematics and engineering. Examining a broader array of individual, contextual, and social factors is crucial to unpacking and discerning students' meaning-making processes from their narratives. Taken as a whole, her story contributes to the growing body of literature that portrays achievement from the meaning-making processes and particular perspectives of Black students. Their meaning making could serve to better contextualize the inequities that exist in the school system (i.e., race, class, sexism, ageism, etc.).

In sum, analyzing Tinesha's life narrative within the larger narratives in which the experiences of Black, high-achieving mathematics and engineering college students are embedded provides a better appreciation of what it means to be Black and academically successful in contexts where Black students are few in number and where negative societal and school beliefs about their abilities and motivation persist. The examination of these phenomena opens the door for more holistic portrayals and examinations of these valuable students.

References

Anthony, E. J. (1974). The syndrome of the psychologically invulnerable child. In E. J. Anthony & C. Koupernik (Eds.), *The child and his family: Children at psychiatric risk* (pp. 529–544). New York, NY: Wiley.

Antonio, A. 2001. The role of interracial interaction in the development of leadership skills and cultural knowledge and understanding. *Research in Higher Education, 42*(5), 593–617.

Banks, J. A., & Banks, C. A. (1993). *Multicultural education: Issues and perspectives.* Boston, MA: Allyn and Bacon.

Bowman, P., & Howard, C. (1985). Race-related socialization, motivation, and academic achievement: A study of black youths in three-generation families. *Journal of the American Academy of Child Psychiatry, 24*(2), 134–141.

Buttny, R. (1999). Discursive constructions of racial boundaries and self-segregation on campus. *Journal of Language and Social Psychology, 18,* 247–268.

Carlone, H. B., & Johnson, A. (2007). Understanding the science experiences of successful women of color: Science identity as an analytic lens. *Journal of Research in Science Teaching, 44*(8), 1187–1218.

Carter, P. L. (2003). Black cultural capital, status positioning, and the conflict of schooling for low-income African American Youth. *Social Problems, 50*(1), 136–155.

Chavous, T. M., Bernat, D., Schmeelk-Cone, K., Caldwell, C., Kohn-Wood, L. P., & Zimmerman, M. (2003). Racial identity and academic attainment among African American adolescents. *Child Development, 74*(4), 1076–1090.

Chenail, R. J. (1994). Qualitative research and clinical work: "Private-ization" and "publication." *The Qualitative Report, 2*(1), 1, 3–13.

Cross, W. E. (1991). *Shades of black: Diversity in African American identity.* Philadelphia, PA: Temple University Press.

Cunningham, M., Swanson, D. P., Spencer, M. B., & Dupree, D. (2003). The association of physical maturation with family hassles in African American males. *Cultural Diversity and Ethnic Minority Psychology, 9,* 274–276.

Delgado, R. (1995). Storytelling for oppositionists and others: A plea for narrative. In R. Delgado (Ed.), *Critical race theory: The cutting edge.* Philadelphia, PA: Temple University Press.

Delgado, R. (2000). Storytelling for oppositionists and others: A plea for narrative. In R. Delgado & J. Stefancic (Eds.), *Critical race theory: The cutting edge* (pp. 60–70). Philadelphia, PA: Temple University Press.

Delgado, R. & Stefancic, J. (2001). *Critical race theory: An introduction.* New York, NY: New York University Press.

DuBois, W.E.B. (1973). *The souls of black folk.* New York, NY: Kraus-Thomson.

10

EXPLORING EDUCATIVE POSSIBILITY THROUGH THE PROCESS OF LEARNING IN YOUTH SPORTS

Na'ilah Suad Nasir

Introduction

A track and field team is practicing on an overcast day in Northern California. There are about 40 high school athletes and three coaches spread about various parts of the track. Hurdlers are practicing jumping over hurdles on one part of the track, long distance runners are running laps, sprinters are on another part of the track, and the field events athletes (discus, shot-putters, and jumpers) are in the middle. The coaches float to different parts of the field, where young people are working. They watch, critique, give instructions, and offer feedback and encouragement. The athletes and the coaches are all African American. Their practice occurs in what is considered a very tough part of the city, and occasionally one can hear a dog bark or a child cry. Other younger children ride by on bikes or stop to watch the athletes for a moment.

In the middle of the track, the jumpers are practicing launching themselves as far as they can into a pit of sand. One jumper, a slightly heavyset 10th grader, seems to concentrate deeply as she takes a running start, then, when she reaches the right mark, jumps as far as she can into the pit. She falls forward onto her hands and knees in the sand and lets out a squeal. She seems a bit embarrassed by the fall. The coach, who is standing with his arms folded across his chest, watching, responds by saying, "Good. Good job. That's how you are supposed to land, alright?" The student answers, "Yeah." The coach walks back to where she lands in the sand and says, "That's about 12. I want you at 13, alright?" The student responds and the coach reminds her that she will be jumping in the meet tomorrow.

This excerpt illustrates several important aspects of learning settings that hold educative possibility. First, learners have multiple opportunities to practice the skill that they are learning, and that practice occurs with consistent feedback from more knowledgeable others. But perhaps what is most important is what happens first in the interaction between the learner and the coach. After the initial effort to make the jump, the learner fell, which could have been construed by the learner as a failure. This potential failure and demonstration of incompetence was immediately reframed as a success when the coach says, "That's how you are supposed to land." The potential of displaying incompetence is a source of psychological risk in any learning setting, and in this interaction, the coach mitigated that risk by redefining what a successful performance would look like. Learners face multiple kinds of risk in learning settings, from the kinds of psychological risk in this setting to broader kinds of sociological risk related to neighborhood, socioeconomic status (SES), and stratified opportunity structures. One important aspect of learning spaces that are rich with educative possibility is how they mitigate and help learners manage risk.

This chapter is about youth sports settings as one kind of space of educative possibility.[1] However, it is mostly about thinking differently about learning settings. Many learning scientists would agree that the ways we typically organize for learning in school spaces at best fail to engage learners deeply and give them access to important subject matter and, at worst, actually inhibit learning. Learning scientists are increasingly beginning to acknowledge learning as a fundamentally human process (O'Connor & Penuel, 2010) that is deeply tied to volitional, emotional, relational, and developmental processes. Learning occurs in interactions between people and within cultural and social spaces that can have an important influence on the content, nature, and process of learning (Cole, 1996; Rogoff, 1999, 2003). Further, learning is ubiquitous; it happens everywhere, whether or not there is intention to teach or to learn, as we go about the activities of our daily lives (Gutierrez & Rogoff, 2003; Lee & Majors, 2003; Majors, 2003; Moll & González, 2004; Nasir, 2000; Rose, 2004).

This characterization of learning is more expansive than the ways we have typically seen learning designed for in schools and classrooms (Tyack & Cuban, 1995; Varenne & McDermott, 1998). The reason for this is at least twofold. First, schooling spaces have been quite resistant to change for several decades, and despite strikingly successful efforts at redesigning them, economic and institutional forces have worked to keep more traditional ways of doing school in place. For instance, over the past 100 years there have been many striking efforts to create schools that focus on deep, authentic learning, rather than "drill and kill" methods (Tyack & Cuban, 1995). However, these efforts have been short-lived, despite their success.

Second, some have argued that supporting deep and effective learning for all students is at cross-purposes both with the history and goals of schooling in our society (Varenne & McDermott, 1998). In other words, if one important purpose of schooling is to replicate class stratification (Bowles & Gintis, 1973), then creating learning settings that support successful learning for a wide range of students would be nothing short of revolutionary. While there may be significant impediments to creating learning settings in schools that are transformative, schools, as institutions, are important sites for social change. Out-of-school learning spaces may offer important lessons to help facilitate that change.

I've noted that this chapter uses youth sports organizations as spaces of educative possibility. I view these organizations as just one example of nonschool learning spaces where developmental capacities are supported and nurtured, thus better fostering both learning and identities as learners. I do not argue that all youth-sport learning spaces share the kinds of positive characteristics that I point out in these settings, rather that these characteristics, wherever they are found, are critical to the design of positive, productive learning spaces for young people. I also focus on African American youth in this chapter—not because I view these youth as another species of learner that needs something different than what any other learner would need, but rather because African American youth, along with other youth from marginalized groups, tend to have fewer such opportunities made available in schools (Darling-Hammond, 2000; Darling-Hammond, Williamson, & Hyler, 2008; Ladson-Billings, 2006; Oakes, 1990, 2004), and because they tend to be viewed as unable or unwilling to learn (Drake, 1997).

It is also critical to note that while I describe youth sports settings as spaces of inclusion for the youth that I studied they may also have been spaces of exclusion for others. It is likely that these youth sports spaces were gendered, heteronormalized, and (dis)abled in ways that were likely symbolically exclusionary and violent to those who don't conform to the dominant performativities of these spaces. Additionally, to some degree, young people self-select into youth sports teams, though athletes in each of these settings represented a wide range of skill levels and levels of commitment to their sport. This acknowledgement is critical, because social spaces are never neutral, and access for some may constitute lack of access for others. The final caveat here is that the findings I report in this chapter come from studies of youth sports settings in which adults explicitly sought to positively support the development of young people. Thus, these settings are structured in ways that create particular organizational forms in line with this goal. Obviously, not all youth sports settings have this goal, and in that way, the settings I describe in this chapter are not representative of all youth sports contexts.

Within the youth sports settings that I describe, coaching and coaches play a particularly salient role in the lives of young people. Coaches often serve not only as people who teach a set of sports-related skills but also as mentors, guides, and caring adults in youths' lives (Duncan-Andrade, 2010; Nasir & Cooks, 2009). The presence of such caring adults has been shown to make a critical difference in the lives of youth, especially youth from marginalized communities (Gordon & Song, 1994).

My primary goal for this chapter is to draw on theory in the learning and development research I have done in informal learning spaces and to argue for the importance of two kinds of related processes in educational spaces. The first process is supporting students in developing identities of competence and identities as learners in a domain. The second process is supporting students in the mediation and management of multiple kinds of psychological and environmental risks.

Theoretical Framing: Identity and Risk in Learning

Issues of identity and risk are central to learning. In this section, I highlight three sets of ideas that support a deeper understanding of how processes of risk and identity relate to learning: Spencer's phenomenology variant of ecological systems theory (PVEST) (Spencer, Dupree, & Hartmann, 1997; Spencer, 1999, 2006, 2008), Lee's (2007) cultural modeling, and Nasir's (2002) treatment of the ways in which identity, goals, and learning relate to one another.

Margaret Beale Spencer (Spencer, 1999, 2006, 2008; Spencer & Hartmann, 1997) argues that all humans face risk in one form or another. The experience of risk is not limited to youth in urban communities. In other words, risk is inherent to the human condition: to be human is to be at risk. Thus, an important developmental task is the management of risk at multiple levels. For instance, youth face environmental risk, like high crime rates and poorly funded schools, and they also face psychological risks, like negative stereotypes about one's ethnic group. Spencer further argues that developmental outcomes can be understood as being related to the amount of risk in relation to the number of protective factors. In other words, various psychological, cultural, social, and environmental factors work together to mediate and support us in managing the various kinds of risks that we face daily. Protective factors might include a supportive family that creates a daily routine to buffer the effects of the immediate environmental risk, or a stable identity that connects youth positively to school.

In addition to the normative set of risks, to be African American in this country imposes added risks for youth, even more so if they grow up in underresourced urban neighborhoods, which are places where public schools are poorly resourced and understaffed (Darling-Hammond, 2000). Ladson-Billings has referred to what she calls the *education debt* (Ladson-Billings, 2006), a term she uses to name the long history of the denial of adequate educational resources to African Americans. In addition to poor schools, multiple environmental risks threaten the safety and well-being of youth, including risks associated with being a member of a marginalized group, which is a proxy for one's community having endured a long history of discrimination and oppression in both the governmental and the private sectors, including housing, employment, and environmental toxins.

According to Spencer (2006, 2008), youth respond in moments of stress with *reactive* coping mechanisms; that is, they find ways to preserve their sense of self in situations where they feel psychologically threatened in some way. Over time, patterns of reactive coping evolve into *stable* coping mechanisms; that is, they get taken up as a part of one's long-term, stable identity or sense of self. The reactive coping mechanisms can be adaptive for positive life outcomes and school success, or they can be maladaptive, meaning they can lead to negative life outcomes and school failure. The identities that emerge from these coping mechanisms can similarly be adaptive (identifying as someone who is good at school and who overcomes challenges) or maladaptive (identifying as someone who doesn't care about school or life).

While Spencer does not study learning, the developmental processes she describes clearly have important implications for learning. If we think about learning as an outcome, it is likely that the kinds of negative risk and identity cycles she describes would have a detrimental affect on learning, whereby youth who develop identities as people who are not engaged in school likely will not achieve to their intellectual potential. Alternatively, youth who have developed what Spencer calls stable coping responses that might involve seeing school engagement as an important part of their identity would likely be more positively engaged in school and learning. However, we might think about learning not simply as an outcome but as a key element in a cycle of disruption. To further explore this, I draw on the work of Lee (2007) and Nasir (2002).

Carol Lee (2007) focuses on "cultural displays in the service of learning." She takes as her premise that culture is at the center of how we interact with one another and how we engage with the world. She views learning as inherently cultural in nature and makes the case that we learn best when what we are learning connects with the knowledge we hold in our cultural repertoires. For Lee, learning is a complex endeavor—one that involves multiple layers and is related to the developmental and identity processes described by Spencer. Lee described cultural modeling as an instructional approach that builds on youths' cultural data sets to support high-level thinking and learning in a discipline. She writes, "Cultural Modeling aims to provide instructional organization that makes ways of engaging in the work of the disciplines familiar, and provides supports for the instances when the learner is unsure" (2007, p. 29). Thus, cultural modeling is a method of conducting classroom instruction and a sense of honoring and building on the cultural knowledge of youth in that instructional process.

Further, Lee shares Spencer's concern with the ways in which youth, in particular youth from marginalized communities, navigate aspects of their lives, multiple and sometimes conflicting settings, and contend with the challenges imposed by poverty, White supremacy, and urban neighborhoods. However, she is focused on how learning takes shape in and through classroom interactions and views learning as a means by which to support positive academic identities of students, and as a way to support youth in successfully managing difficult circumstances.

Lee hints at the role of identity in learning, and describes learning as being subtly related to developmental processes like coping and the negotiation of self and knowledge. I have written explicitly about the relation between identity and learning, and the ways that learning settings can support the developmental and identity needs of learners (Nasir, 2002; Nasir & Hand, 2008; Nasir, Warren, Rosenbery, & Lee, 2006). I have argued that learning, identity, and goals are intimately related to one another and co-construct one another as learners take part in learning settings. Specifically, I have argued that identity, goals, and learning can be conceptualized as three prongs of a triangle, with bidirectional arrows between each two points. There are three important assertions in this model. The first is that learning creates identity, and identity creates learning. I write, "As members of communities of practice experience more engaged identities, they learn new skills and bodies of knowledge, facilitating new ways of participating, which in turn, helps to create new identities relative to their community" (Nasir, 2002, p. 239). Thus learning and identity are viewed as reciprocal processes that support one another.

The second proposition is that learning creates goals, and goals create learning. Learning involves both coming to understand new problems and reconceptualizing old problems. When problems are understood in new ways, new goals emerge in problem solving. New goals require further learning as one seeks to accomplish these new goals.

The third assertion is that identity creates goals, and goals create identity. In other words, as one comes to take up new identities, new kinds of problems emerge, and new kinds of goals. Conversely, engaging in pursuing these new practice-linked goals further supports emerging identities with that domain.

These three mutual relationships between identity, goals, and learning offer the potential to bring together discussions of risk and identity in Spencer's work and discussion of culture and learning in Lee's work. As I've noted, the identities students construct in relation to school have the potential to inform their participation in learning settings. My model supports the idea that there is likely a reciprocal relation between students' identities in school, their learning, and their goals with respect to their learning and schooling. Drawing on Spencer, we can conceptualize this as occurring in a less adaptive reactive form, whereby young people react to the multiple negative stressors, including those in school, to develop identities as people who don't identify with school and thus fail to engage in and learn in their classes. The lack of engagement further strengthens their identities as poor students, and they seek feelings of competence in other settings. We can also conceptualize this as occurring in a more adaptive, stable, coping response, where youth have access to protective factors in school, for instance, instruction that is consistent with a cultural modeling frame, where their cultural knowledge is taken seriously and where they adapt by developing a positive identity of themselves as students. This identity supports engagement in learning settings, and thus learning, which fosters new learning goals and a strengthening of their identity as students.

The critical idea here is that we can conceptualize positive learning environments as having the potential to *disrupt* negative identity cycles that can exacerbate underachievement in school. Learning contexts that take one's culture seriously can be a source for positive identity—this highlights the power of local learning spaces to help youth realize their potential and to be sites of educative possibility. In other words, access to positive learning spaces is, in and of itself, a protective factor that helps mediate some of the risks associated with living and attending schools in urban contexts. In the following sections of this chapter, I draw on data from two studies of youth sports—one study of two high school basketball teams, and another study of a high school track and field team—to illustrate how youth sports can be spaces in which young people are supported in developing identities as learners and in managing multiple kinds of risk. As these settings provide opportunities for positive identity and competence development and the mitigation of risk, they become sites of educative possibility.

Context of the Studies

Learning and Identity in Basketball

The study on basketball focused on the nature of learning in the sport and examined the social organization of learning in basketball for players in two schools in different school districts. This work also sought to understand the identities players were constructing in and through their learning of basketball. Methods included observation (video and field notes) of players in basketball settings, and interviews on math and basketball learning, achievement, and students' identities. One of the schools, Roseville,[2] was a large public high school in an urban district, while the other, Academy, was a private school that ran without charging tuition in a grossly underserved urban neighborhood in a midsized city. Both schools served predominantly or exclusively African American and Latino students, and both were located in areas where there were a high proportion of families living under the poverty line. The school in the large urban district at the time of our study enrolled just under 2,000 students, almost all of whom were African American or Latino with low incomes. At this school, 58% of students had GPAs below a C, and only 8% of the students were reading at the national average.

Learning and Identity in Track and Field

This study focused on how teaching and learning happened for high school African American students and track coaches in the context of track and field. Data included observations of track practices and games as well as informal and formal interviews with track athletes. Data also included weekly analysis sessions with the coach and audiotaped interactions between athletes and coaches during track meets and practices. The athletes attended school in the same large district, though in a different school, as one of the basketball teams. The school, Hills High, served more than 2,200 ethnically and economically diverse students, Grades 9 through 12. At the time of our study, its student population was 50% African American, 20% Asian American, 17% Latino, and 13% White. Fifty-two percent of the students were accepted to 4-year colleges upon graduation, and 38% attended community colleges. In many ways, however, these statistics are misleading.

While many of the Asian and White students enjoyed strong academic outcomes, advanced placement courses, and transition to college, most of the Latino and African American students were tracked into the remedial courses and were not enjoying these same outcomes. For instance, in the year of our study, while 70% of White students were in the 50th percentile in reading, only 33% of African American students were. In mathematics, 68% of White students were in the 50th percentile or above, while that number was 30% for African American students.

District-wide, the dropout rate for African American students was over 60%, and the average GPA for African American high school students was 1.6. In all three settings, student athletes were required to maintain a minimum GPA (the exact GPA requirements varied). Thus, student athletes tended to have higher GPAs than the general student population.

Supporting Identity and Managing Risk in Youth Sports

I have argued that when learning spaces support students in developing identities as competent learners, they also help mitigate psychological risk in the learning context. However, in addition to mitigating psychological risk, youth sports settings also work to mitigate environmental or sociological risks. In the following sections, I draw on data from the study of high school basketball and the study of high school track and field to illustrate the ways in which learning interactions in these settings support students' developing identities as learners and as competent participants, thus mitigating psychological risk. Then I broaden my lens to explore how these settings also work to mitigate the sociological risk that young people face.

Supporting Learning Identity and Mediating Risk Within *the Learning Space*

A close look at learning interactions in both basketball and track and field demonstrates that learning is organized in ways that supported athletes' identities as learners, position them as competent learners, and mitigate the risk and vulnerability associated with being a novice in a practice.

For instance, consider this interaction from track, in which a group of female hurdlers are learning to three-step, which means jumping hurdles and taking only three steps between each hurdle. The learners are new at this technique and are finding it difficult to execute. In the following interaction, one of the athletes is preparing to run the hurdles when the coach walks up from another part of the track.

Coach J: What we're going to do now. We're three stepping, we're three stepping. (He walks toward girls). What do I mean by three stepping? What do I mean by three stepping?

Lila: You land and you go one, two, three (raises lead leg out in front of her).

Coach J: You know exactly what I mean.

T: One, two, three, take.

Coach J: There you go.

T: One two three take.

Coach J: There you go. You all getting it. (Smiling.)

T: And I go, one, two, three, four, take.

Coach J: I'm making you.

T: Coach (jokingly).

Coach J: I'm making you'all hurdlers. I'm making you all hurdlers.

In the first line, the coach marks what "we're" doing as three-stepping, and then elicits their understandings of what three-stepping is. The athlete, Lila, responds with both an intellectual understanding and the physical movements (as she moves her legs to demonstrate). Interesting that she doesn't just say "you take three steps"—she talks through it as if she were actually doing it, indicating that part of what it means to learn in this setting is to physically execute. That her response is appropriate is evident in the coach's reply "You know exactly what I mean." Then another student elaborates, making the language even more specific, "One, two, three, take." He affirms this, and the student repeats this form and applies it to her own form, "And I go one, two, three, four, take." This provides an extended opportunity to evaluate the performance that she has just executed, and to understand it in a new way, presenting multiple resources for learning. In the final line, the coach ties their demonstrated cognitive and physical understanding to an emerging identity, recognizing for them all that they are in the midst of this process, and explicitly *positioning* them as hurdlers. He says, "I'm making you all hurdlers, I'm making you all hurdlers."

In this episode, the coach takes a moment of learning that is difficult for the athletes and offers instruction that makes an identity as a hurdler available to them. He frames learning, failing, and analyzing their own athletic performance as a normal part of the practice of being a hurdler. In part, the mitigation of risk and support for identity that occurs in this episode is due to the nature of the interaction between the coach and the learners. However, the organization of the learning activity in these sports may also contribute both to the support of learning identities and to the mitigation of risk. The following examples from basketball illustrate how the structure of the activity, in addition to the interactions with the coaches, support identities and reduce risk.

In basketball, the players had a lot of responsibility for conducting both games and practices without micromanaging from the coaches. In one practice at Roseville, the researcher observed that the coach took on multiple roles during practice. At some points he was an active participant in the activity; for instance, he stood in front of the basket, blocking shots as players took part in a shooting drill.

At other times he took up the role of a leader, directing the players what drill to do and for how long. At still other times, he seemed to act somewhat like a cheerleader, offering encouragement and giving feedback, yelling out statements to players, like "good block out" or "nice shot, Jones." The practice seemed to have a life and rhythm of its own, and one almost got the impression that it would go on just as it was without the coaches at all. Players worked independently, quietly, and with concentration. They seemed to have run these same drills hundreds of times before.

This description of basketball practice at Roseville illustrates the way that the participant structure of the basketball practice supports the full engagement of players, gives them responsibility as learners and players, and facilitates them when offering one another feedback on their play. Readers might also note that the practice, like the track practice, seems to run without much direction from the coach. The coach's role seemed to be to give the initial instruction to get the players started on the activity, then to watch from the sidelines and offer feedback on ways to improve their play. The next episode occurred in a practice midseason at Academy, where the team was preparing for a game the following day. The structure of the practice was representative of a typical day.

> Coach sets up a full court paired running drill. Jacob is paired with Victor, and Ayo is with Carl. This drill is also quiet, with Coach C watching silently from the sidelines. The boys are guarding each other, but again, each seems intent on only their own role. Jacob misses a shot, hops up, and shouts, "Damn!" This is quite noticeable because it is the first word spoken in about 5 minutes, except for Coach C's soft intermittent comments. Kevin flamboyantly dunks on his partner, and screams. They all cheer and yell for him. The talk of the dunk continues through the next round. On this round, Kevin misses a shot, and then the next shot. He walks by Jacob, shaking his head. "I'm tired, man." Jacob gives a quick, tight nod of his head, but is watching the players currently on the court.

Several moments in this episode are relevant to thinking about identity and the mediation of risk in relation to learning in youth basketball. First, the practice runs without much direction from the coach, other than his setting up the initial drill and setting the stop clock. The players engage the drills fully, because they share the goal of learning so as to be prepared for the upcoming game. Their identities as players are assumed in the very structure of the activity and then conveyed in the expectations for their level of participation. Second, the players help to train one another, and they give each other feedback on their play. Finally, it is noteworthy that Kevin, when explaining why he is not making his shots, offers the explanation to another player—the point guard and leader of the team, who acknowledges the explanation with a nod of his head but continues to model full engagement in the drill. This subtle movement also conveys to Kevin that it is okay that he has missed these shots—and that missing shots is a part of the game.

The following episode also illustrates the ways that players not only looked to the coaches for key feedback, but they also looked to one another and were both learners and teachers. This structure of the activity afforded opportunities for players to develop identities as competent, since they had lots of opportunities to help one another become better players and to offer advice to others during games and practices.

> Coach C is very directive during this drill, giving specific instruction. "Step right here." "Move back two steps." At one point, Coach C stops the play and says, "I'm worried about our tendency to keep our head down." They spread out, executing a man-to-man defense. A player in a thin white T-shirt runs into the wall after a hard drive to the basket. He falls down exaggeratedly and looks around. He gets no attention, so he gets up, okay. Coach C watches the players, making few comments, except for the occasional, "Hustle," or "Get back." There are two missed shots in a row, and Norton states, "Missed layups, can't have that." After a missed pass, Coach C yells, "Gotta come get it!" Norton yells, "Way to hustle, Carl."

This example shows how the coach provides scaffolding and feedback during the practice sessions, giving players detailed feedback on the plays and their execution of them. In addition to this feedback by the coach, players also offer one another feedback, as when Norton comments on the missed layups or compliments Carl on his hustle. In this instance, Norton takes responsibility as a leader and teacher.

The assertion that youth seem to feel an ownership over their learning and see themselves and their teammates as teachers of one another is evident in their responses during interviews. For instance, one player, Brian, describes how he learns from the other players on the team so seamlessly that he doesn't even always remember from whom he learned what.

> I mean, I can't really directly say, but, because I don't know how to say it, but it kind of rubs off, and you don't hardly know it—I got that from him, or he taught me to do this. Because everybody on the team learns from different people every day, even though they younger you still may, they might know something you don't know.

When players talk about their learning, they talk about it as a blend of learning techniques and principles of game play and learning about themselves—further evidence that learning in the sport is related to their developing identities as learners of the sport and as competent participants in the game. Consider, for example, how Jonathon described his learning when asked by the interviewer to report some of the things he'd learned this season:

> [I've learned] to have patience with other people and, well, that was my big thing because I didn't have patience. And then as I learned, like as a point guard you have to have patience because you're like the main thing, like on the court, you get the plays started, nothing starts unless you start it. So like earlier this year, I was getting frustrated with some of the other players. I just learned to take my time, slow down, and work with them to make it work.
>
> *When the interviewer asks how he learned that, he continues to respond.*
>
> Well, I got talked to a couple of times by Coach, so, and then I just started picking it up, I just started watching other point guards and stuff. I do that a lot, I just watch other players; I think that's as good as me or better than me. And I use what they do and add it to mine.

In this quote, Jonathon articulates the range of things he has learned this season. He includes learning about technique—citing the ways he has learned from other players and learned about himself. He explains that he learned to have more patience and that patience was central to his becoming a point guard. When players see themselves as learners in the sport, they are more likely to view potential failures as opportunities to learn. Thus failure no longer looms as a psychological risk, and engaging in the practice, even during moments of "failure," is safe.

Supporting Youth in Managing Environmental *Risk*

In both of the youth sports learning settings thus far, coaches and the participant structures of the practices have supported the learning identities and competence of the athletes in multiple ways. I have argued that the kinds of learning interactions in these youth sports, and the ways that youth talk about their learning in these activities, offers evidence of the minimization of psychological risk for young people. In other words, as youths' identities as learners and as members of these communities are strengthened, their risk of feeling less than competent and developing the kinds of reactive coping strategies that Spencer (2006, 2008) described decreases.

However, as I've noted, risk for African American urban youth is multilayered and not limited to the kinds of exchanges that occur within their learning settings in sports or in school. There are significant sociological risks such youth face, including having to navigate underresourced schools that may fail to provide information and academic preparation for college, neighborhoods that may be physically and psychologically unsafe, and the presence of the drug trade and harassment by law enforcement. Coaches in the youth sports settings that I studied were active in working to support students in navigating these sociological risks effectively.

One basketball coach spoke passionately about the kinds of environmental risks his students and players faced:

> If I were to take a poll in my class how many people have seen somebody go to jail, have them raise their hand, how many people have family members in jail? Most of them would raise their hand. How many people have family members who are on crack or who sell dope? Everyone would pretty much raise their hand. ... Most of the kids are so, they've had so many negative experiences. ... It's daily, it's a constant struggle. If you don't have the basic necessities, how can you do well in school? One kid's dad went to jail; he's going to jail for 2 or 3 years, and his mother and dad live together, all his life. One kid's grandmother died, one kid's dad died, one kid just got out of jail, at one point he was charged with armed robbery. Another kid was on probation because maybe he, earlier in the year, was up here selling drugs. Another kid, this kid, relative to everybody else, just had bad grades. One kid got kicked off the team for fighting with a teacher. He got back into school because the charges were dropped because it was actually the teacher who provoked it. Many of them do not have a strong academic skill set, so they force themselves to do school work. They go to a school where some classes are real strict, and other classes, it's real lenient or they may not even have a teacher. Another couldn't afford, he was going to have to get a job because he couldn't afford to go to college next year. ... Just a ridiculous amount of stuff.

In this quote, the Roseville coach describes a range of risks that his players face, including family members in jail or on drugs, involvement themselves with the drug trade, uneven access to quality instruction in their school, and financial constraints that limit their opportunity to attend college. These are significant risks, and this coach implies that many of his players are facing these kinds of risks, and many of them will have more than one of these challenges simultaneously. This coach was from the same neighborhood as many of the students and felt that he understood their challenges firsthand.

The coach at the Academy also spoke of the types of challenges that his students faced, and while he was not from a neighborhood like the one he coached in and didn't share the same racial background as his players, he spoke of his own realization about the existence of structural inequality as a high school student when he saw the other athletes that he played with not have opportunities to go on to college after graduation.

Given this understanding of the kinds of environmental risks that students must contend with, what do coaches do to help students manage these high levels of risk? The track and field coach sees a significant part of his job as involving not only training young people as track athletes but also helping them raise their academic performance while in high school and transition into college. As a part of this envisioned role, he made phone calls to college athletic recruiters, supported students' in their college applications, checked their grades regularly, and talked to them about college life and the requirements to get into college.

The track coach's focus on college was a part of a broader agenda to help young people develop the habits of mind and comportment that would foster their success in school and in society. He explicitly instructed students on how to shake hands, look adults in the eye when speaking to them, and on how to be articulate when talking to the media. On a trip to a meet in another state, the coach was walking across a college campus with the team. There were very few other African Americans on the campus, and the track coach explicitly taught the students how to say good morning to every person (the people were almost entirely White) that they passed on the campus. In other words, the coach was engaged in an active socialization of the athletes, with respect to how to interact with people in other communities. In addition to support with respect to how to engage with others in the world, the track coach also maintained communication with youth and their parents and intervened when young people or their families were in crisis. As an example, when one of the male athletes got kicked out of his home by a parent, the coach helped him find another relative with whom he could stay for the duration of the school year, and then mediated conversations between the student and the parent.

The basketball coaches also worked hard to help players manage the multiple sources of risk. In the quote below, the basketball coach described one way that he sought to encourage youth to make good choices, given the range of risky choices that they could make. He wrote individual letters to students and mailed them to their homes. In these letters he encouraged youth, as players, as students, and as developing young people. The coach described these letters and one young person's response to them.

> One of the best things I had this year, this kid, was a kid who sold dope, he graduated. I mean, during the whole season he had a 4.0, the whole time. And he played his best basketball, and made it to the payoffs. And when they gave him his certificate, he was one of five people with a 4.0. When they asked him what his inspiration was, he said my mom, my auntie, Coach R, and Coach D. Sometimes you don't really know how much it means to him, but one time I went over to his house, and I would write letters, and he had all the letters taped up on his bedroom closet door. ... Letters about how he has to change and about basketball. ... So he read it, and put it on his wall.

This coach reports that the letters he had written to one of his players were, unbeknownst to him, so important to the young person that he had taped them on the wall of his bedroom. This incident illustrates both the deep level of personal work that the coach did to help youth manage the multiple stressors in their lives and the way that this support was taken up and valued by this student.

The track athletes clearly saw their coach in the role of support person as well. One athlete says of her coach,

> He put his whole energy into helping us—trying to get us to do good for us to succeed in life, basically. ... Like he'll—like if you're having a problem whatever, he'll be like, "Come talk to me." Or if not then get one of the other coaches to come and talk to you. And he'll even come up in his own free time—come up here, talk to the teachers for you. So if you'll need to get a grade changed or anything like that, he'll be willing to come up here and get it changed—if your parents can't.

This athlete saw her coach in a parent-like role—someone that would help you through your personal problems, and someone who would also help with academic issues, like trying to get a grade changed. A male athlete reiterated this sense that the track coach was an academic support to athletes. He said, "[Me and coach] have a good relationship. Like at first he really got on me 'cause my grades are low. Well he gets on me all the time. I think we've gotten a lot closer since my 10th-grade year." Another female athlete emphasized the way that the coach was a support for her on personal issues:

> I tell him a lot of stuff. You know, it's like sometimes if I feel that I can't go to my daddy 'cause he might hit me or something, like I'm scared he's gonna fuss at me—I just tell Coach. And he give me advice. He help me get through things."

She, too, seems to see the coach as somewhat of a parental figure—someone she can talk to when she is scared to talk to her father.

However, providing this level of support was not without its challenges. The coach at Roseville talked about the tension between the kinds of attention and support that the basketball players got and the potential jealousy that others in the school community felt about this special treatment for the athletes:

> With the hoop players, a lot of kids feel like the hoop players get more attention and more help than everybody else. I don't know. So, this year for example, with the team, they get like, they got shoes; they went on trips, so on and so forth. And they're always in my room, always, you know. But these kids are the same kids as everyone else, it's just that they have somebody who can, if a problem happens, they can go directly to that person, and they know that stuff will get done. And that person is going to check on those kids constantly, like I've called them at home when they are not at school, check with teachers about their grades. We're about to have study hall again next week. All different types of things. So, as a result, the other kids are just not having their own personal survival person.

The portrayal of the basketball players having their own "personal survival person" is a striking one, which speaks to both the perceived need for multiple kinds of support for students and the paucity of available support in the school community for students.

The coaches in these youth sports settings often took up this role of personal survival person for the young people that they coached and mentored. In doing so, they supported youth in managing multiple kinds of risks in their environments, from a lack of college counselors, to problems at home, to the potential dangers in their neighborhoods. They provided a combination of emotional and practical support to help young people traverse multiple complex settings and to develop positive identities and succeed in school.

This chapter has offered a perspective of youth sports as providing support for the mitigation of risk at two levels: psychological risk that is inherent in any learning setting when one is positioned as a novice, and environmental risk that youth faced in their schools and neighborhoods and as people from a marginalized group in society. As such, it makes a statement about the intersection of race, learning, and educative possibility.

One problem with the ways educators have tended to think about race and learning is that we have viewed race as a characteristic of an individual that somehow prevents them from learning (through culture, perhaps). However, when we view race as a way that our society organizes access to experiences, we see more clearly how race limits access to positive learning spaces (especially in schools). The nature of a learning space that is rich with educative possibility does not change depending on the race of the learner, however. African American and Latino youth tend to both have fewer opportunities to engage in such learning spaces, and to face significant barriers to positive identity-development learning due the multiple kinds of challenges that being African American and Latino poses in this country.

The youth sports settings in this chapter worked to both mitigate and help youth in managing the multiple sources of risk that they were challenged with in their lives. At the same time, these spaces provided settings where youth could be vulnerable, where their failures were often redefined as learning successes, and where they had multiple resources to support their learning. The critical point here is that educative possibility does not lie solely in populations of learners whose protective factors outweigh their sources of risk; it also lies in redefining the work that must happen in learning spaces so that learners can have access to rich learning, even when they are faced with multiple and significant sources of risk.

Notes

1. In this chapter I focus on organized sports; however, many of the processes and interactions I describe also characterize informal sports and afterschool settings. One example

of this is the type of teaching and learning that occurs in informal park sports, such as basketball, as well as other informal games, such as dominoes.
2. All names of schools and youth are pseudonyms.

References

Bowles, S., & Gintis, H. (1977). *Schooling in capitalist America: Educational reform and the contradictions of economic life.* New York, NY: Basic Books.

Cole, M. (1996). *Cultural psychology: A once and future discipline.* Cambridge, MA: Harvard University Press.

Darling-Hammond, L. (2000). New standards and old inequalities: School reform and the education of African American students. *Journal of Negro Education, 69*(4), 263–287.

Darling Hammond, L., Williamson, J. A., & Hyler, M. (2008). Securing the right to learn: The quest for empowering curriculum for African American citizens. *Journal of Negro Education, 76*(3), 281–296.

Drake, S. C. (1987). *Black folk here and there.* Los Angeles: Center for Afro-American Studies.

Duncan-Andrade, J. (2010). *What a coach can teach a teacher.* New York, NY: Lang.

Gordon, E. W., & Song, D. L. (1994). Variations in the experience of resilience. In M. Wang and E. Gordon (Eds.), *Educational resilience in inner-city America.* Mahwah, NJ: Lawrence Erlbaum Associates.

Gutierrez, K., & Rogoff, B. (2003). Cultural ways of learning: Individual traits of cultural repertoires of practice. *Educational Researcher, 32*(5), 19–25.

Ladson-Billings, G. (2006). From the achievement gap to the education debt: Understanding achievement in U.S. schools. *Educational Researcher, 35*(7), 3–12.

Lee, C. D. (2007). *Culture, literacy, and learning: Blooming in the midst of a whirlwind.* New York, NY: Teachers College Press.

Lee, C. D., & Majors, Y. (2003). "Heading up the street": Localized opportunities for shared constructions of knowledge. *Pedagogy, Culture and Society, 11*(1), 49–67.

Majors, Y. (2003). Shoptalk: Teaching and learning in an African American hair salon. *Mind, Culture and Activity, 10*(4), 289–310.

Moll, L., & González, N. (2004). Engaging life: A funds of knowledge approach to multicultural education. In J. Banks & C. McGee Banks (Eds.), *Handbook of research on multicultural education* (2nd ed., pp. 699–715). New York, NY: Jossey-Bass.

Nasir, N. (2000). "Points ain't everything": Emergent goals and average and percent understandings in the play of basketball among African-American students. *Anthropology and Education Quarterly, 31*(3), 283–305.

Nasir, N. (2002). Identity, goals, and learning: Mathematics in cultural practice. In N. Nasir & P. Cobb (Eds.), *Mathematical thinking and learning, 4*(2/3), 213–248.

Nasir, N., & Cooks, J. (2009). Becoming a hurdler: How learning settings afford identities. *Anthropology & Education Quarterly, 40*(1), 41–61.

Nasir, N., & Hand, V. (2008). From the court to the classroom: Opportunities for engagement, learning, and identity in basketball and classroom mathematics. *Journal of the Learning Sciences, 17*(2), 143–161.

Nasir, N. S., Warren, B., Roseberry, A., & Lee, C. (2006). Learning as a cultural process: Achieving equity through diversity. In K. Sawyer (Ed.), *Cambridge handbook of the learning sciences* (pp. 489–504). New York, NY: Cambridge University Press.

Oakes, J. (1990). Opportunities, achievement, and choice: Women and minority students in science and mathematics. *Review of Research in Education* (Vol. 16, pp. 153–222).

Oakes, J. (2004, June). *Inequality, stratification, and the struggle for just schooling.* Talk delivered at the annual meeting of the International Conference of the Learning Sciences, Los Angeles, CA.

O'Connor, K., & Penuel, W. R. (2010). *Research on learning as a human science.* New York, NY: Teachers College Press.

Rogoff, B. (1993). *Apprenticeship in thinking.* New York, NY: Oxford University Press.

Rogoff, B. (2003). *The cultural nature of human development.* New York, NY: Oxford University Press.

Rose, M. (2004). *The mind at work.* New York, NY: Viking.

Spencer, M. (1999). Social and cultural influences on school adjustment: The application of an identity-focused cultural ecological perspective. *Educational Psychologist, 34*(1) 43–57.

Spencer, M. B. (2006). Phenomenology and ecological systems theory: Development of diverse groups. In W. Damon & R. Lerner (Eds.), *Handbook of child psychology: Vol. 1. Theoretical models of human development* (6th ed., pp. 829–893). New York, NY: Wiley.

Spencer, M. B. (2008). Fourth annual Brown lecture in education research—Lessons learned and opportunities ignored since Brown v. Board of Education: Youth development and the myth of a color-blind society. *Educational Researcher, 37,* 253–266.

Spencer, M. B., Dupree, D., & Hartmann, T. (1997). A phenomenological variant of ecological systems theory (PVEST): A self-organization perspective in context. *Development and Psychopathology, 9,* 817–833.

Tyack, D., & Cuban, L. (1995). *Tinkering toward utopia: A century of public school reform.* Cambridge, MA: Harvard University Press.

Varenne, H., & McDermott, R. (1998). *Successful failure: The school American builds.* Boulder, CO: Westview.

11

WE ARE THE ONES

Educative Possibilities in Youth Poetry

Korina Jocson

> We are the ones we have been waiting for.
> June Jordan, "Poem for South African Women"

In the past two decades, youth poetry has gained tremendous momentum in and out of school. Literary arts organizations such as Youth Speaks and Urban Word NYC have led the way to instantiate local, regional, and national youth poetry slam competitions, with increased participation from thousands of youth across the United States. In the spring of 2008, the Home Box Office (HBO) cable network began a documentary series called Brave New Voices, named after the national slam competition that takes place every summer. This growing literary movement as part of a larger culture points to the potential of poetry in the lives of young people. June Jordan's (1980) words "We are the ones we have been looking for" (from a poem written for women in their struggle against apartheid) evoke hope and connote social action. In this chapter, I discuss some possibilities in youth poetry as enacted by partners in education. The perspective I offer not only recognizes poetry as a medium of expression but also affirms the importance of writing that makes explicit uneven relations of power. The language in poetry, as I will illustrate, exposes social realities that are often steeped in the margins. Drawing on an ethnographic study on youth poetry, I highlight a group of teachers' experience in a school-university partnership and provide practical suggestions for educators interested in similar pedagogies in other contexts. First, I begin with a treatment of poetry as part of a larger culture.

Poetry in the 21st Century

Poetry is not a new phenomenon, but it has (re)emerged more inclusive and more visibly connected to politics than ever.[1] For instance, President Obama's inauguration consisted of a celebration of the arts with world-renowned musical guests and artists. It also featured a commissioned poem entitled "Praise Song for the Day" by Elizabeth Alexander, a professor at Yale University. The moment was not the first of its kind. Robert Frost shared his poem for the inauguration of President John F. Kennedy, and Maya Angelou and Miller Williams delivered theirs at the first and second inauguration of President William "Bill" Clinton, respectively. But Obama's choice of Alexander seemed a conscious attempt to reach out to a particular school of black poetry—represented by Cornelius Eady, Toi Deracotte, Carl Philips, Nathaniel Mackey, and Yusef Komanyakaa—that distinctly blends poetics and cultural politics, and that is both complex yet accessible in many of its references to readers of color. These poets are the children of the Black literary and performance poets of the 1960s and 1970s, just as Obama himself is. At such a highly visible event, talented artists fill the stage and let their craft do its work. On a smaller scale, and complementary in spirit, are the local, regional, and national venues where emerging writers, who range in age and hail from various cities and towns, share their passion, thought, and experience.

Literary arts organizations such as Youth Speaks, based in San Francisco, and Urban Word in New York City lead the way in serving youth ages 13 to 19, providing them with mentorship and learning opportunities through afterschool writing workshops, internships, and, most of all, formal spaces for sharing their works in front of large audiences. Their approach to spoken word poetry has been modeled after successful programs such as Poets in the Schools and June Jordan's Poetry for the People, influencing in current times the teaching of poetry in classrooms and the proliferation of other programs outside of school (see Fisher, 2007; Jocson, 2005; Kim, in press; Weiss & Herndon, 2001). Innovative in its approach, Brave New Voices (with representative teams from San Francisco, New York, Chicago, Hawaii, Santa Fe, Fort Lauderdale, Ann Arbor, and Providence, to name a few) now includes a Brave New Teachers program. Training sessions and workshops have become a critical component of the weeklong festival.[2] Aside from its popularity among hip-hop, theater, and literary arts circles, Brave New Voices is also a documentary series on the HBO cable network.[3] The provocative topics represented on stage, projected on a single or multiple microphones, are complex and often personal. Social issues and forms of inequality, as encountered by these teens, take the form of words, gestures, intonation, and, in some instances, coordinated group performance. The power of this collective voice in one room is bracing. Not long ago, emerging and seasoned poets alike graced the same stage in an HBO series called *Russell Simmons' Def Poetry Jam,* hosted by rapper and actor Mos Def. Successful in its late-Friday-night time slot, the show ran for six seasons. The BNV slam competition and documentary series demonstrate a resurgence of literacy as a means for young people not only to write about their lives and share their words with a large audience but, more important, to craft life trajectories with a literary cadence that challenges social norms and inequalities. The writing is a celebration of life and its meanings.

Putting such passion, thought, and experience into the language of poetry has real-world implications; it is indicative of the everyday practices of young people. Featured poems from the 2009 slam competition include titles such as "Fish, Grits & Buttermilk Biscuits" by 18-year-old African American Britney Wilson, a BNV poet from New York. The challenge of having cerebral palsy intertwined with the courage to break social molds takes on a particular force as she describes her own battles, ambitions, and dreams. Another poem, "Change," by 19-year-old African American B. Yung, also a BNV poet from New York, points to the historical struggles of being a young Black male in American society. He performed his 4-minute poem, which includes the notable line "every time I write a poem my paper bleeds," at the Urban Word NYC Slam Finals.[4]

Other examples of poetry come in a variety of multimedia formats. Chinese Taiwanese American Kelly Tsai's "By-Standing: The Beginning of an American Lifetime," a five-minute spoken word video and winner of the War and Peace Award from Media That Matters, was featured in its Seventh Annual Film Festival in New York.[5] The following excerpt signals humanity and responsible action in a multiracial society:

> My friends, my family, my lovers, myself
> We who slip back into what our lives were like before
> Making our convictions seem trendy
>
> Yesterday, I went to study "happy" people at Navy Pier
> People who are regular people
> They don't go to rallies or conferences
> They don't talk about war
> They wait for a sunny day and go to Navy Pier
> They don't talk about politics between them
> They just hold hands and smile beneath their sunglasses
> They eat ice cream that they paid too much money for
> They come together because they need each other
> They decided to be thankful for that today
> They take advantage of the opportunity to love
> They are lucky and everyone in this world should be as lucky
>
> Never, nowhere, anywhere: this is why no war.

Similarly, numerous spoken-word artists have produced their own videos and used YouTube, MySpace, Facebook, and other social media sites to share or distribute their work. Armed with such new media technology, artists have a growing interest in taking poems from the page to the stage and onto the screen. They employ a language of critique (Giroux, 2000) and form alliances through critical solidarity in very creative (and sometimes viral) ways (Jocson, in press).

As poetry continues to transcend physical and technological boundaries, it is essential to remember the potential power of words in the movement toward individual and social transformation. My own research affirms the idea that poetry can be used as a form of critical literacy, both inside and outside school (Jocson, 2008). That is, rooted in poems are literate practices that assess texts to understand relations of power that inform them. What is written or performed often represents the messiness of social relations and practices in everyday life. As a medium of expression, poetry can be one means for moving educators a step closer to improving educational practices and, ultimately, can accelerate literacy achievement for traditionally underserved students. It creates learning environments that allow youth to take part more fully in their own learning process. Likewise, it can give adults a way to make sense of youth's social worlds—to enter everyday imagination and lived experiences. The late professor, activist, and poet June Jordan, whose work at the university extended into the community, including a church that served the homeless, a state prison, a women's correctional facility, and an urban high school, capitalized on the power of poetry. In my encounters with youth poets and other emerging writers, I have discovered that the dialogue that takes place through writing is sometimes a necessary reflection to ease the pain of experience with courage and clarity. Sometimes, it is about releasing fantasies and taking pleasure in the sublime. Sometimes, it is about the jovial randomness that springs up daily in our lives, the kid itching to jump out at the chance to play, laugh, and love or be loved. Sometimes, it is about indignation and getting passed it without harping on anger and deepening wounds. Sometimes, it is about learning *from* and *with* each other, despite the messiness. Such complexities in social relations and practices are often where schooling can supplement the potential for learning.

To illustrate this potential, the next section takes a turn toward educative possibilities. It highlights the experiences of English teachers who capitalized on the power of poetry in the context of an urban high school–university partnership, through the Poetry for the People (P4P) program, in northern California. P4P was first established on the University of California campus in 1991, to use poetry as a form of critical discourse and to promote artistic and political empowerment among otherwise historically denied or disenfranchised populations. It comprises three courses (introduction, writing, and practicum), open to both undergraduate and graduate students. In 1996, a partnership with a local high school began to allow for 3- to 6-week long, curriculum-based poetry writing workshops in English classrooms. University students in the practicum course of the P4P program worked closely with high school English teachers to facilitate these workshops in their respective classrooms. The experience of these teachers in the P4P program reveals the value of poetry in youths' lives and points to the importance of partners in education.

What Teachers Had to Say

"I Actually Learned, Too"

Teachers deemed P4P as a form of professional development. The poems and instructional materials, compiled in a reader format, provided concrete ways of exploring writing traditions and styles. Additionally, teachers expressed benefiting from P4P's pedagogical approach in recognizing youth's poetic voice and its transferability to other forms of writing. Noted was learning how to tap into the multiple writing voices of students and how to specifically use their poetic voices as a departure point for exploring other genres of writing, such as short stories, essays, and speeches. It was deliberate to cover poetry at the beginning of the year (as opposed to the end) because it provided an opening for exploring writing throughout the year.

"Taking a Backseat"

P4P as a school-university partnership benefited teachers in two ways. First, it offered time and flexibility. Instead of single-handedly facilitating instruction and devising lesson plans, teachers were able to focus on building better relationships with their students. There were unique opportunities for interacting with students and examining student writing more closely.

Second, P4P reinforced the relevance of community in teaching and learning. College student-teacher-poets from various racial and cultural backgrounds in the same classroom as high school students and their teacher allowed for an alternative way to negotiate writing. From the printed reader consisting of multicultural poems, to small group writing workshops, to the final reading event held at local community venues, P4P provided multiple resources and contexts for its participants to engage poetry in very relevant ways (for more details on P4P's organization and pedagogy, see Muller & Poetry for the People Blueprint Collective, 1996). For teachers, this meant taking a backseat and learning along with their students.

"Why Pretend These Things Aren't Important?"

Teachers also noted the influence of college student-teacher-poets, particularly their shared knowledge about youth popular culture and their ability to connect with students. One teacher called this connection "invisible work." It was key to tap into the potential for conversation about students' lives that subsequently formed the basis of their writing. Additionally, college student-teacher-poets helped to create a college-going culture in the classroom and demystified the idea that going to college or taking on leadership roles is only for certain people. Teachers recognized the importance of this type of social dynamic, in which they, too, participated.

Some Educative Possibilities

There is no prescription for integrating empowering literacies and pedagogies in the classroom. As demonstrated by teacher partners in P4P, there are many possibilities that can make a difference in students' engagement with poetry if one is willing to experiment. The question is, "How might poetry and poetry writing modeled after P4P's beliefs in artistic and political empowerment look in today's classrooms?" The following are some suggestions to serve as an impetus for a particular interaction with writing. Every context is different, and no single classroom is ever the same as the next. Educators and youth advocates must decide for themselves what is appropriate for the contexts they occupy.

How Do I Begin?

For many, the challenge sometimes is figuring out where or how to begin. One thing I have learned from teachers who had P4P in their classrooms at different times of the year is that there is no perfect time. Timing depends on one's curriculum and one's objectives for the academic year. Perhaps one way to think about timing is to configure one's unit during a time of the year when a particular theme lends itself easily to incorporate poetry. Several teachers scheduled their poetry unit for April (National Poetry Month), when the buzz is loudest and acts as a major catalyst for excitement. Others criticized this approach, preferring poetry earlier in the year and treating it as a conduit for exciting students about writing from the onset. For these teachers, it was a way to connect with students, create a learning community and build trust that opened up different possibilities for the rest of the year.

Whether one chooses to incorporate poetry early or late in the year or somewhere in between, it is important to plan ahead and determine specifically when and for how long to cover a theme or topic. Some may prefer an integrated approach—meaning incorporating poetry into different curricular strands throughout the year. This may pose additional challenges in terms of alignment, but it is certainly a possibility. For both approaches, a good place to start is selecting the topics. P4P's topics such as profiling, democracy, home, love, and urgency have been useful and resonated with many students (see Jocson, 2009). Providing exemplary poems written by youth in the program such as the one below is key.

Wastes Away

As he twists and turns through life
His soul spins from divine to unkind
Will he forever be punished
For past sins of his lifetime

As he dies I see the whites of his eyes
Burn red from greed
He feels the need to lie, cheat and steal

All to make that bill he thinks
He needs so badly

But doesn't he see that while he's a G
His gun is destroying equality for you and me?
Doesn't he realize that he's erased the tracks
Made by the broken backs
Of his ancestors

But as he proceeds his family bleeds
The pain which he causes
And as time pauses
He falls into a cycle of ill-begotten dreams
That shatter like glass

That last for a lifetime
He says he cherishes his life
But cold enough to take another
Demand his family to love each other
But slap around his baby's mother

He's running for cover
As the cold, hard wind of reality hits his face
And the sun rises up, shines away
The last strand of darkness
He hides from the light
Afraid that his mask will decay
And dare I say
He wastes away

How Do I Ignite and Sustain Students' Interest?

Applying elements of surprise to one's classroom practice is not easy. When it is done with students in and out of school literacy and with cultural practices in mind, then engaging students in poetry and poetry writing may be welcomed with open arms. By elements of surprise, I mean anticipatory activities and discrepant events to change things up. By that, I mean doing something new, something fresh, something that would grab students' attention, something that would seem totally "off" from classroom norms and habits, something that would bring together new faces in the classroom, or something even as simple as a shocking line or verse. Something new certainly does not require the presence of actual people, such as "hotshot" guest poets or, as had been the case with P4P, student-teacher-poets facilitating teaching, reading and discussion of poetry, and writing workshops in the classroom. Something new does not require an established university program to enter high schools and collaborate with teachers. I would suggest, however, employing similar approaches to teaching and learning by incorporating students' cultures and prior knowledge, including various elements of hip-hop, spoken word, film, television, and other popular cultural texts. By this, I mean being conscious about one's selection given the range of styles, artists, and subgenres in each cultural form. It might take some level of familiarity to select works relevant to students, but the wide range should not dissuade anyone from trying. There is no right or wrong selection as long as it is an informed one, careful to acknowledge without patronizing young people and their (sub)cultures. With this in mind, my point is simple.

Playing a song or a recorded performance by a spoken word artist at the beginning of class, even before uttering a single word to explain why such an event is happening, might provide the kind of unexpectedness, the kind of freshness, the kind of surge that would command immediate attention. There are many individual albums and anthologized works that educators and youth advocates can elect to purchase at particular record stores, shows, and other local events. With today's advanced technologies, poetry readings and spoken word performances are also available online or through individual or collective artists' websites, making it easier to access them for classroom use. HBO's *Def Poetry* television series can serve as another resource, with its mix of poets from different ethnic groups and different styles from different contexts in the United States. Past episodes on video or DVD format are available for purchase. Numerous clips are also accessible via YouTube.

This approach to literacy instruction would require educators and youth advocates to pay attention to the current and changing trends in music, film, television, and online capabilities. This would also require them to keep up to date with local youth groups and literary arts organizations, even attending relevant events from time to time or checking out different publications. Several teachers with whom I have worked in the San Francisco Bay Area have used these timely instances to spark beginning conversations with other educators to establish sustained relationships with community organizations and programs. These relationships have linked these teachers to additional human resources from the surrounding community in an effort to engage their students in poetry and other types of writing in the classroom. The links trigger beginnings and, ultimately, grow into a community of practice. That is how I have connected with a number of amazing teachers and advocates of youth, a further indication that informal partnerships are being established in a collective effort to innovate classroom practices. It is one indication that education is ubiquitous and can open up various possibilities.

Far from comprehensive, Table 11.1 includes a number of examples and multimedia resources for classroom use. Listed are recommendations from students and teachers dating back to 2004. Additional resources produced by more recent poets and spoken-word artists may be found on YouTube, Facebook, and other online social networks. These resources are often the result of do-it-yourself media production, which again suggests that education is ubiquitous in new media times.

Table 11.1 Examples of youth poetry resources for classroom use

Text and Media	Authors/Sources
Textbooks and anthologies	Brewbaker and Hyland's *Poems by Adolescents and Adults*; Michaels' *Risking Intensity*; Muller and the P4P Blueprint Collective's *June Jordan's Poetry for the People: Revolutionary Blueprint*; Reed's *From Totems to Hip-Hop*; Simmons' *Def Poetry Jam on Broadway*
Books and chapbooks	Hodge's *For Girls With Hips*; Forman's *Renaissance* and *We Are the Young Magicians*; Keys' *Tears for Water*; Park's *The Temperature of This Water*; Sanchez's *Shake Loose My Skin*; Shakur's *The Rose That Grew From Concrete*
Spoken word, rap, alternative, and other lyrical music—artists	Taalam Acey; Jimmy Santiago Baca; Common; Aya de Leon; Eminem; Ani de Franco; Lauryn Hill; Danny Hoch; Immortal Technique; India.Arie; Ise Lyfe; Jay Z; Norah Jones; Sarah Jones; KRS-One; Talib Kweli; The Last Poets; Mos Def; Mystic; Nas; Ozomatli; Pedro Pietri; Rakim; The Roots; Ursula Rucker; Jill Scott; Kanye West
Films and videos	Richard LaGravenese's *Freedom Writers*; Marc Levin's *Slam*; Gus Van Sant's *Finding Forrester*; Peter Weir's *Dead Poets Society*; Theodore Witcher's *Love Jones*; Yanofsky's *Poetic License*
Television shows	Home Box Office's *Brave New Voices* and *Def Poetry*; Black Entertainment Television's *Lyric Café*
Literary magazines	*American Poetry Review; Indiana Review: Kenyon Review; Missouri Review; New American Writing; North American Review; Ploughshares; Poetry; Poets and Writers; Tin House; The Sun Times; ZYZZYVA*
Websites—organizations	American Academy of Poets: www.poets.org The Poetry Center of Chicago: www.poetrycenter.org Urban Word NYC: www.urbanwordnyc.org Youth Speaks: www.youthspeaks.org
Websites—authors	Sandra Cisneros: www.sandracisneros.com Martín Espada: www.martinespada.net June Jordan: www.junejordan.com Uchechi Kalu: www.uchechikalu.com Ishle Park: www.ishle.com Saul Williams: www.saulwilliams.com

How Do I Innovate and Address Standards at the Same Time?

Assessing poetry coincides with the current national focus on testing, standards, and accountability. The work of P4P, for instance, lends a particular perspective to

English language arts standards related to (a) *applying concepts* such as theme, purpose, and audience in students' production of poetry; (b) *using spoken and written language* in various forms to communicate knowledge; (c) *reading a wide range of poems* written by multicultural authors from various traditions as a consistent activity for scaffolding student work; and (d) adhering to specific writing guidelines as a means of teaching the importance of *revision in the writing process* (International Reading Association/National Council of Teachers of English, 1996). Notable in P4P's work at the high school level is a chance for students, teachers, student-teacher-poets, and other members of the school to become part of an authentic audience for students' poetry in the classroom. The audience then grows in size as parents, friends, and members of the larger community become part of a public reading event, a place where each attendee receives a complimentary anthology to take home and continue to share with others. For students, it is a chance to represent their words and their worlds. It is a chance to convene and engage a larger audience in a dialogue—a chance to speak out.

To further assess student poetry, a writing rubric with an emphasis on purpose, intensity, subject, and craftsmanship may be useful as an evaluative tool. Although some educators may disagree, those who elect to use a writing rubric might involve students as peer evaluators, or invite other teachers as partners in enacting a democratic means of assessing student work. Students' and teachers' experiences are shaped by both social interactions and discourses outside of the classroom. It would be advantageous to recognize knowledge and expertise that may not necessarily be sanctioned by school rules, norms, and standards. Certainly, there are myriad ways to rethink what is possible in 21st-century classrooms. For some who are interested in critical literacy, P4P's approach to writing as a form of artistic and political empowerment might be worth exploring in English language arts and across content areas. Or perhaps extending learning beyond classroom walls through writing workshops and activities with members of the community might also be considered. For others, it might be worthwhile to see what happens when students choose their best work for publication in class anthologies and examine along with their peers what it means to write for multiple audiences. Those involved in project-based learning approaches might find it worthwhile to incorporate evaluation that is not solely based on testing and grades. It might be possible to assess student portfolios and other performance-based work across time, place, and genres. Perhaps even forms of external assessment with input from parents and other community members might be included. There are no limits to effective literacy instruction, as there are no limits to shaping innovative practice.

How Can I Be Better at What I Do?

Innovation is about experimentation. As I have noted, how a person experiments should be based on well-informed choices. To do that means to see education in everyday processes. It means doing seemingly mundane yet concrete things.

For example, talk with young people. Ask them about what is "in" or what is "hot." Find out about what they are reading, watching, or listening to, both inside and outside of school. Read current literature on adolescent literacy. Attend local events related to youth poetry and spoken word. Visit local stores to keep up to date with students' interests, perhaps in music or even in fashion. Ask students about the latest films, television shows, music videos, video games, and podcasts. Also, observe and inquire about the latest technological gadgets that are popular among youth. Surf the Internet and stay curious about "what's new." Take an interest in youth organizations in your area. Again, ask. Talk to colleagues and others in the larger community about available resources—whether human, material, or otherwise. Check out places where young people spend their leisure time, both in and out of school. Showing a genuine interest when inquiring or uttering that you will actually be there; that might help. Watch what happens in these places. Take notes. Connect these social worlds with the worlds of your classroom. Ask yourself, "Is this working?" Be reflective. Try other things. Go to the movies. Flip the channels on your television set. Ask your kids or your cousins, nieces, and nephews about what is happening in their world. Again, be reflective. Browse through magazines from a local newsstand. Pick up the latest books in the young adult section in a local bookstore. Start a conversation with youths seated in the aisles (and who are probably so engaged by the text that their eyes are glued to the page, reading, and they are not paying attention to you). Inquire about what is good and exciting. Chances are they would provide key information and point us toward the right direction. Chat and share ideas with other allies. Like minds could lead to the building of informal and formal networks, thus building a community of practice. Be bold. Ask difficult questions, "What is it that I know and still don't know?" "How do I build on what I know in new ways?" "How can young people help me get there?"

What Might This Look Like in Teacher Education?

For those in teacher-education programs, several features of poetry writing and instruction modeled after P4P may be helpful to consider. These features echo June Jordan's vision of using words as weapons in the continued fight for a democratic society. They move us toward a critical literacy education that demands more not only from ourselves but also from those with whom and for whom we work (Morrell 2005, 2007). Following are features of poetry that, at a minimum, if practiced with inquiry-based approaches, break the grounds of critical literacy education:

- Poetry as a medium for relating everyday realities
- Poetry as a safe space for building community, including youth and adults
- Poetry as a tool for naming and recognizing the voices of historically denied populations

- Poetry as a timeless genre that in the context of spoken word and hip-hop culture can lead to the exploration of different genres of writing
- Poetry as an individual- or a group-oriented activity that can lead to a person's own or collective discovery of multiple writing voices, styles, and talents that are transferable to multiple discursive spaces
- Poetry as a reflection of love, hope, and humanity

These features are not limited to teacher education or to the notion of school. Given poetry's broad appeal, it would be advantageous to also rethink educative possibilities in nonschool spaces, such as literary-arts organizations, public libraries, parks, camps, churches, and community centers, among others. The possibilities are many if education is viewed comprehensively.

Poetry as Comprehensive Education: What Now?

Writing is integral to the lives of young people. For some, poetry as a recurring activity takes the form of onstage performances and slam competitions. For others, poetry graces video screens and websites; sometimes it remains in the pages of notebooks yet to be shared with another. The call for improved and innovative pedagogies is upon us. What can we do differently if education is indeed ubiquitous and comprehensive? How can advocates of poetry and those invested in youth development in various learning environments contribute? What kinds of policies would support existing programs or create new ones? These are some questions that continue to drive individual and collective efforts in literacy, arts, and urban education. For youth whom I have encountered, poetry has been one means of making sense of their social worlds, both inside and outside of school. Their crafting of words is an invitation to embrace an un/structured literate practice filled with educative possibilities.

Notes

1. Parts of this chapter have appeared in a different argument. In an essay titled "Poetry in a New Race Era" (Jocson, 2011), I discuss a connection between poetry, race, and politics.
2. For more information about each organization, visit their websites: Youth Speaks (http://www.youthspeaks.org) and Urban Word NYC (http://www.urbanwordnyc.org). For details about BNV's Annual Slam Competition, visit their website (http://www.bravenewvoices.org).
3. These and several other poems from teams Ann Arbor, Fort Lauderdale, Hawaii, Philadelphia, San Francisco, and Santa Fe are featured on HBO's website (www.hbo.com). Full episodes of the BNV series, accompanied by woven narratives about each poet, may also be viewed via HBO On Demand or purchased as a DVD set.
4. The video *By Standing: The Beginning of an American Lifetime,* by Kelly Tsai, can be accessed via http://www.mediathatmattersfest.org/films. The poem can be accessed via http://www.yellowgurl.com.

References

Fisher, M. (2007). *Writing in rhythm: Spoken word poetry in urban classrooms.* New York, NY: Teachers College Press.

Giroux, H. (2001). Theory and resistance in education: Towards a pedagogy for the opposition. Westport, CT: Bergin & Garvey.

International Reading Association/National Council of Teachers of English. (1996). *Standards for the English language arts.* Urbana, IL: National Council of Teachers of English.

Jocson, K. M. (2005). "Taking it to the mic": Pedagogy of June Jordan's Poetry for the People and partnership with an urban high school. *English Education, 37*(2), 44–60.

Jocson, K. M. (2008). *Youth poets: Empowering literacies in and out of schools.* New York, NY: Peter Lang.

Jocson, K. M. (2009). Steering legacies: Pedagogy, literacy and social justice in schools. *The Urban Review, 41*(3), 269–285.

Jocson, K. M. (2011). Poetry in a new race era. *Daedalus: Journal of the Academy of Arts & Sciences, 140*(1), 154–162.

Jocson, K. M. (in press). Remix revisited: Critical solidarity in youth media arts. *Pedagogies: An International Journal.*

Jordan, J. (1980). *Passion: New poems (1977–1980).* Boston, MA: Beacon.

Kim, R. (in press). *Spoken art pedagogies: Youth, critical literacy & a cultural movement in the making.* Unpublished doctoral dissertation. University of California, Santa Cruz.

Morrell, E. (2005). Toward a critical English education: Reflections on and projections for the discipline. *English Education, 37*(4), 312–322.

Muller, L., & Poetry for the People Blueprint Collective (Eds.). (1995). *June Jordan's Poetry for the People: A revolutionary blueprint.* New York, NY: Routledge.

Weiss, J., & Herndon, S. (2001). *Brave new voices: The Youth Speaks guide to teaching spoken word and poetry.* Portsmouth, NH: Heinemann.

Toward a Public Policy Agenda on Comprehensively Conceived Education

12

THE CHALLENGES OF DEVELOPING A ROBUST KNOWLEDGE BASE ON COMPLEMENTARY EDUCATION

Toward a Policy-Relevant Research Agenda

Jacob Leos-Urbel and J. Lawrence Aber

Introduction

This volume is evidence of an increasing awareness that, in order to increase student success and narrow the achievement gap that exists along racial and socio-economic lines, public policy must extend beyond the traditional school house and classroom. Although quality schools are a crucial factor in children's learning and development, researchers have long known that a multitude of family and other out-of-school influences play an even larger role. Our current base of knowledge about which types of programs are most effective in complementing or supplementing in-school learning is limited, and research in this area faces numerous constraints. In this chapter we consider the challenges of designing and conducting research on complementary education and suggest strategies for developing a more robust knowledge base in order to inform public policy.

First, we briefly explore the importance of thinking about education comprehensively, define terms, and lay out the scope of our discussion. Next, we outline some of the major challenges to researching comprehensively understood education and provide a brief selective overview of the existing knowledge base to highlight its strengths and remaining gaps. We devote the remainder of the chapter to developing a proposal for a policy-relevant research agenda in comprehensive education that more effectively addresses the challenges and constraints in the field.

Looking Beyond the Classroom: Education Policy as Broader Than Schooling Policy

At least since the Coleman Report in 1966, there has been an understanding that children's experiences outside of school have serious implications for their academic success. Researchers commonly find that schooling accounts for no more than one-third of the variation in children's academic achievement (Rothstein, 2004). Poverty can influence children's education and development in myriad ways, for example, through poorer health, greater mobility, and fewer neighborhood resources (Aber, Jones, & Raver, 2007). Differences in learning along socioeconomic lines emerge both before children start elementary school and during the time when school is out of session. In some contexts, differences in learning before entering school have been found to explain approximately one-third of the academic achievement gap, with differences in learning during the summer explaining the remaining two-thirds of the academic achievement gap (Alexander, Olson, & Entwisle, 2007).[1]

Although school constitutes the lion's share of publicly funded programming for children, other programs aim to help prepare children for school, complement their school-day experiences, enhance families and communities in their ability to support children, and help youth as they transition to adulthood. As discussed previously in this volume, a comprehensive conceptualization of education encompasses all intentional learning experiences, both inside and outside of school. Complementary or supplementary[2] education refers specifically to learning and development that takes place outside of the classroom. Our discussion in this chapter focuses on complementary education and, in particular, on the domains of complementary education where there has been considerable public policy action and research.[3]

Complementary education, as treated here, encompasses early childhood education, afterschool and summer programs for elementary and middle school students, postsecondary programs for youth, and comprehensive community initiatives. Although programs for these age groups are often treated separately, they share important commonalities from both a policy and research perspective. First, they operate outside of the traditional school classroom, although their success is often measured against the goal of improving cognitive or academic outcomes. At the same time, they often have additional goals ranging from promoting children's social and emotional development to providing appropriate care and supervision while parents work. This array of policy goals and occasional tension between academic and nonacademic measures is common to complementary education as a field. These varying goals influence programmatic and policy design as well as conclusions regarding success or failure.

The study of complementary education also involves an underlying question of the extent to which ensuring that all children have access to educational and developmental activities outside of school is considered a public responsibility. In contrast to schooling, in which all children have a legal right to at least a minimal level of government-funded education, complementary or supplementary education programming occupies a relatively grey policy space. While there are large-scale policy efforts in these areas, the level of public versus private responsibility for meeting children's educational and developmental needs outside of the classroom is less well defined, and the legal frame, dedicated financing, and physical infrastructure are less well developed.

Although free public schooling is available for all children, supplemental education such as early childhood education, afterschool programs, summer programs, and other community initiatives is available to some but not all low-income families. Also, middle-class parents often pay for these services, which may further complicate considerations of the extent to which providing for children's education and development outside of the classroom is considered a public responsibility. The result is a lack of *developmental equity*, which places low-income children at a comparative disadvantage, especially during the stages of life in which public investments in children are lowest, including before kindergarten and after high school (Aber & Chaudry, 2010; Aber et al., 2007).

Finally, complementary education programs, as conceived here, share a common set of challenges with regard to research and evaluation. These include continued questions of which outcomes programs should be held accountable for lack of clarity and agreement about exactly what inputs and activities should be thought of as constituting complementary education, as well as difficulty establishing the causal impact of complementary education. In the remainder of this chapter we discuss these challenges, the existing base of research evidence in the complementary education literature, and strategies for future research.

Why Is Research in Complementary Education Complex?

Research in complementary education is challenging for a number of reasons. First, as noted previously, complementary learning programs often have multiple goals, both academic and nonacademic, and there is a lack of clarity and agreement regarding the outcomes of interest in determining whether programs "work." Research has largely focused on academic or cognitive measures, at least in part because they are already measured by schools and school systems and are of clear interest to policy makers and others. However, an understandable sense of urgency to close the academic achievement gap may lead to overemphasis on test scores as well as unrealistic expectations for the magnitude of the effect of a given complementary education program. At the same time, the "noncognitive" achievement gap, including constructs such as social skills, persistence, and self-esteem, is less well understood, albeit of great importance for ultimate success in the workplace (Heckman & Rubinstein, 2001; Rothstein, 2004). Nonacademic outcomes are not routinely measured in the same way that test scores are, and it may be less clear how to interpret them from a policy perspective.

There is also a lack of clarity regarding the inputs that should be thought of as constituting complementary education. The definition of complementary education as encompassing all learning and development that takes place outside of school makes sense conceptually, but a more operational definition is needed to guide policy makers and researchers. There is a wide array of possible inputs in complementary education, and the domain is not nearly as well mapped as in-school education, where the range of inputs is considerably more bounded. It may be especially challenging to specify this range of inputs and identify variation in complementary education because the ratio of familial versus societal investments is much higher than in schooling. Further, while most research in complementary education focuses on a specific program or activity, each is just one piece of a larger set of activities that foster children's out-of-school learning and development, or supplementary education.

Research in complementary education also faces considerable methodological challenges in making causal inferences regarding the impact of programs and policies. In many ways these challenges stem from the voluntary nature of most complementary education programs. There are myriad ways that children can spend their time outside of the classroom, and those not participating in a given complementary education program could be participating in a similar or even higher-quality program or activity elsewhere, or in no program at all. Therefore, it is difficult to know what we are comparing the effectiveness of a given complementary education program to or, in research terminology, what the counterfactual is. Conceptualizing the counterfactual is further complicated by the less bounded temporal and spatial nature of complementary education, as well as the many other factors that may influence or moderate the impact of complementary education programs on children's outcomes.

Figure 12.1 provides a simple model for thinking about the relationship between complementary education and child outcomes, and the complexities inherent in assessing the effectiveness of complementary education programs. Paths (a) and (b) indicate that factors such as the availability and quality of complementary education, the likelihood of take-up, and the level of participation (i.e., dosage) may all be influenced by family, community, and school characteristics. Paths (c) and (d) demonstrate the direct impact of family, community, and school on child outcomes. Path (g) represents the impact of complementary education on child outcomes, while paths (e) and (f) indicate that the impact of complementary education on child outcomes may be moderated by family, community, and school influences.

Children who choose to take up and participate in a given program may be different from those who choose not to participate (e.g., different levels of motivation), which limits the comparability of treatment and comparison groups when trying to isolate the impact of the program. Random assignment can help deal with this selection bias, but there have been relatively few true experiments in complementary education research. Research in complementary education also faces important tradeoffs between internal and external validity. In true experiments, which can yield high internal validity, the study sample or program conditions may differ from the program as a whole. For instance, in one of the few true experiments in the afterschool literature, the evaluation of the federal 21st Century Community Learning Center (21st CCLC) program, the study

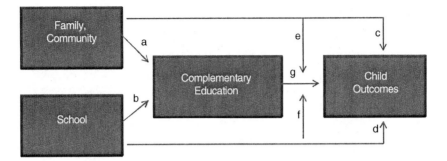

Figure 12.1 Influences on the relationship between complementary education and child outcomes.

was limited to programs that were oversubscribed, yielding a sample that differed considerably from the population of program participants nationwide (James-Burdumy, Dynarski, & Deke, 2007).

In addition to deciding whether to take up complementary education, children and families also choose how much to participate. Many complementary education programs experience relatively low attendance rates by participants. Researchers have pointed to low program attendance (i.e., insufficient dosage) as one possible explanation for limited findings (Gardner, Roth, & Brooks-Gunn, 2009; James-Burdumy et al., 2007). While low attendance has often been treated as a research challenge, it is also a policy and managerial issue that warrants further attention. Finally, in some cases, complementary education programs may simply not be long or intense enough to yield the expected effects, and many studies may not have sufficiently large samples to detect smaller effects (due to cost and other logistical factors). For example, while the evaluation of the 21st CCLC program did not find effects on participants' academic outcomes, the expected effect size may have been too large, given the actual increase in instruction time and that the study did not have sufficient power to detect smaller effects (Kane, 2004).

Current Research Base

Next we provide a brief overview of the literature in complementary education, focusing on early childhood education, out-of-school programming for school-age children, programs for youth, and comprehensive community initiatives. While this by no means encompasses everything that could fit within the conceptual definition of complementary education, it does focus on the domains where there has been the most policy action and research. This review is selective and is intended to provide a general picture of the state of the research, including evidence for the effectiveness of complementary education programs as well as remaining questions and gaps in the literature.

Early Childhood Education

The strongest evidence that supplementary education programs can be effective comes from the early childhood education literature. Early childhood education is also the area of complementary education where there has been the greatest policy response and the most rigorous research. Nonetheless, both policy and research responses are still inadequate to meet the existing need. Experimental evaluations of a small number of intensive programs that operated in the 1960s and 1970s find impressive effects. Participants in the comprehensive Perry Pre-school program in Ypsilanti, Michigan, demonstrated higher IQs than controls, and although these effects disappear by third grade, beneficial effects on earnings, employment, and arrests have persisted for participants through age 40. Similarly, participants in the experimentally evaluated Abecedarian preschool program in Chapel Hill, North Carolina, demonstrated effects on IQ that were still evident 15 years later, entered college at two and a half times the rate of those in the control group, demonstrated lower rates of teen parenthood and marijuana use, and were more likely to have skilled employment in early adulthood (Campbell et al., 2008; Duncan, Ludwig, & Magnuson, 2007).

Studies of large-scale early childhood education programs, most notably Head Start, which primarily serves low-income 3- and 4-year-olds, point to the potential benefits of these programs, but the interpretation of research findings has been subject to debate. Many early nonexperimental studies of Head Start found positive short-term cognitive effects that faded out over time. Notably, some studies indicate that this fade-out is greatest among children who go on to attend the poorest schools (Currie & Thomas, 2000). The experimental *Head Start Impact Study* (U.S. Department of Health and Human Services, 2010) also found few positive persisting effects, although some argue that estimates of program effects should account for actual program participation rather than simple assignment to the treatment or control group (Ludwig & Phillips, 2008). In addition, an experimental study of the Early Head Start Program, which serves children under the age of 3, found positive cognitive and noncognitive impacts for participants, and parents reported reading to their children more and spanking them less (Love et al., 2002). A growing body of research in prekindergarten programs also suggests positive program impacts on children's cognitive development (Gormley & Gayer, 2005; Gormley, Phillips, Adelstein, & Shaw, 2010).

Out-of-School Time

Evidence of the effectiveness of afterschool programs is not as strong. A recent report by the Harvard Family Research Project, which advocates a systemic approach to out-of-school time that integrates school and out-of-school supports, concedes that "the field is limited in its ability to make causal claims about the effectiveness of participation in after-school programs" (Weiss, Little, Bouffard, Deschenes, & Malone, 2009). One of the few experimental studies of afterschool programs (James-Burdumy et al., 2007), the evaluation of the federal 21st Century Community Learning Centers Program mentioned previously, has generated considerable debate. Perhaps surprisingly to its supporters, the study found no impact of 21st CCLC on academic outcomes or the amount of time that children spent unsupervised. However, several observational studies do point to academic benefits of afterschool participation, although the level of internal validity of these studies is often not as high (see, for instance, Lauer et al., 2006; Vandell, Reisner, & Pierce, 2007).

There is also some evidence suggesting that afterschool programs may have positive effects on children's social and emotional development. A meta-analysis of both experimental and quasi-experimental studies of programs with an explicit mission to promote children's personal and social development in areas such as problem solving, conflict resolution, self-control, leadership, responsible decision making, enhancement of self-efficacy, and self-esteem found that youth who participated in these afterschool programs significantly improved in feelings, attitudes, and behavioral adjustment, as well as in their school performance (Durlak, Weissberg, & Pachan, 2010). Notably, of the programs included in the meta-analysis, only those that met a specific set of quality criteria were associated with positive outcomes for youth, while those that did not meet the criteria did not yield positive outcomes. These "SAFE" criteria include a *sequenced* set of activities to promote skills, *active* forms of learning, program components *focused* on developing personal or social skills, and *explicit* targeting of specific social or personal skills. Another quasi-experimental evaluation, studying the San Francisco Beacons program, found that participants demonstrated better self-esteem than a comparison group of nonparticipating students, although the authors note that the groups differ in important ways and therefore the definitiveness of the findings is limited (Walker & Arbreton, 2004).

Finally, there is some research evidence indicating that academic learning can in fact take place during the out-of-school hours, albeit in more school-like settings. For example, an experimental evaluation of the Building Educated Leaders for Life's 6-week summer program for children entering Grades 1 through 7 found that children in the treatment group learned about 1 month's worth of reading skills more than the control group (Chaplin & Capizzano, 2006). Another study that randomly assigned elementary school students within the same afterschool program to receive enhanced academic instruction (delivered by certified teachers with low teacher-to-student ratios) found a small positive and significant impact for math achievement but no impact for the reading module (Black, Doolittle, Zhu, Unterman, & Grossman, 2008). Neither evaluation found program effects in social and emotional domains, such as academic engagement or social behavior.

Youth

Evaluations of youth programs have largely looked at employment and earnings as outcomes of interest. While the evidence of long-term program effectiveness is limited, there are some positive findings. An experimental evaluation (Schochet, Burghardt, & McConnell, 2008) of the Job Corps program, the largest training program for disadvantaged youths in the country, found increased educational attainment and increased earnings and reduced criminal activity for participants. However, these effects were small, and the earnings gains faded out for most participants. Reviews of other rigorous studies also find positive effects of youth-development programs in the short term (Bloom, 2010). Other current programs, such as YouthBuild, which helps youth work towards high school diploma or GED while learning job skills by building homes for homeless and low-income families, are promising although not yet rigorously evaluated (Bloom, 2010; Hahn, Leavitt, Horvat, & Davis, 2004).

Comprehensive Community Initiatives

Most of the research discussed above has focused on individual supplementary education programs or policies (e.g., an early childhood education program, an afterschool program) that are usually targeted to children of a specific age or stage of development. There also have been efforts to support and complement children's in-school learning more broadly, through "comprehensive community initiatives" that provide a wider array of services and include a broader age-range of children. The Harlem Children Zone (HCZ) and the federally funded Promise Neighborhoods (modeled after HCZ), which aim to support children "from cradle to college," are perhaps the most well-known current incarnations of the comprehensive community initiative approach. As the comprehensive community initiative field grew considerably in the 1980s and 1990s, researchers struggled with how best to evaluate their effectiveness and largely settled on a "theory of change" approach, which evaluated program activities and intended outcomes yet largely did not solve the challenge of establishing causality (Connell & Kubisch, 1998). Currently, despite the appeal of and excitement around the Harlem Children's Zone and Promise Neighborhoods, there has been little rigorous research regarding their effectiveness. One study, which definitively concluded that the HCZ improved students' academic test scores, and suggested that the school rather than the bundle of other community services and resources was primarily responsible for the gains, has been the subject of some debate (Dobbie & Fryer, 2009).

Discussion of Existing Research and Gaps in Knowledge

The existing research base in complementary education is anchored by relatively strong evidence of the potential to improve a variety of outcomes over the long term, from a small number of early childhood education studies conducted decades ago. The evidence from studies of early childhood education implemented on a larger scale suggests positive impacts but in many cases is not as definitive. There also is suggestive evidence of the potential for out-of-school-time programs for school-age children to have positive impacts on academic and behavioral outcomes, but there is quite limited ability to date to make causal claims. Research on programs for youth yields evidence of short-term effects on earnings. Finally, the research on comprehensive community initiatives lags behind most in terms of both rigor and positive findings.

Thus, despite promising leads, the current knowledge base lacks sufficient evidence of what components of complementary education work, and for whom. Given this lack of scientific evidence, a major debate in the field regarding the proper activities and goals for complementary education programs (i.e., the extent to which they should look more or less like school) has been largely ideological. While some argue that children struggling academically need more school, others argue quite the opposite that children need opportunities to learn and develop in other ways. This lack of agreement about program goals and structure may serve to limit the expansion of complementary education (Brecher, Brazill, Weitzman, & Silver, 2009).

This question of whether to focus on the work of improving "academics" versus the "fun" of social–emotional learning has often been treated as an either/ or decision. Some research does, in fact, suggest that there may be tradeoffs between the goals of improving cognitive and academic skills for children on the one hand, and improving social and emotional skills on the other. For instance, some nonexperimental studies in early childhood education find that participation in center-based preschool and pre-K programs may increase both academic skills and behavior problems (Belsky et al., 2007; Magnuson, Ruhm, & Waldfogel, 2007). However, there also is some research evidence suggesting that a focus on children's social and emotional development can have positive effects on their academic performance (Durlak et al., 2010).

Research in complementary education for the most part has focused on a fairly narrow set of outcomes, with a considerable emphasis on cognitive and academic test scores, most often looking over a short time frame. However, when considering the theory of change for many complementary education programs that focus on a wide range of activities, many of which are not academic, it may not be surprising that the evidence supporting an immediate increase in tests scores is limited. Instead, based on program theory and activities, we may primarily expect, at least in the short term, effects on social and emotional development. Further, we have a limited understanding of the medium- and longer-term impacts of many complementary education programs, and whether programs may still have longer-term positive influences on life outcomes, even in the absence of short-term improvements in test scores.

The existing research base also is limited in its ability to help us understand the selection into and differential take-up of complementary education programs. Why do some children decide to participate in complementary education programs and others do not, and how do participants differ from nonparticipants? We have a fairly limited understanding of the counterfactual environment in complementary education research, which has enormous implications for determining whether programs "work." There is a need not only for greater understanding of what the counterfactual is but also for discussion of how the nature of the counterfactual influences determinations of whether policies are worthwhile.

Finally, there is a need to consider what the appropriate unit of analysis is when thinking comprehensively about education. It is clear that complementary education is made up of multiple programs and activities, both formal and informal, serving children of differential stages of development, from early childhood to late adolescence. Thus far, research in complementary education has largely focused on these individual and age-specific components of complementary education, for instance, evaluating the effectiveness of one program compared to whatever children would have been engaged in otherwise. While this approach is relatively straightforward, an alternative approach could treat the community as the unit of analysis and examine both the extent to which children's complementary education needs are met and whether communities adequately provide a truly comprehensive educational experience.

Toward a Policy-Relevant Research Agenda

Our brief review of the research suggests the continued need to design and implement effective complementary education to help close gaps left even by very effective schools. But given the limited research to date on complementary education, the nation faces a considerable challenge. In this final section of the chapter we suggest strategies for future research in complementary education that could help address some of the complexities and gaps in the current research base discussed above.

Balanced Research Portfolio

A policy-relevant research agenda aimed at building the knowledge base in complementary education should consist of a balanced research portfolio, including descriptive, analytic, and causal research. Descriptive research is needed to provide information about what young peoples' complementary education experiences are like, who is participating, and what they are doing. Descriptive research is also needed to guide us in thinking more deeply about the various types of "learning" that are important for children, and to better understand the settings where learning activities take place. Such research could also help us think about the inputs and activities that constitute complementary education and build our knowledge regarding how programs are actually implemented on the ground (Fixsen, Naoom, Blase, Friedman, & Wallace, 2005).

Future analytic research can help us to better understand what characteristics are associated with children and families selecting and participating in complementary education programs or opting out, and control for these selection factors when assessing the effect of variation in complementary education inputs. Such analytic research can help in targeting programs to the populations that need them most and ensuring that program activities are appropriate for the types of children who participate. Analytic research can also help us identify and understand potential causal mechanisms at work in improving children's outcomes through complementary education programs, while at the same time maintaining a high level of external validity and representativeness of programs and policies as they are implemented under real-world conditions.

Finally, additional research that can make plausible causal estimates of program effectiveness, with a high level of internal validity, is needed to inform the policy process. Causal research that attempts to open up the "black box" by investigating the mediators and processes by which complementary education benefits children is needed. Further, it is important to highlight the distinction between causal analysis of the effectiveness of an individual program, and the potential to improve the knowledge base in comprehensive education through random assignment studies of more comprehensive community initiatives.

Strategies for Addressing Research Constraints

In the previous sections we outlined the considerable complexities inherent in conducting research in complementary education. These include (a) determinations of appropriate outcome measures, (b) the question of whether to focus only on components of complementary education or attempt to understand holistic profiles of complementary/comprehensive education at the community level, (c) the challenge of knowing what the counterfactual is, (d) selection bias in program take-up, and (e) actual fidelity of implementation and program dosage. While challenging, future research efforts can considerably improve our understanding of complementary education.

Research in complementary education should encompass a wide range of outcome measures, including academic test scores, if appropriate, but also other measures of children's learning and development. Wherever possible, researchers can take advantage of administrative data already being collected to examine policy-relevant measures such as school attendance, credit accumulation, grade retention, suspension, and graduation. Research that tracks students over time, taking advantage of existing administrative data, can provide important information about program impacts on children over the medium and longer terms at the population level.

As mentioned above, research in complementary education faces persistent questions such as "what is the counterfactual?" Future research should pay increased attention to answering this question by studying comparison-group activities in order to better understand what the complementary education program of interest is being compared to. Also, although challenging, efforts to collect better administrative data on parents, such as education and income, in a manner that maintains privacy and confidentiality, would greatly improve researchers' ability to control for these important factors and identify the effect of complementary education programs, independent of the myriad other factors that influence children's learning.

Although not unique to complementary education, selection bias is a real challenge to our ability to definitively determine program success. To strengthen the internal validity of nonexperimental and quasi-experimental studies of the influence of comprehensive education, more research is needed on those child, family, community, and policy factors that influence both selection into comprehensive education and dosage of comprehensive education. Strong theory and research on these selection processes will go a long way in improving both the rigor and the policy relevance of analytic research.

In addition to strengthening nonexperimental and quasi-experimental research, more and better "true experiments" in comprehensive education are needed. Researchers, in collaboration with policy makers and program providers, must look for opportunities for random assignment when testing innovative interventions of unknown effectiveness or when demand simply exceeds supply. The ethical, political, and communication obstacles to true experiments in complementary education are solvable (Boruch et al., 2004). Place-based, rather than individual-level random assignment may offer advantages under certain circumstances, including the ability to better understand the peer effects of an intervention. Natural experiments, in the form of policy changes in complementary education offerings, may provide opportunities for research that is less threatened by selection bias.

Certainly, in the current budget climate, federal and state governments will face difficulties in mounting costly new demonstrations of comprehensive education initiatives such as Promise Neighborhoods. One way to reduce annual costs and enhance knowledge development at the same time is to plan to roll out initiatives over a period of years and randomly assign neighborhoods to starting the initiative in different years. Creative ways to reduce the economic and logistic burdens of place-randomized trials will help the field develop a stronger knowledge base of the causal impact of comprehensive education initiatives on children and youth.

As noted above, children and families that are given the option to participate in complementary learning programs do not always take up the offer. While it is important to understand how programs and policies operate in the real world, including the fact that not all eligible children will participate, it is also important to understand how programs affect those who actually do attend. Researchers are developing increasingly sophisticated methods for accounting for the fidelity of program implementation, by modeling actual take-up and reestimating program effects. In addition, future qualitative research could help us to better understand the reasons that some children and families decide to take up complementary education programs and others do not. Also, by examining the activities of non-participants, qualitative research can improve our understanding of what complementary education programs are being compared to (i.e., the counterfactual), which will inform expectations of program impacts.

Finally, there are a number of practical challenges that must be addressed in order to advance rigorous research on comprehensive education.

1. Comprehensive education initiatives are "delivered" by a very broad range of agencies, funded in very diverse ways. Consequently, it is quite time- and resource-consuming for researchers to develop research collaborations with comprehensive education "providers." Some jurisdictions have attempted to meet this and related challenges by creating cross-agency, cross-researcher forums for the development of relationships and exchange of ideas (e.g., the child and family policy research forum, jointly convened by New York University and the Agency for Children's Services in New York City Government).

2. Studies of comprehensive education require careful investigation of multiple processes and outcomes, which are the purview of a wide range of academic and intellectual disciplines. Some universities and policy research centers have sought to address this challenge by creating interdisciplinary research institutes that strive to build bridges between relevant academic disciplines as well as between the worlds of research, policy, and practice (e.g., NYU's Institute of Human Development and Social Change; the Consortium of University-based Child and Family Policy Research Centers).

3. Because comprehensive services are funded by different agencies within and across federal and subfederal levels of government, and because the research is best pursued in a transdisciplinary fashion, it is not the exclusive purview of any single funder who feels responsible. At the federal level, problems of cross-agency coordination are being addressed, for example, by the Early Learning Interagency Policy Board, which is jointly chaired by leaders from the Department of Health and Human Services and the Department of Education. Also, a critical role in advancing a creative and rigorous research agenda on comprehensive education can be played by key philanthropies that can fund across organizational and/or topical boundaries (e.g., W. T. Grant, Spencer, Wallace, and Gates). Similarly, corporate philanthropies have made important investments in complementary education (e.g., see Chapter 5 for a discussion of the Jacobs Engineering Group's community investments in San Diego), and are in a strategic position to fund research addressing the impact of if these programs on educational and social outcomes.

Conclusion

We began this chapter by noting the growing evidence of strong out-of-school influences on children's academic and social-emotional development and the increasing efforts to address these influences via comprehensive education initiatives. As achievement gaps along racial and socioeconomic lines stubbornly persist, and as America's need for a better educated populace continues to expand in an increasingly global economy, the knowledge gap on comprehensive education becomes a larger and larger impediment to action. While significant, all of the challenges in developing a robust knowledge base on complementary education are tractable, although it will require intellectual creativity, political will, and social organization to meet them.

Notes

1. Alexander et al. (2007) look at differences in reading scores along socioeconomic lines in Baltimore city schools, and therefore their findings apply to the academic achievement gap within this relatively low-income urban context. This research does not, for example, imply that any achievement gap between students in the city and surrounding suburbs would be attributable to preparation levels at school entry and summer experiences only.
2. We use these terms interchangeably throughout this chapter.
3. It is important to note that some treat this issue even more broadly. For example, the Campaign for Educational Equity's Comprehensive Educational Opportunity Project's definition of *comprehensive education* includes early childhood education, preventative physical and mental health care, afterschool and summer programs, and family engagement services. While this definition encompasses other services that are important and necessary to ensure that children are ready and able to learn, we have chosen to focus our discussion in this chapter on programs that aim to promote education more directly.

References

Aber, J. L., & Chaudry, A. (2010). *Low-income children, their families and the great recession: What next in policy?* Washington, DC: The Urban Institute.

Aber, J. L., Jones, S., & Raver, C. (2007). Poverty and child development: New perspectives on a defining issue. In J. L. Aber, S. Bishop-Josef, S. Jones, K. McLearn, & D. Phillips (Eds.), *Child development and social policy: Knowledge for action* (pp. 149–166). Washington, DC: American Psychological Association.

Alexander, K., Olson, L., & Entwisle, D. (2007). Lasting consequences of the summer learning gap. *American Sociological Review, 72,* 167–180.

Belsky, J., Vandell, D. L., Burchinal, M., Clarke-Stewart, K. A., McCartney, K., & Owen, M. T. (2007). Are there long-term effects of early child care? *Child Development, 78*(2), 681–701.

Black, A. R., Doolittle, F., Zhu, P., Unterman, R., & Grossman, J. B. (2008). *The evaluation of enhanced academic instruction in after-school programs: Findings after the first year of implementation.* (NCEE 2008–4021). Washington, DC: National Center for Education Evaluation and Regional Assistance, Institute of Education Sciences, U.S. Department of Education.

Bloom, D. (2010). Programs and policies to assist high school dropouts in the transition to adulthood. *The Future of Children, 20*(1), 89–108.

Boruch, R., May, H., Turner, H., Lavenberg, J., Petrosino, A., de Moya, D.,...Foley, E. (2004). Estimating the effects of interventions that are deployed in many places: Place-randomized trials. *American Behavioral Scientist, 47*(5), 608–633. doi: 10.1177/0002764 203259291

Brecher, C., Brazill, C., Weitzman, B. C., & Silver, D. (2010). Understanding the political context of "new" policy issues: The use of the advocacy coalition framework in the case of expanded after-school programs. *Journal of Public Administration Research and Theory, 20*(2), 335–355. doi: 10.1093/jopart/mup008

Campbell, F., Wasik, B., Pungello, E., Burchinal, M., Barbarin, O., Kainz, K., ... Ramey, C. (2008). Young adult outcomes of the Abecedarian and CARE early childhood educational interventions. *Early Childhood Research Quarterly, 23*(4), 452–466.

Chaplin, D., & Capizzano, J. (2006). *Impacts of a summer learning program: A random assignment study of Building Educated Leaders for Life (BELL).* Washington, DC: The Urban Institute.

Connell, J., & Kubisch, A. (1998). *Applying a theory of change approach to the evaluation of comprehensive community initiatives: Progress, prospects, and problems.* Washington, DC: The Aspen Institute.

Currie, J., & Thomas, D. (2000). School quality and the longer-term effects of Head Start. *Journal of Human Resources, 35*(4), 755–774.

Dobbie, W., & Fryer, R. (2009). *Are high quality schools enough to close the achievement gap? Evidence from a social experiment in Harlem* (NBER Working Paper No. 15473). Cambridge, MA: National Bureau of Economic Research.

Duncan, G., Ludwig, J., & Magnuson, K. (2007). Reducing poverty through preschool interventions. *The Future of Children: The Next Generation of Antipoverty Policies, 17*(2), 143–160.

Durlak, J., Weissberg, R., & Pachan, M. (2010). A meta-analysis of after-school programs that seek to promote personal and social skills in children and adolescents. *American Journal of Community Psychology, 45*(3/4), 294–309.

Fixsen, D., Naoom, S., Blase, K., Friedman, R., & Wallace, F. (2005). *Implementation research: A synthesis of the literature.* Tampa: National Implementation Research Network, Louis de la Parte Florida Mental Health Institute, University of South Florida.

Gardner, M., Roth, J. L., & Brooks-Gunn, J. (2009). Can after-school programs help level the playing field for disadvantaged youth? *Equity Matters: Research Review* (No. 4). New York, NY: The Campaign for Educational Equity.

Gormley, W., & Gayer, T. (2005). Promoting school readiness in Oklahoma: An evaluation of Tulsa's pre-K program. *Journal of Human Resources, 40*(3), 533–558.

Gormley, W., Phillips, D., Adelstein, S., & Shaw, C. (2010). Head Start's comparative advantage: Myth or reality? *Policy Studies Journal, 38*(3), 397–418.

Hahn, A., Leavitt, T. D., Horvat, E. M., & Davis, J. E. (2004). *Life after YouthBuild: 900 YouthBuild graduates reflect on their lives, dreams and experiences.* Somerville, MA: YouthBuild USA.

Heckman, J., & Rubinstein, Y. (2001). The importance of noncognitive skills: Lessons from the GED testing program. *The American Economic Review, 91*(2), 145–149.

James-Burdumy, S., Dynarski, M., & Deke, J. (2007). When elementary schools stay open late: Results from the national evaluation of the 21st Century Community Learning Centers Program. *Educational Evaluation and Policy Analysis, 29,* 296.

Kane, T. (2004). *The impact of after-school programs: Interpreting the results of four recent evaluations.* New York, NY: William T. Grant Foundation.

Lauer, P. A., Akiba, M., Wilkerson, S. B., Apthorp, H. S., Snow, D., & Martin-Glenn, M. (2006). Out-of-school time programs: A meta-analysis of effects for at-risk students. *Review of Educational Research, 76,* 275–313.

Love, J. M., Kisker, E. E., Ross, C. R., Schochet, P. Z., Brooks-Gunn, J., Paulsell, D., ... Brady-Smith, C. (2002). *Making a difference in the lives of infants and toddlers and their families: The impacts of Early Head Start.* Washington, DC: U.S. Department of Health and Human Services.

Ludwig, J., & Phillips, D. (2008). Long-term effects of Head Start on low-income children. *Annals of the New York Academy of Sciences, 1136,* 257–268.

Magnuson, K., Ruhm, C., & Waldfogel, J. (2007). Does prekindergarten improve school preparation and performance? *Economics of Education Review, 26*(1), 33–51.

Rothstein, R. (2004). *Class and schools: Using social, economic, and educational reform to close the black-white achievement gap.* New York, NY: Columbia University, Economic Policy Institute, Teachers College.

Schochet, P., Burghardt, J., & McConnell, S. (2008). Does Job Corps work? Impact findings from the National Job Corps Study. *American Economic Review, 98*(5), 1864–1886.

U.S. Department of Health and Human Services. (2010). *Head Start impact study.* Washington, DC: Author.

Vandell, D. L., Reisner, E. R., & Pierce, K. M. (2007). *Outcomes linked to high-quality after-school programs: Longitudinal findings from the study of Promising Afterschool Programs.* Report to the Charles Stewart Mott Foundation, University of California, Irvine.

Walker, K., & Arbreton, A. (2004). *After-school pursuits: An examination of outcomes in the San Francisco Beacon Initiative.* Philadelphia, PA: Private/Public Ventures.

Weiss, H., Little, P., Bouffard, S. M., Deschenes, S. N., & Malone, H. J. (2009). *The federal role in out-of-school learning: After-school, summer learning, and family involvement as critical learning supports.* Cambridge, MA: Harvard Family Research Project.

13

A BROADER AND BOLDER APPROACH FOR NEWARK

Lauren Wells and Pedro Noguera

Newark Liberty International Airport is major a hub of international commerce and transportation. Covering over 425 acres, Newark Airport is one of the leading skyways into the New York metropolitan area and is the third-busiest airport in the United States. In 2006 alone, 35,764,910 passengers and 95,658 pieces of airmail passed through its terminals. Ironically, very few of these individuals ever enter the city for which the airport was named. Similarly, three interstate highways pass through and around the periphery of the city: Interstate 78, Interstate 280, and the New Jersey Turnpike. Like the airport, they serve as conduits for a considerable flow of commuter traffic and are essential to the economic well-being of the metropolitan area. These thoroughfares pass over, around, and through Newark, but the city and its residents are marginal to much of this activity.

Despite the fact that Newark is major commuter hub along the Northeast corridor and the largest city in the state of New Jersey, the city and its residents are economically and politically marginal to the state and the region. Newark, like Detroit, Baltimore, Buffalo, and several other postindustrial urban centers in the United States, has been mired in a cycle of decline for many years. While many of the affluent White residents who once called Newark home (like the current governor Chris Christie) point to the riot of 1967 as the beginning of the city's descent, economist point to the combination of processes that commenced at the end of World War II—suburbanization, deindustrialization, and globalization—to explain why Newark, like other urban areas in the Northeast and Midwest, became stuck in a cycle of economic deterioration in the latter part of the 20th century (Sassen, 1988; Wilson, 1978, 1987.

Today, Newark is one of several American cities trapped in a vicious cycle of economic depression that has relatively little to do with trends in the national economy. Years before the current national recession, unemployment rates in Newark were well above 10% and, in the poorest neighborhoods of the city, the number of families with children living below the poverty line was as high as 28% (Association for Children of New Jersey, 2009). Business leaders and elected officials, including the mayor, Cory Booker, have attempted to break this cycle by promoting economic development projects designed to stimulate the economy and rejuvenate downtown. They have also made a concerted effort to reduce the crime rate by hiring a large number of police officers and employing modern policing tactics that have proven effective elsewhere.[1] However, so far, these efforts have not succeeded in revitalizing the city and resuscitating it from the cumulative effects of deindustrialization, disinvestment, and middle class flight.

There is a growing awareness that if Newark is to experience a sustained economic and social renaissance, it must develop new strategies for developing its human capital, by educating its citizens and doing more to ensure their well-being. Transforming schools, so that they are more effective in providing young people in Newark an education that can make it possible for them to participate fully in the economic rebirth of the city, is widely recognized as essential. However, the record of school reform in Newark is one of unfulfilled promise and repeated failure (Anyon, 1997; Council of the Great City Schools [CGCS], 2007). For years there has been a growing recognition among community stakeholders who have grappled with the challenges confronting Newark's schools that something more is needed than yet another set of reform fads. Over the last 20 years, Newark has participated in numerous national educational reform experiments, but these have yielded negligible results.[2] Schools in Newark exhibit all of the features typically associated with large urban school districts throughout the United States, where failure and decay have been pervasive—high drop-out rates, low student achievement measures, poor attendance, high rates of disciplinary infractions, and so forth (Payne, 2008). The persistence of failure has contributed to a growing awareness that any effort to improve schools in Newark must be carried out in concert with strategies that address economic and social conditions confronting children, families, and the neighborhoods where they reside.

In this chapter we analyze such an effort and explore the challenges that will be confronted as the work proceeds. Called the Broader Bolder Approach to Education (BBA),[3] this ambitious reform project has been launched as an attempt to develop a comprehensive school reform strategy through a variety of school-based interventions that will address issues and challenges arising out of the distressed social contexts in which families and public schools are situated. The goal of the BBA is to bring school reform efforts into alignment with social service provision, economic development, and civic engagement in order to ensure that efforts to transform schools are not undermined by environmental hardships or the lack of attention to quality control in educational practices and interventions. A central component of BBA is to expand learning opportunities for students through quality early childhood education and by extending the traditional school day, and by enriching the curriculum to insure that students are provided with an education that is relevant to the economic, political, cultural, and social life of the city, the nation, and the world in the 21st century. It also seeks to build critical partnerships that will make it possible to strengthen the capacity of schools to respond to student needs and for community interests to come together in ways that allow parents and their allies to hold schools and those who lead them accountable for academic outcomes.

The Need for a Broader and Bolder Approach

The theory of action guiding the BBA is that by transforming schools in Newark it will be possible to address many of the social and economic challenges that have prevented residents of the city from experiencing a superior quality of life. Specifically, the BBA strategy aims at combining research-based educational strategies with school-based social services, afterschool programs, and interventions to increase the capacity of schools to respond to issues that are endemic to the social and environmental context (i.e., the need for health, nutrition, jobs, safety, etc.). The assumption is that such an approach will make it possible for schools in Newark to be in a better position to meet the needs of the students they serve. It is also assumed that successful implementation of a full-service reform model will improve the ability of schools to prepare students to meet the demands of a rapidly changing knowledge-based economy and increase the likelihood that public education in Newark will play a role in reducing poverty and improving social conditions over time.

This is clearly an ambitious agenda. After all, for the last 20 years most social scientists and urban planners who have studied poverty alleviation have argued that economic development must precede other efforts aimed at bringing about improvement in quality of life (Danziger, 1994/2004). In part, this is because improvements in public services—transportation, housing, parks, recreation, and so forth—require funding that is usually supplied by local property taxes. Without a substantial increase in the number of businesses offering high-wage jobs in Newark, public funding for schools or other public services is more likely to shrink than increase in the near future. Additionally, past experience has shown that when school reform projects are dependent on external funding from public or private sources, sustaining change is nearly impossible.[4]

While the need for more jobs in Newark is clear, it does not appear likely that a major infusion of capital and jobs will occur in the near future. In fact, the very conditions that make change necessary—high crime, pervasive poverty, and low levels of educational attainment among residents—make it unlikely that Newark will attract businesses capable of producing the jobs that are needed. Rather than wait for a transformation of the local economy, the BBA strategy is based on the theory that it may be possible to spur economic development and improve the quality of life for a greater number of residents by transforming the schools. Though this proposition has never been tested on such a large scale before, the theory behind BBA is based on the recognition that education is both a *cause* of many of the problems that plague the city and a potential *solution* to those problems.

The BBA strategy aims at transforming schools through the development of the civic capacity of Newark. Stone, Henig, Jones, and Pierannunzi (2001) and others (Noguera, 2003; Orr, 2007) have defined civic capacity as the creation of a series of strategic partnerships between schools, businesses, universities, hospitals, local government, and a broad array of neighborhood-based service organizations. Such partnerships are designed to increase local support for schools and enhance the social capital of students and their families. Policy advocates of civic capacity building have argued that providing schools with substantial increases in external support is the most cost-effective means to deliver the resources and support they need. The theory holds that such support will lead to greater accountability, better functioning schools, and higher levels of student achievement.

As is true in many other high-poverty urban areas, a combination of social, economic, and political problems has historically constrained efforts to improve schools in Newark. These problems are also at the root of many of the current challenges confronting its residents. In high-poverty cities like Newark, where the children attending public schools are primarily from low-income Black and Latino families, social isolation and economic marginalization have an enormous influence upon employment opportunities, health and welfare, aspirations and behavior, and the noncognitive traits typically associated with academic success (Bryke, Sebring, Allensworth, Luppescu, & Easton, 2010; Wilson, 1987). Past ex- perience in Newark (and several other cities) has shown that when educational reforms fail to take into account the various ways in which environmental fac- tors influence students and schools, sustainable improvements in student academic outcomes are difficult to achieve (Noguera, 2003; Payne, 2008; Rothstein, 2004). The BBA strategy seeks to mitigate the detrimental effects of the environment by developing the capacity of schools to respond to student needs and by drawing on support and resources from local institutions.

The BBA strategy also seeks to transform the way in which urban public schools typically serve low-income children of color and their families. In many communities across the country, there is a complacency that is prevalent in public schools. Conditioned by years of failure, by low expectations, by a high degree of disorder and dysfunction and a lack of internal or external accountability, failure, in many public schools, is normalized (Noguera, 2003). As Charles Payne writes in *Getting What We Ask For,* schools with a track record of failure often lose any in- centive to improve because they rationalize failure as the inevitable consequence of serving impoverished children (Payne, 1984). Years of failure in Newark schools have had similar effects upon many of the staff employed there and the normaliza- tion of failure can be seen in (a) high absentee rates among staff (Newark had the highest teacher absentee rate in the State of New Jersey in 2009); (b) tolerance for student absenteeism and tardiness (at two of the "better" high schools in Newark it is a common practice not to take attendance until after 10 a.m. in order to maximize the number of students who will be counted present, because large numbers arrive after the start of school at 8 a.m.); and (c) the lack of attention to quality control in the implementation of interventions and programs designed to help students. The BBA will address complacency and the normalization of failure in schools by using data to carefully monitor student progress and the ways in which programs are implemented. The goal will be to respond immediately to evidence that programs are not implemented with fidelity or are not achieving the goals that have been set.

Successfully implementing such a strategy will be difficult due to a variety of obstacles and constraints that are present within the political and economic environment of Newark. Although there is a small but significant number of high performing/high poverty schools (Education Trust, 1999), there are almost no examples in the United States of school districts that have achieved significant improvements following years of failure (CGCS, 2007). Nonetheless, a growing body of research in urban education suggests that there may be no viable alternative to the BBA approach. A study on the impact of school reforms in Chicago found that gains in school performance were least likely in schools that served the most disadvantaged populations, precisely because these schools were overwhelmed and unable to respond effectively to student needs (Bryke et al., 2010). Research has consistently shown that without a comprehensive strategy there are a variety of contextual conditions—inadequate housing, a broad array of health challenges, high crime and violence, high unemployment—that will impact and undermine student achievement and school performance.

Adverse social and economic conditions within a community will impact the performance of a school in at least three important ways:

1. They influence the amount and quality of academic and social support students receive outside of school, at home from parents and other relatives, or elsewhere. A vast body of research has shown that family income, parent education, and child rearing practices significantly impact developmental and academic outcomes for children (Jencks, 1972; Rothstein, 2004; Weiss, 1988). Sociologist James Coleman coined the term *social closure* to describe the mutually reinforcing partnerships that exist in healthy schools and communities between parents and the staff of schools. These relationships promote and strengthen values and norms that support student achievement and often serve as an essential ingredient of school success (Coleman, 1998). In cities like Newark, social closure is generally weak or nonexistent between parents and schools because parents often lack the skills to support their children academically, and relations between parents and schools are characterized by distrust and even antagonism (Lareau, 2003; Lawrence-Lightfoot, 2003; Noguera, 2003).

234 Lauren Wells and Pedro Noguera

2. Environmental conditions influence the health, nutrition, safety, and overall psychological and emotional well-being of young people. Research shows that the quality of life and the overall health of the neighborhoods where children reside have considerable bearing on academic and developmental outcomes (Adelman & Taylor, 2002; Syme, 2004). Without the resources to support or a strategy to protect children from the harmful effects of dangerous and even toxic communities (Greenberg & Schneider, 1996), schools can be overwhelmed and unable to respond to the nonacademic needs of the children. For example, several studies on federally funded Head Start programs have shown that the benefits of early childhood education can be undermined if children do not receive ongoing support, both within and outside of school, after they enter kindergarten (Karoly, Kilburn, & Cannon, 2005). Similarly, a study on the long-term consequences of infant exposure to substance abuse has shown that such children are no more likely to experience school failure than are nonaffected children who live in the same neighborhoods, because the harmful effects of the environment are even more detrimental than early exposure to drugs (Karoly et al., 2005).

3. Environmental conditions influence the ability of parents and schools to develop the social capital that makes it possible to draw upon local resources to further student learning and promote healthy development. Schools in high-poverty communities often function in isolation from other community agencies (churches, social service agencies, recreation centers, etc.) either because school staff lack relationships with these community-based organizations or because they perceive the neighborhood as hostile and potentially dangerous. In many poor urban areas, schools are the most stable social institutions (largely because of public funding), while potential partner organizations often lack resources or capacity or simply do not exist (Tabb, 1970; Wilson, 1987). In a worse-case scenario, schools may even erode the social capital for the communities they were intended to serve if those who work within them resist efforts to build partnerships with families and neighborhood-based organizations, either from fear, bias, or a lack of awareness that help is needed (Noguera, 2003; Wacquant, 2002).[5]

Recognizing the importance of the relationship between environmental factors and academic performance, BBA in Newark makes a deliberate effort to mitigate the harmful effects of conditions that undermine student performance by building a system of support for schools, drawing on the resources of local institutions. Through strategic partnerships with local corporations, nonprofits, and health centers, BBA will develop a support system for schools designed to increase their ability to respond positively to student needs. The theory of action guiding BBA is that obstacles to school improvement that emerge from the local context will be countered by the strategic deployment and coordination of community resources. A combination of qualitative and quantitative data collected as the project is implemented will be used to test the viability of this proposition.

Overcoming History: Failure and Marginalization in Newark

In Newark, economic decline and educational failure have a long, intertwined history. Founded in 1666, over 100 years before the birth of the nation, Newark is one of the oldest cities in the United States. Strategically located at the mouth of the Newark River, the city became an important center for commerce and, later, industry, due to its easy access to New York Harbor and the Atlantic. By the turn of the 19th century, Newark developed both rail and port systems that made it possible for it to serve as a regional hub of manufacturing and commercial activity. By World War II, Newark was a thriving retail and political center. Several major department stores, cultural centers, and hospitals were located in its downtown, and the presence of a variety of state and municipal buildings made Newark the most important administrative and legal center in northern New Jersey. With a population composed of White ethnics (Jews, Italians, Slavs, etc.), and a mix of working-class and professional households, Newark exhibited the characteristics typically associated with a healthy metropolitan area (Gans, 1962) until the early 1960s. Though African Americans were present in Newark for hundreds of years, their numbers did not increase significantly until the Great Migration in the 1940s and 1950s (Lehman, 1996). The Latino population of Newark did not expand until the 1970s. Today, Latinos constitute the fastest-growing segment of the state's population (U.S. Census, 2010).

Between 1950 and 1967, Newark's White population declined from 363,000 to 158,000. During the same time period, the city's Black residents increased from 70,000 to 220,000 (Chernick, Indik, & Sternlieb, 1967). Beginning in the 1960s, housing policy in Newark appears to have been designed to deliberately keep poor African Americans concentrated in segregated neighborhoods. Five new housing projects were built in Newark's central ward during the 1960s, and low-income African American households comprised 95% of the residents in these new developments (Anyon, 1997; Sasaki, 1994). Similar patterns of segregation emerged in the eastern and southern sections of the city during the same period. Although African Americans migrated to northern cities like Newark in pursuit of jobs, poverty and unemployment in segregated neighborhoods were high from the time they were developed. Cut off from jobs in the northern industrial sections of the city and subject to discrimination in the downtown retail sector, the stage was set for a social upheaval, as resentment festered in neighborhoods where opportunity and mobility were scarce (Price, 1980).

As was true for Detroit, Cleveland, and several other U.S. cities at this time, the riots of 1968 were sparked by the assassination of Martin Luther King Jr. on April 3. However, as was true in many of other cities that experience unrest, a history of discrimination and egregious incidents of police brutality provided the local trigger for indignation and upheaval (Price, 2007). The riots were a watershed for Newark. From May 3 to May 26 there were several clashes between African American residents and the local police.[6] Throughout this period, businesses and homes were burned and looted in the central ward. It took the deployment of troops from the National Guard and 14 days of military occupation to restore a semblance of order. In the wake of this upheaval, Newark experienced a steady exodus of White residents and capital. Over the next few years, the city was dramatically transformed into one that was primarily poor, Black, and economically depressed.

For more than a generation, since 1967, Newark has been ranked among the top 10 poorest cities in the nation with a population over 250,000 (U.S. Census Bureau, 2010). In 2009, the per capita income of Newark residents was $17,372 compared to the $50,919 for households in the state (U.S. Census Bureau, 2010). The median household income, $35,963, was half of the statewide median household income of $70,398. According to the U.S. Census Bureau, 25% of Newark residents lived below the federal poverty level, almost four times the average for the state (U.S. Census, 2010). However, the New Jersey Poverty Research Institute, which calculates a poverty rate based on geographic variations in the cost of living across the state, indicated that the true poverty rate for Newark was closer to 50% (Pearce, 2008). Today, Newark is a "majority minority" city. According to the 2000 Census Report on Newark, 54% of its residents are identified as Black (this includes immigrants from the Caribbean and Africa) and another 30% are Latino (the majority are Puerto Rican, but there are also large numbers of residents from the Dominican Republic, Mexico, Brazil, and Central America). Whites make up only 24% of the city's residents, and most are concentrated in the northern ward.

It has taken over 40 years, but for the last 4 years Newark finally appears to be in the midst of a period of rebirth and rejuvenation. There are clear signs of economic development and improvement to the city's housing market and infrastructure, and new hotels, sporting arenas, and cultural centers in the downtown area have become powerful symbols of change. Although several neighborhoods in Newark are still characterized by high rates of crime and poverty, the demolition of older, low-income housing and the construction of new housing developments has brought evidence of gradual change even in these areas. The current economic crisis pushed the unemployment rate in Newark from 9% to 16% in 2009 (U.S. Census Bureau, 2010), but there has also been a gradual increase in the middle class as professionals have moved into new condominiums and apartments in the north ward.

With this mix of indicators, Newark can be described as a city on the edge. It sits precariously on the border between continued gradual progress and improvement and the possibility that it will fall back into a state of entrenched poverty and economic blight. There is a growing consensus among stakeholders in Newark that if the progress is to continue, schools in Newark must be substantially improved. With 42% of adults over 25 lacking high schools diplomas, and a mere 9% in possession of bachelor's degrees (U.S. Census Bureau, 2000), Newark is in need of a strategy to develop its human capital. Yet, despite the clear need for improvement, educational change has been difficult to achieve.

In her seminal work, *Ghetto Schooling* (1997), Jean Anyon provides a thorough historical examination of the dynamic relationship between urban school reform, changing demographics (particularly with respect to the race and class makeup of the city), and the political economy of Newark. Her analysis reveals how the calculated economic and political decisions made by the city's leaders between the 1940s and the 1970s left the city and school district "bankrupt and dysfunctional." The combination of corruption and systematic disinvestment in the public school occurred as the Black population grew. As was true in many other cities across the country, politicians in Newark viewed schools and other public operations as a source of patronage. Rather than focusing on whether children received a quality education, those responsible for the school were far more concerned with who controlled the jobs and the contracts issued by the school district (Anyon, 1997).

The election of Ken Gibson as mayor of Newark in was yet another watershed for Newark. Occurring in the aftermath of the riots, Gibson was one of the first African Americans elected to lead a major U.S. city. Despite the symbolic importance of the election, patronage and corruption remained rampant in public institutions. Even as African Americans assumed leadership positions in public institutions, graft, corruption, and nepotism continued to be rampant throughout the city (Louis, 1975). Throughout the 1980s and 1990s, a series of reform efforts were initiated in the schools with great fanfare. However, these efforts came and went without much evidence of improvement. Anyon (1997) attributes the failure of these measures not only to the climate of dysfunction that characterized the district, but also to the singular focus of the reform efforts that accompanied the *Abbott v. Burke* Supreme Court rulings (discussed in the following section) on educational systems alone: "By isolating city school from their urban context, and then aiming funding only at the educational institutions, are we not 'missing one whole side of the barn?'…we need to broaden our sights and focus, in addition, on the problems of what the New Jersey Supreme Court called the 'economic and social disaster areas' that are our nation's cities" (p. 148.).

What is illuminating about Anyon's work, for our purposes, are the ways in which her analysis of school failure makes clear that school reform in Newark has repeatedly proceeded in the absence of consideration of the ways in which the racial, political, and economic context of the city affects the well-being and education of children. The BBA initiative is designed not to make the same mistake.

Race, Class, and Educational Reform in Newark

In 1990, the New Jersey Supreme Court's ruled that the education provided to poor students in school districts throughout the state was inadequate due to gross inequities in school funding, and it called for a new funding formula to make up for a history of injustice. *Abbott v. Burke* was a groundbreaking court ruling because it acknowledged the impact of racial and class inequities on the quality of public education in urban schools and attempted to address them by mandating greater equity in school finance. The scope and impact of the *Abbott* decision on the landscape of public school finance and educational reform in high-poverty, urban school districts throughout New Jersey was dramatic. From 1990 to 2008, the New Jersey Supreme Court issued a series of mandates, requiring the State Department of Education to equalize funding between suburban and urban districts and to provide supplemental funds for programs that would reduce the educational disadvantages associated with poverty. In many districts this included the provision of full-day preschool and kindergarten, lower class sizes, afterschool and summer programs, and a variety of other reforms designed to improve schools. Together, these mandates constituted the most targeted and sustained effort aimed at improving schools in Newark, and many other urban districts in New Jersey, over the last 25 years.

As a result of funding from *Abbott,* preschool enrollment in Newark increased for 3- and 4-year-olds from 44% in 2000–2001 to 74% in the 2005–2006 school year. Class size for students in Newark's elementary schools between 1994 and 2004 decreased and remained below averages for all other New Jersey districts. By 2004, over 90% of all Newark Public School (NPS) elementary and secondary teachers were fully certified and deemed highly qualified teachers, according to the federal No Child Left Behind Act (Education Law Center [ELC], 2005). Increased funding for educational interventions gradually had a positive impact on student achievement outcomes. The percentage of students performing at or above proficiency on the fourth-grade state assessment doubled for both English language arts (ELA) and mathematics between the 1998–1999 school year and the 2003–2004 school year. Eighth graders also achieved small but steady increases on both ELA and mathematics assessments during the same period (ELC, 2005).

With increased funding made possible by *Abbott,* new programs proliferated and some academic indicators improved as a result of increased funding. Despite some positive trends, educational outcomes experienced by alarming numbers of Newark's youth remained dismal during much of this period. Four-year graduation rates remained below 60%. Over 40% of students were unable to pass the ELA section of the state graduation exam (New Jersey High School Proficiency Assessment) in 2008–2009, and over 60% did not pass the mathematics section. Explanations for the failure of the *Abbott*-funded reforms to produce a more significant impact either on the overall quality of education or student performance were plentiful. In some circles, student deficits and lack of motivation were blamed, while for others, low standards and expectations were treated as the villain. Swinging back and forth between individual and structural explanations of factors that undermine student achievement, many observers fail to take into account the interaction between children and their social environment. As a result of this failure, the programs and policies that have been put in place to improve the conditions of schools and bring about high student achievement have generally had a negligible impact. In Newark, this has even been true when reforms have been supported by massive infusions of new funds. The reforms are in effect not unlike the airplanes that fly across the Newark skyway and the cars that bypass the city along its highways. The reform efforts operate at a symbolic and surface level and are largely disconnected from the depths of Newark's poverty and marginalization. Without substantially more attention to the development of human capital, accountability, quality control versus compliance, and a very clear focus on how educational reforms will be coordinated in concert with other reforms, it is unlikely that NPS will experience the transformation they so desperately need. The new reforms must result in substantive improvements in learning conditions if they are to truly benefit the students and prepare them with the skills and knowledge they need to be economically, socially, and politically relevant in today's world. If NPS is to develop a system of public education where all students can achieve and be successful, it must coordinate its educational strategies and become responsive to the social context in which the public schools are embedded.

An Ecological Framework for Change

The BBA reform agenda in Newark is rooted in an ecological framework, one that explicitly recognizes that creating classrooms, schools, and school systems where children of all ages and backgrounds thrive requires a focus on the social and economic factors that influence schools and children. In a city like Newark, where poverty is concentrated and has been reproduced across generations, the social conditions that arise from poverty: poor health, high crime rates, substance abuse, and so forth—present formidable challenges to school reform. The BBA approach is designed to provide educators and those who collaborate with them with the skills and resources to mitigate the risks that might otherwise undermine their efforts to meet their learning needs. It acknowledges that "fixing schools" in high-poverty neighborhoods must include strategies that make it possible to respond to the wide range of challenges that affect child development and learning and the performance of schools and classrooms. Breaking with past precedent, reformers in Newark have embraced a strategy that should make it possible to address what we have known for years: Children's lives are situated within ecological systems that are made up of complex histories, processes, relationships, and institutions that shape their development.

Not surprisingly, such an approach certainly has critics and opponents. Shortly after the Broader and Bolder Approach was announced as a policy agenda, another national group of educational leaders and policy makers launched what they called the Coalition for Civil Rights and Education (CCE). Led by an unusual combination of prominent public figures (Joel Klein, Chancellor of New York City Schools, Newt Gingrich, former House Republican Leader, and civil rights activist Reverend Al Sharpton), the CCE described education as the most important civil rights issue of the 21st century and called for affirming the principles of No Child Left Behind (e.g., standards-based reform and accountability through high-stakes testing). The CCE also suggested that any effort to shift the focus of school reform to efforts aimed at reducing poverty or improving the health and welfare of children were nothing more than an attempt to use poverty as an excuse for not educating all children at high standards.

Despite its critics, the BBA strategy is moving forward and gaining momentum as a broad array of stakeholders in Newark agree to support the approach even in the face of bridging complex interests, political dynamics, and entrenched patterns of isolation. Much of the reason for this broad support lies in the recognition that all other approaches have failed. Although called by other names, the schools alone strategy advocated by the CCE has been the strategy pursued by Newark Public Schools (and most other urban school districts) for the last 30 years. With funds provided to the Newark Public Schools as a result of the *Abbott v. Burke* rulings, schools have been rebuilt, new technology has been introduced, afterschool and preschool programs have been implemented, but none of these costly measures has had the impact upon academic and developmental outcomes of children that has been hoped for. Leaders from city government, hospitals, local nonprofits, private foundations, and the private sector have now affirmed their support for BBA. It has become clear that in Newark, the ecological framework in which the strategy is rooted is increasingly recognized as the only way that sustainable progress in public education will be achieved.

The BBA strategy draws on lessons learned from research carried out in a variety of fields on the social and emotional needs of children and from the best practices of current reform initiatives. This research suggests that a more comprehensive approach is needed to increase academic outcomes for poor students and to improve the schools that serve them (Blau & Currie, 2006; Comer, 1988; Dryfoos, 1993; Rothstein, 2004; Waldfogel & Lahaie, 2007). The community schools movement, which provides students (and often their families) with access to mental health and other socials supports at school sites, is but one example of how service organizations have partnered with schools in high-poverty urban areas to address the social needs of children (Dryfoos, Quinn, & Barkin, 2005). In a recent book, David Kirp cites the full service schools developed by the Children's Aid Society and Communities in Schools as models that have proven successful in helping schools meet both the academic and nonacademic needs of children (Kirp, 2011). A growing body of research shows that when schools can offer students access to a variety of social services (i.e., licensed social workers or psychologists, nurse practitioners, or dental services), academic and developmental outcomes for children can improve (Darling-Hammond, 2010). Similarly, research shows that extending the school day before and after traditional school hours, as well as requiring students to attend school on Saturdays and lengthening the school year, can have a tremendous impact on achievement (Gladwell, 2008; Mathews,

2009). When carried out in tandem, these practices make it possible for schools to meet the wide variety of needs that typically undermine student learning and child development. While there is no guarantee that such an approach will succeed in raising student achievement and significantly improving the performance of schools in Newark, the long history of failure shows that reform strategies that ignore student needs have not worked.

Conclusion

To a large degree, the Broader Bolder Approach to school reform in Newark is an experiment designed to challenge existing policy assumptions about what it takes to improve urban schools. Though the project draws lessons from past mistakes in school reform, it is still clear that achieving success will not be easy. In November 2009, Chris Christie became the first Republican to win a statewide election since 1997, ousting Governor Jon Corzine. Since assuming office, Governor Christie has vowed to "take back New Jersey," by decreasing spending, cutting taxes across the board, and appointing an education commissioner who would lift the cap on charter schools. Not long after his election, Newark superintendent Dr. Cliff Janey, a major supporter of BBA, was informed that his contract would not be renewed after it expired in June 2011.

The state budget passed by the new administration for the 2010–2011 fiscal year cut aid to New Jersey's public schools by $802 million (Runquist & Alloway, 2010). In Newark these reductions created a $42 million budget gap, sparking district budget cuts that resulted in the elimination of numerous positions and programs. In the midst of these rising fiscal and school staffing challenges, the New Jersey State Department of Education issued a list of 34 persistently low-achieving schools across the state that were required to implement one of four federal school intervention models; one-third of the schools on this list were in Newark.

In such an economic climate, the need to align education and social services has become even more necessary, but doing so is even more challenging. Mayor Booker will now have considerable influence over the appointment of the next superintendent. Given his support for vouchers and charter schools, it is not clear what this will mean for BBA and public schools in Newark. Despite this uncertainty, the BBA initiative in Newark continues to move forward. With a broad-based advisory board composed of civic leaders and representatives of major social institutions and local organizations (such as Rutgers University, the Newark Alliance, The Essex County United Way, and the Abbott Leadership Institute, the Newark Teachers Union, local philanthropic organizations such as The Victoria Foundation, The Nicholson Foundation, and The Prudential Foundation), it should be possible to continue the work despite the political changes. Additionally, parents, students, teachers, and community members have been engaged in various ways, including participation in the development of the school improvement plan for Central High School as well as in a 3-year strategic planning process that included these traditionally marginalized stakeholders. Finally, the principals of the seven BBA schools have coalesced around the initiative in a way that is unprecedented, committing to a reciprocal accountability structure through which they will share resources, discuss common problems, and promote leadership development that research has shown is necessary to lead systemic change in urban schools systems (Fullan, 2007).

Only time will tell if the BBA strategy will work. There is a clear sense of what hasn't worked, but this is no guarantee that the BBA strategy will be more effective and make it possible for schools to overcome their history of failure. The BBA strategy is committed to transparency and accountability to the funders and stakeholders in Newark and the community being served. This will not necessarily increase the chance of success, but it will make it much harder to simply blame others if it doesn't.

Notes

1. Shortly after his election, Mayor Booker appointed Garry McCarthy, a veteran of New York City's police force, as the chief of the Newark Police Department in the hope that Newark, like its larger neighbor across the Hudson, might experience a substantial decline in its crime rate. See the Newark City website (http://www.ci.newark.nj.us/government/city_departments/police_department/about_the_director.php).
2. Some of the major reforms over the last few years include project GRAD, the creation of small learning communities at high schools, the implementation of new math and literacy curricula, and investments in technology to enhance teaching and learning. For a discussion of these initiatives and an analysis of their impact, see *Raising Student Achievement in the Newark Public Schools*, a Report of the Strategic Support Team of the Council of the Great City Schools, submitted to the Newark Public Schools by the Council of the Great City Schools (2007).
3. The Broader and Bolder Approach is a policy statement that was issued by a coalition of scholars, policy makers, and educational leaders in 2008. The BBA statement called for three major revisions in federal education policy: expanded access to preschool, health care, and afterschool programs. For a detailed discussion of the BBA plan, go to www.boldapproach.com.
4. Several of the past school reforms in Newark that were carried out over the last 10 to 20 years were made possible by funding from the State of New Jersey as a result of the *Abbott v. Burke* court decision of 1990. Expanded access to preschool, afterschool programs, and smaller class sizes were some of the programs made possible by Abbott. Continuation of these programs has been suspended as a result of a recent court ruling.
5. The breakdown of partnerships between schools and community-based organizations often occurs due to a lack of clear understanding about the nature and terms of the collaboration. For a discussion of frequent conflicts between schools and CBOs, see *Identity and Youth Development* (McLaughlin & Heath, 1995) and *Obstacles to Strong School-Community Partnerships*, by Joyce Dryfoos (Children's Aid Society).
6. In Mayor Cory Booker's most recent State of the City address, he cited several signs of progress, including new jobs and housing units.

References

Adelman, H., & Taylor, L. (2002). Toward a comprehensive policy vision for mental health in schools. In M. Weist, S. Evans, & N. Lever (Eds.), *Handbook of school mental health: Advancing practice and research* (pp. 24–43). Norwell, MA: Kluwer.

Anyon, J. (1997). *Ghetto schooling: A political economy of urban educational reform.* New York, NY: Teachers College Press.

Association for Children of New Jersey. (2009). *Newark kids count 2009: A city profile of child well-being.* Newark: Association for the Children of New Jersey.

Blau, D., & Currie, J. (2006). Pre-school, day care, and after-school care: Who's minding the kids? In E. Hanushek & F. Welch (Eds.), *Handbook on the economics of education* (pp. 63–71). Amsterdam, The Netherlands: North Holland.

Bryke, A. S., Sebring, P. B., Allensworth, E., Luppescu, S., & Easton, J. Q. (2010). *Organizing schools for improvement: Lessons from Chicago.* Chicago, IL: University of Chicago Press.

Chernick, J., Indik, B., & Sternlieb, G. (1967). *Newark New Jersey: Population and labor force, spring 1967.* New Brunswick, NJ: Rutgers University–Newark.

Coleman, J. S. (1998). *Foundations of social theory.* Cambridge, MA: Belknap Press of Harvard University Press.

Comer, J. P. (1988). Educating poor minority children. *Scientific American, 259*(5), 24–30.

Council of the Great City Schools. (2007). *Raising student achievement in the Newark public schools* (Report of the Strategic Support Team of the Council of the Great City Schools). Washington, DC: Council of Great City Schools.

Danziger, S. (Ed.). (2004). *Confronting poverty: Prescriptions for change.* Cambridge, MA: Harvard Education Press. (Original work published 1994)

Darling-Hammond, L. (2010). *The flat world and education: How America's commitment to equity will determine our future.* New York, NY: Teachers College Press.

Dryfoos, J. (1993). Schools as places for health, mental health, and social services. *Teachers College Record, 94*(3), 540–567.

Dryfoos, J. G., Quinn, J., & Barkin, C. (2005). *Community schools in action: Lessons from a decade of practice.* New York, NY: Oxford Press.

Education Law Center. (2005). *Tracking progress engaging communities: Newark Abbott Indicators summary report.* Newark, NJ: Author.

Education Trust. (1999). *Dispelling the myth: High poverty schools exceeding expectations.* Washington, DC: U.S. Department of Education.

Fullan, M. (2007). *Leading a culture of change.* San Francisco, CA: Jossey-Bass.

Gans, H. (1962). *The urban villagers.* New York, NY: The Free Press.

Gladwell, M. (2008). *Outliers: The story of success.* New York, NY: Little, Brown.

Greenberg, M., & Schneider, D. (1996). *Environmentally devastated neighborhoods: Perceptions, policies, and realities.* New Brunswick, NJ: Rutgers University Press.

Jencks, C. (1972). *Inequality: A reassessment of the effect of family and schooling in America.* New York, NY: Basic Books.

Karoly, L. A., Kilburn, R., & Cannon, J. S. (2005). *Early childhood interventions: Proven results, future promise.* Santa Monica, CA: RAND Corporation.

Kirp, D. (2011). *Kids first: Five big ideas for transforming children's lives and America's future.* San Francisco, CA: Jossey-Bass.

Lareau, A. (2003). *Unequal childhoods: Class, race, and family life.* Berkeley and Los Angeles: University of California Press

Lawrence-Lightfoot, S. (2003). *The essential conversation: What parents and teachers can learn from each other.* New York, NY: Ballantine Books.

Lehman, N. (1996). *The promised land: The great black migration and how it changed America.* New York, NY: Vintage Books.

Louis, A. M. (1975, January). The worst American city. *Harper's Magazine, 67–71.*

Mathews, J. (2009). *Work hard be nice: How two inspired teachers created the most promising schools in America.* Chapel Hill, NC: Algonquin Books.

Noguera, P. (2003). *City schools and the American dream: Reclaiming the promise of public education.* New York, NY: Teachers College Press.

Orr, M. (2007). *Transforming the city: Community organizing the challenge of political change.* Lawrence: University of Kansas Press.

Payne, C. (1984). *Getting what we ask for: The ambiguity of success and failure in urban education.* Westport, CT: Greenwood Press.

Payne, C. (2008). *So much reform, so little change: The persistence of failure in urban schools.* Cambridge, MA: Harvard Education Press.

Pearce, D. (2008). *Not enough to live on: Characteristics of households below the real cost of living in New Jersey.* New Brunswick: Legal Services of New Jersey Poverty Research Institute.

Price, C. (1980). *Freedom not far distant: A documentary history of Afro-Americans in New Jersey.* A joint project of the New Jersey Historical Society and the New Jersey Historical Commission, American Chemical Society.

Price, C. (2007). How the riots changed Newark. *The Star Ledger on Newark Riots.* Retrieved from http://www.nj.com/newark1967/

Rothstein, R. (2004). *Class and schools: Using social, economic, and educational reform to close the black-white achievement gap.* Washington, DC: Economic Policy Institute.

Runquist, J. and Alloway, C. (2010, March 17). N.J. school district officials say Gov. Chris Christie budget cuts will force program, staff cuts. *Star Ledger.* Retrieved from http://www.nj.com/news/index.ssf/2010/03/nj_gov_chris_christie_budget_c.html

Sasaki, Y. (1994). "But not next door": Housing discrimination and the emergence of the "second ghetto" in Newark, New Jersey, after World War II. *Japanese Journal of American Studies, 5,* 113–135.

Sassen, S. (1988). *The mobility of labor and capital: A study in international investment and labor flow.* Cambridge, UK: Cambridge University Press.

Stone, C., Henig, J., Jones, B., & Pierannunzi, C. (2001). *Building civic capacity: The politics of reforming urban schools.* Lawrence: University of Kansas Press.

Syme, S. L. (2004). Social determinants of health: The community as empowered partner. *Preventing Chronic Disease: Public Health Research, Practice, and Policy, 1*(1), 1–4.

Tabb, W. (1970). *The political economy of the black ghetto.* New York, NY: W. W. Norton and Company.

U.S. Census Bureau. (2010). *American community survey, 2009.* Washington, DC: Author.

Wacquant, L. (2002). Taking Bourdieu into the field. *Berkeley Journal of Sociology, 46,* 180–186.

Waldfogel, J., & Lahaie, C. (2007). The role of preschool and after-school policies in improving the school achievement of children of immigrants. In J. E. Lansford, K. Deater-Deckard, & M. H. Bornstein (Eds.), *Immigrant families in contemporary society* (pp. 137–156). New York, NY: Guilford Press.

Weiss, L. (1988). *Class, race and gender in American schools.* Albany: State University of New York Press.

Wilson, W. J. (1978). The declining significance of race: Blacks and changing American institutions. Chicago, IL: University of Chicago Press.

Wilson, W. J. (1987). *The truly disadvantaged: The inner city, the underclass, and public policy.* Chicago, IL: University of Chicago Press.

14

SCHOOL REFORM

A Limited Strategy in National Education Policy

Edmund W. Gordon and Paola C. Heincke

Since the 1950s, federal and local governments in the United States have used several approaches to increase the academic productivity of schools and the diverse populations served by the nation's schools. Most of these initiatives have been directed at improving the functioning of schools and at uncoupling the characteristics of children from the effectiveness of schooling, and little progress has been made in reducing those differentials in achievement. We argue that the continuing emphasis on school reform should not be the treatment of choice.

This is an exciting period for the field of education in the United States. Despite one of the most serious economic downturns in the history of the nation, at the level of national government we see evidence of the recognition of the critical importance of effective education to nation building, to national security, to the nation's competitive position in the world, and to our functioning as a democratic society. Whether during a Republican or Democratic administration, there is at least "lip service" given to the importance of education as a national priority.

Under President Obama's administration we are seeing unprecedented budget allocations for education, and concern for education, broadly defined, appears on the agendas of several of the departments of federal government. We also see that in the statehouses of the 50 states the costs of education account for sizeable proportions of all local government budgets. This circumstance presents monumental challenges to the U.S. education enterprise to deliver on this nationally recognized demand. The field of education is even more seriously challenged to use this unusual circumstance to reshape the education enterprise into a more effective and efficient system. As a longtime student of, and an active participant in, the development of the U.S. education enterprise for the past 65 years, I wish that I could be more optimistic concerning the possibility that we will meet this challenge and take advantage of this opportunity. I fear that the heavy emphasis currently being placed on traditional and some refined approaches to school reform is both insufficient and inappropriate to the realities of the problem. I am convinced that there are limits to what schools can do alone and to what we can achieve through school reform. In his book, *Waiting for a Miracle,* my colleague and friend, Professor James Comer, claims that we are "waiting for a miracle" when we wait for our schools (alone) to solve this problem (Comer, 1997).

More than 100 years ago, we began to realize that, as important as are good hospitals to the health of the people in this nation, excellent hospitals are neither good indicators of the nation's health nor are they effective in the production of a nation of physically healthy people. The public health movement emerged with its emphasis on sanitation, potable water, garbage and sewage removal, affordable medical care, and, eventually, on the attitudes and behaviors of the people whose health is of concern. In other words, efforts were put not only into trying to improve the hospitals but also into developing the infrastructure that permits people to be healthy and into educating people to develop attitudes and behaviors that will keep them healthy, such as nutritional habits, exercise, and the avoidance of toxins like tobacco, alcohol, airborne pollutants, animal fats, and stress. Obviously, the public health approach to health maintenance has not eliminated health and medical problems for all people, especially low-income minorities. It may be that the public health approach is a necessary but insufficient condition for the development of a healthy U.S. populace. However, significant improvement in public health has contributed to major improvements in the health of the nation. It may be that a similar approach should be taken with education. I argue that we need to give more attention to the ways in which the behaviors of people and the infrastructure of the nation support academic development.

I am pessimistic about the school reform movement, because I believe that while focusing so heavily on schools our nation is neglecting the most crucial targets of intervention, if improved academic achievement is the goal. In addition to wide access to good schools and competent teachers we, as a society, desperately need to strengthen the capacities of families and the communities of which they are a part to support the academic and personal development of students. I welcome the attention to school reforms and the better financing of schooling. I am less enthusiastic about the emphasis on accountability that rests so heavily on the performance of students on standardized tests. I have no doubts that all of us can benefit from a clear understanding of the common and universal goals toward which we are working. However, I do not believe that we can solve the nation's education problems through the focus on improving schools alone, when our children do not have the adequate support outside the school that can help them to maximize the benefits of the experiences that occur in the school.

We know that high levels of academic achievement are associated with more than good schools. Several studies (Bloom, 1976; Bryke & Schneider, 2002; Clark, 1983; Coleman et al., 1966; Committee on Developments in the Science of Learning, Commission on Behavioral and Social Sciences and Education, National Research Council, 1999; Gordon, 1999; Sexton, 1961; Wilkerson, 1979; Wolf, 1966) indicate that the roots of effective education can be attributed to many conditions, contexts, and places. The causes of development are concrete, existential, and symbolic. These several factors seem to come together in socioeconomic status (SES) and its ubiquitous association with higher academic achievement. Higher status families appear to be better able to extract and provide for their children the conditions, forms of capital, and supports for academic learning that we associate with higher academic achievement. We see a relationship between higher SES and health maintenance that is similar to the relationship observed between SES and academic achievement. Good hospitals and good schools are necessary but appear to be insufficient to ensure the good health or effective education of the nation's people. We need the school reforms, and it is entirely appropriate that our national government lead the charge for school reform. I fully endorse many of the serious efforts at improving the delivery of and access to good schooling for all segments of our population. Over the past 65 years, I have seen the education enterprise in the United States try to respond to the problem and continuing challenge of academic underproductivity with at least eight movements, but the society has strangely neglected sustained effort at a ninth. The following are among our highly promoted efforts:

1. School desegregation
2. Compensatory and preschool education and targeted remediation
3. Various school reform strategies
4. New standards, and now common standards for academic achievement and attainment
5. Accountability grounded in a focus on standardized achievement tests data, with little or no expressed concern for *responsibility* or for the constraining impact of the dominant assessment technologies on teaching and learning transactions
6. National standards for teacher quality, with little attention given to the important role of trustful relationships and their adjudication between those who teach and those who learn
7. Data-driven decision making, but with limited attention to relational systems of program, staff, and student data management, which enable accountability *and responsibility* while *informing* intervention and its improvement
8. Complementary, supplementary, and comprehensive education, with limited attention to the complementarities between the learning and teaching that occur out of schools and the teaching and learning that occur inside of schools—education as a continuum of preparation for and engagement in opportunities to learn in diverse and ubiquitous settings for teaching and learning

All of these reflect the conscientious efforts of our society and our schools to arrive at solutions to the problems of adequately educating diverse populations of young people in a democratic nation. Neglected in these movements, though, have been sustained efforts at strengthening the capacities of families and the communities in which they live to actively support the academic and personal development of learning persons.

My colleagues and I have embraced the idea of "thinking comprehensively about education." I have defined comprehensive education as inclusive of schooling and of all the family and community-based activities and learning experiences in support of academic and personal development that occur outside of the school, and I suggest that we can attribute high academic achievement to exposure to these types of developmental activities and experiences—as much so as to the formal academic curriculum taught in schools. Several researchers have observed a significant gap in academic achievement between African American and Latino students and their European American and Asian American counterparts at all socioeconomic and class levels (Coleman et al., 1966; College Board, 1999). It is possible that the roots of this so-called achievement gap lay in the combination of characteristics of schools and the different ways that families and communities support the academic and personal development of their children.

Yet, those of us who have studied such initiatives as I have indicated above know that, despite unusual effort, we have not been able to solve the problems associated with the academic underproductivity of some segments of the population and the schools that serve them. Some gains are associated with each of these efforts at the reform of schooling, but, in general, school reform does not appear to provide the solution. There may be no single focus solution because we are dealing with multifaceted, dialectically interacting factors, and not just the character and quality of schools.

Given the long history of research that documents the strong association between socioeconomic status and academic achievement, it is ironic that, except for the brief and insufficient effort at the "war on poverty" (1965–1968), little or no attention is being given to improvement in the family income and conditions of life as an approach to the improvement of educational outcomes. Just as family planning is related to family income, with number of children declining as family income increases, it appears that academic achievement increases as family income increases. As with so many of our social problems, solutions are not so simple. Data from the Black middle class are troublesome on this issue. Miller (1995), Coleman et al. (1966), Gordon (1999), and others report data that suggest serious academic underproductivity from Black middle class families. The children from Black middle class families who have earned at least one college degree tend to have scores on the SAT that are similar to the SAT scores of White families who have only completed high school. With respect to developed academic ability, the income and class status of these Black families does not protect them sufficiently from lower than otherwise expected academic achievement.

These data suggest that two different problems are operating. On the one hand, well-resourced families in technologically advanced societies tend to find ways to prepare their children to meet the demands of the society that is working for them. We need to adequately resource all families. The second problem may be even more complex. When we turn to the inter- and intrapersonal problems associated with caste and cultural identity that are possibly at the root of the academic underproductivity of some cultural and ethnic minority groups in the United States, we are faced with dynamic, dialectical, and bidirectional processes that are so intertwined as to defy solution through social engineering. Yet, if they sometimes operate to preclude the development of high levels of intellective competence, they must be addressed if effective education is to be universally achieved. Effective learning seems to require good teaching, but it also requires appropriate learning behavior and environmental support for the same. Even though Coleman (1966), Comer (1997), Miller (1995), other scholars, and I have been calling attention to the fact that what happens in the communities and homes of learners is an important part of the problem, since 1965 no segment of the society has been willing to openly engage this problem. Some of us are afraid to open that door for fear that the victims will be blamed; others of us fear that it is too complex; and, of course, some elements of the society just don't care.

The National Study Group on Supplementary Education aka Comprehensive Education has recently prepared its report, following 3 years of deliberation. In a policy statement (Gordon & Nettles, 2010) prepared for the Study Group, the recommendations that follow were advanced. It is recommended that at all levels of government and community organization we should

- facilitate the informed engagement of parents, guardians, and other interested adults in (actively) supporting children's full academic and personal development;
- develop a new framework for accountability and responsibility, with high quality and transparency;
- implement comprehensive educational opportunities that include out-of-school learning opportunities and in-home and peer-group supports for academic learning;
- support research, evaluation, and dissemination of innovations and promising indigenous practices occurring at the local level;
- provide incentives for community partnerships to align and coordinate learning opportunities and supports; and
- integrate an explicit complementary learning framework into the center of the education reform discussion and provide adequate funding and support to implement these efforts at exploiting the complementarities between the learning and teaching opportunities that occur out-of-school and the teaching and learning transactions that occur in school.

During the past several months, educators flying the banner of A Broader, Bolder Approach to Education (BBA) have advocated for a similar perspective (see Chapter 13 of this volume). BBA argues that the nation must recognize that education is not coterminus with schooling and that good education systems must approach the development of children holistically. The Obama administration has included in its education agenda the Promise Neighborhood initiative, a declared intent to replicate the inspired work of Geoffrey Canada at the Harlem Children's Zone (HCZ). The experiment that begins with planning grants for 20 communities to develop interventions modeled after the HCZ is on target, but a greater commitment and more money will be necessary. I estimate that several such projects will cost much more than the $200 million that has been discussed. The $20 million that was once proposed is about one-third of the yearly cost of the model currently demonstrated in Harlem. Controversy has arisen concerning the wisdom of such an investment in the absence of empirical evidence of the relationship of such wrap-around services to the improvement of academic achievement and personal development. However, I take the position that we more affluent and, perhaps, more educationally sophisticated parents know that the optimal development of our children requires more than good schools can provide. I can see no reason why children from low income and marginalized families need any less support. If anything, such children may require more.

If high academic achievement rests, in part, on active support from the communities and families from which children come to school, it appears rational that we strengthen the capacities of communities and families to follow Jim Comer's advice and do more of the developmental lifting ourselves. I grew up in rural, segregated North Carolina at a time when, in many communities of Blacks, we took what we could get from our underresourced schools and *built scaffolds,* to use Angela Glover Blackwell's (2002) term, around our children to protect them and to enable them to climb, develop, and grow—intellectually, politically, and socially. We have no choice but to do so again and on a much larger scale to include more people of color and other socially marginalized children.

We need many initiatives to move us in that direction. It appears that no one solution will be sufficient. I am convinced that all solutions will need to address the problems related to persistent poverty and the absence of access to communities of opportunity. Well-developed people are one of the by-products of communities that are rich in developmental opportunities. One tangible next step is the creation and adequate funding of the Promise Neighborhoods initiative. Another is the expansion of the effort of the National Urban League through its Excellence and Equity Initiative. Through this initiative, the National Urban League seeks to change the culture of selected communities with respect to the importance of high academic achievement as judged by world class standards of educational achievement. Still another is the strengthening of the United Negro College Fund's (UNCF) advocacy for college-level education for increasingly larger numbers of our children. UNCF has embraced the notion that in the

21st century, readiness for admission to the labor force is synonymous with readiness for admission to college. The standard is moving toward recognition that in technologically advanced societies intellective competence, comparable to that which we associate with completion of college, is essential to upward mobility. Another idea is the creation of centers like the ones in Rockland County, New York, where the State University of New York (SUNY) Rockland Community College has undertaken to implement a model for a Comprehensive Education and Family Resource Center, to provide families and communities with technical assistance and the resources necessary to strengthen their capacity to actively support the academic and personal development of children. The Community College and its Comprehensive Education and Family Resource Center are trying to change the culture for education in the communities of marginalized people to help them become high performance learning communities, where high academic achievement matters and denizens know how to exercise human agency and support academic and personal development.[1]

In addition to these developments, consideration should be given to the more extensive involvement of our faith-based institutions in the delivery of out-of-school learning opportunities. Faith-based institutions have long been recognized as being among the pillars of low-income minority communities. Without supporting these institutions in the use of such services for the propagation of their faiths, they could be powerful sources for the delivery of supplementary education and youth development services. Still another example can be borrowed from the early days of Head Start and the War on Poverty, where federally funded programs of family and community development morphed into grassroots political action. These fledgling community organizations and their movement into political action, I think, contributed to the sense of collective agency that was associated with the strengthening of families and the communities in which disadvantaged children lived. Given the deliberate, politically inspired movement of the federal government away from these kinds of programs, we may not be able to again provide government support, but the targeted populations could be educated to the need and encouraged to explore the contribution of collective agency and political action to the advancement of academic and personal development in children and youth. Our federal government may have a natural vehicle through the U.S. Department of Housing and Urban Development (HUD). Not only does HUD have responsibility for housing, it also includes in its mission responsibility for the reduction of the negative impacts of poverty. These combined responsibilities, for improved housing and reduced impact of poverty, force a concern with the strengthening of the capacities of communities and families to support the development of the people who are housed and who are members of these families and communities.

These examples suggest the need for public policy and indigenous community commitment to a public-health approach to the achievement of human agency and intellective competence. Given the epidemic proportions of the problems of low academic achievement and intellective underdevelopment in our society, we may need to push for a national program and Federal Office of Affirmative Development of Intellective Competence (Gordon & Bridglall, 2007). Such an office, within the U.S. Department of Education or in the U.S. Department of Housing and Urban Development, could be focused on better enabling our communities and the families that reside in them to actively support the academic and personal development of children from preconception through the completion of college, while the U.S. Department of Education continues the focus on school reform. We still need good schools and good teachers, but good schools and teachers need the active support of communities and families to effectively educate all of our children. The focus on school reform is a limited strategy in national education policy.

Note

1. The program of the Comprehensive Education and Family Resource Center includes the social marketing of the idea of thinking comprehensively about education—education as inclusive of what happens from before conception, during the infancy, toddler, and adolescent years, through adulthood as it relates to health, nutrition, intellectual stimulation, spare-time activities, role models, good schools, rigorous intellectual and personal demands, and so forth. The model for this resource center, in the tradition of the earlier settlement house movement, provides education for parents and technical assistance to community-based and faith-based institutions interested in providing out-of-school learning experiences for children. The center is an information resource and clearinghouse for relevant information and referral.

References

Blackwell, A. G., Kwoh, S., & Pastor, M. (2002). *Searching for the uncommon common ground: New dimensions on race in America.* New York, NY: Norton.

Bloom, B. S. (1976). *Human characteristics and social learning.* New York, NY: McGraw Hill.

Bryke, A. S., & Schneider, B. (2002). *Trust in schools: A core resource for improvement.* New York, NY: Russell Sage Foundation.

Clark, R. M. (1983). *Family life and school achievement: Why poor black children succeed or fail.* Chicago, IL: University of Chicago Press.

Coleman, J., Campbell, E., Hobson, C., McPartland, J., Mood, A., Weinfeld, F. D., & York, R. L. (1966). *Equality of educational opportunity.* Washington. DC: Department of Health, Education and Welfare.

College Board. (1999). *Reaching the top: A report of the National Task Force on Minority High Achievement.* New York, NY: The College Entrance Examination Board.

Comer, J. P. (1997). *Waiting for a miracle: Why schools can't solve our problems—and how we can.* New York, NY: Dutton.

Committee on Developments in the Science of Learning, Commission on Behavioral and Social Sciences and Education, National Research Council. (1999). *How people learn: Brain, mind, experience, and school.* Washington, DC: National Academies Press.

Gordon, E. W. (1999). *Education and justice: A view from the back of the bus.* New York, NY: Teachers College Press.

Gordon E. W., & Bridglall, B. L. (2007). *Affirmative development: Cultivating academic ability.* Boulder, CO: Rowman & Littlefield.

Gordon E. W., & Nettles, M. T. (2010). *A report of the National Study Group on Supplementary Education aka Comprehensive Education.* Princeton, NJ: Educational Testing Services.

Miller, L. S. (1995). *An American imperative: Accelerating minority educational advancement.* New Haven, CT: Yale University Press.

Sexton, P. (1961). *Education and income: Inequalities of opportunity in our public schools.* New York, NY: Viking Press.

Wilkerson, D. (Ed.). (1979). *Educating all our children: An imperative for democracy.* Westport, CT: Mediax.

Wolf, M. M. (1966). The measurement of environments. In A. Anastasi (Ed.), *Testing problems in perspective* (pp. 491–503). Washington, DC: American Council on Education.

ABOUT THE EDITORS

Ezekiel J. Dixon-Román is an assistant professor of social policy in the School of Social Policy & Practice at the University of Pennsylvania, where he is the director of the Latino Social Service & Policy Initiative. He also holds a secondary appointment in the Graduate School of Education and affiliations with the Center for Africana Studies and Latin American & Latino Studies program. In addition to his university affiliations, he is also a member of the Gordon Commission on the Future of Assessment in Education and a member of the Research Advisory Committee for the American Educational Research Association.

Dr. Dixon-Román's overall research interests are in the sociology of education, cultural studies, policy, and quantitative methods. He is primarily concerned with the reproduction of social differences in human learning and development. More specifically, he is interested in the cumulative/residual effects of inheritance on social differences in human learning and development, how knowledge is constructed and reproduced regarding these differences, as well as identifying the potential resources, practices, and policies that may enable the mediation of these cumulative/residual effects. He is currently working on a single-authored volume, tentatively titled *Inheriting [Im]possibility.*

Edmund W. Gordon is the John M. Musser Professor of Psychology Emeritus at Yale University; Richard March Hoe Professor Emeritus of Psychology and Education at Teachers College, Columbia University; and Director Emeritus of the Institute for Urban and Minority Education (IUME) at Teachers College, Columbia University. He is also the Senior Scholar in Residence at the SUNY Rockland Community College. Professor Gordon's distinguished career spans professional practice, scholarly life as a minister, clinical and counseling psychologist, research scientist, author, editor, and professor. He has held appointments at several of the nation's leading universities including Howard, Yeshiva, Columbia, City University of New York, and Yale. Gordon has been recognized as a preeminent member of the behavioral science disciplines and has been named one of America's most prolific and thoughtful scholars.

He is an elected Fellow of various prestigious associations and was elected member of the National Academy of Education in 1986. Among his most recent honors is the "Edmund W. Gordon Chair for Policy Evaluation and Research," created by the Educational Testing Service to recognize his lasting contributions to developments in education, including Head Start, compensatory education, school desegregation, and supplementary education. In 2005, Columbia University named its campus in Harlem, New York, the Edmund W. Gordon Campus of Teachers College, Columbia University. He is the author of more than 200 articles and 18 books and is currently serving as the Chairman of the Gordon Commission on the Future of Assessment in Education.

ABOUT THE CONTRIBUTORS

J. Lawrence Aber is Distinguished Professor of Applied Psychology and Public Policy at the Steinhardt School of Culture, Education, and Human Development, New York University, where he also serves as board chair of its Institute for Human Development and Social Change. His basic research examines the influence of poverty and violence, at the family and community levels, on the social, emotional, behavioral, cognitive, and academic development of children and youth. Dr. Aber also designs and conducts rigorous evaluations of innovative programs and policies for children, youth, and families, such as violence prevention, literacy development, antipoverty initiatives, and comprehensive services initiatives. He is an internationally recognized expert in child development and social policy and has co-edited *Neighborhood Poverty: Context and Consequences for Children* (1997, Russell Sage Foundation), *Assessing the Impact of September 11th 2001 on Children Youth and Parents: Lessons for Applied Developmental Science* (2004, Erlbaum) and *Child Development and Social Policy: Knowledge for Action* (2007, APA Publications).

Angela Glover Blackwell, founder and chief executive officer, founded Policy-Link in 1999 and continues to drive its mission of advancing economic and social equity. Under Blackwell's leadership, PolicyLink has become a leading voice in the movement to use public policy to improve access and opportunity for all low-income people and communities of color, particularly in the areas of health, housing, transportation, education, and infrastructure. Blackwell is a frequent commentator for some of the nation's top news organizations, including the *Washington Post,* Salon, and the Huffington Post, and has appeared regularly on such shows as public radio's "Marketplace," "The Tavis Smiley Show," "Nightline," and PBS's "Now." Blackwell is the coauthor of *Uncommon Common Ground:*

Race and America's Future (W.W. Norton & Co., 2010), and contributed to *Ending Poverty in America: How to Restore the American Dream* (The New Press, 2007) and *The Covenant with Black America* (Third World Press, 2006). Blackwell earned a bachelor's degree from Howard University and a law degree from the University of California at Berkeley. She serves on numerous boards and served as cochair of the task force on poverty for the Center for American Progress.

Tracey Bryan is a member of the Jacobs Center for Neighborhood Innovation's Strategic Partnerships Team and has authored numerous articles and related print publications detailing the Jacobs Center for Neighborhood Innovation and their work in the Diamond Neighborhoods of southeastern San Diego.

Andrea Yoder Clark is principal and founder of Yoder Clark & Co. Consulting, a consulting firm specializing in community and educational program development, evaluation, and practice. Since its inception, Dr. Yoder Clark has worked with The Salk Institute, The Science Network, The Elementary Institute of Science, The California Department of Education's Statewide Service-Learning Network, Excel Youth Zone, TekSprout, and The SurfAid International School's Program. Dr. Yoder Clark has also written extensively on community development and service-learning and has regularly contributed to the practice-oriented service-learning volume *Growing to Greatness,* published by the National Youth Leadership Council since 2009. In 2007, Dr. Yoder Clark was honored as a Service-Learning Emerging Leader in the field and as a Service-Learning Emerging Scholar in both 2008 and 2009.

Paola C. Heincke is the executive officer of the Gordon Commission on the Future of Assessment in Education. She has worked as an editorial and research assistant to Professor Edmund W. Gordon since 2005. She has served as the coordinator of the National Study Group on Supplementary Education. Previously, Paola worked in corporate affairs, government relations, and corporate communications in Colombia, South America, where she grew up and earned her degree in political science.

Korina Jocson is assistant professor of education in arts and sciences at Washington University in St. Louis. Her research and teaching interests include literacy, youth, and cultural studies in education. Central to her work are sociocultural approaches in examining literacies and media technologies across educational contexts. She has published in various scholarly journals and is the author of *Youth Poets: Empowering Literacies In and Out of Schools.*

Carol Lee is the Edwina S. Tarry Professor of Education and Social Policy, professor of learning sciences, and professor of African American studies at Northwestern University. She has developed a theory of cultural modeling that provides a framework for the design and enactment of curriculum that draws on forms of prior knowledge that traditionally underserved students bring to classrooms.

She is the author of *Signifying as a Scaffold for Literary Interpretation: The Pedagogical Implications of an African American Discourse Genre* and the co-editor, with Peter Smagorinsky, of *Neo-Vygotskian Perspectives on Literacy Research,* published by Cambridge University Press. She has published in numerous journals, is the past president of the National Conference on Research in Language and Literacy, and the past president of the American Educational Research Association.

Jacob Leos-Urbel is an advanced doctoral candidate at New York University's Wagner School of Public Service and a research fellow at the Institute for Education and Social Policy. Prior to coming to NYU, Jake was the Director of Policy Research at the After-School Corporation. His research focuses on programs and policies that operate outside of the traditional school classroom and aim to improve children's educational and other developmental outcomes.

Ebony McGee is assistant professor of diversity and urban schooling in the Department of Teaching and Learning at the Peabody College of Vanderbilt University. She received her PhD in curriculum and instruction with a concentration in mathematics education in 2009 from the University of Illinois at Chicago. Her dissertation, *Race, Identity, and Resilience: Black College Students Negotiating Success in Mathematics and Engineering,* received the Outstanding Dissertation Award from AERA Division G. Her research study investigates successful African American, Asian American, and Latino physical science and mathematics advanced college students and the role of stereotypes and other influences in their postsecondary career and academic decision making. More generally, Dr. McGee's research focuses on the role of racial stereotypes in educational and career attainment, resiliency, identity (racial, mathematics, and otherwise), and identity development and formation in mathematically high-achieving, marginalized students of color.

Na'ilah Suad Nasir is an associate professor in the Graduate School of Education and the African American Studies Department at the University of California, Berkeley. Her program of research focuses on issues of race, culture, and schooling. She is the co-editor, along with Paul Cobb, of *Improving Access to Mathematics: Diversity and Equity in the Classroom,* published in 2006 by Teachers College Press. She is also the author of *Racialized Identities: Race and Achievement for African-American Youth,* published by Stanford University Press. She has published numerous articles in scholarly journals, such as the *American Educational Research Journal, Teachers College Record, Educational Researcher,* and the *Journal of the Learning Sciences.* She is codirector of an IES training grant, *Research in Cognition and Mathematics Education,* and Co-PI of the *LIFE (Learning in Formal and Informal Environments) Center,* an NSF Science of Learning Center. She is also the recipient of the St. Clair Drake Teaching Award at Stanford University, and the Division G Early Career Researcher Award.

Pedro Noguera is the Peter L. Agnew Professor of Education at New York University. He holds tenured faculty appointments in the departments of Teaching and Learning and Humanities and Social Sciences at the Steinhardt School of Culture, Education and Development at NYU. He is also the executive director of the Metropolitan Center for Urban Education and the codirector of the Institute for the Study of Globalization and Education in Metropolitan Settings (IGEMS). Dr. Noguera is the author of seven books and over 150 articles and monographs. His most recent books are *Creating the Opportunity to Learn,* with A. Wade Boykin (ASCD, 2011) and *Invisible No More: Understanding and Responding to the Disenfranchisement of Latino Males,* with A. Hurtado and E. Fergus (Routledge, 2011). Dr. Noguera appears as a regular commentator on educational issues on CNN, National Public Radio, and other national news outlets. He serves on the boards of numerous national and local organizations, including the Economic Policy Institute and *The Nation* magazine. In 2009 he was appointed by the governor of New York to serve as a trustee for the State University of New York (SUNY).

Kimberly Powell is an assistant professor of education and art education at Pennsylvania State University. She has a joint appointment with the Language, Culture and Society program in the College of Education and the School of Visual Arts. Powell's research is concerned with art as an interdisciplinary field informed by performance studies, cultural studies, and educational anthropology. Her work focuses primarily on artistic practice and performance as critical aspects of social change and identity; a comprehensive view of education that recognizes multiple places of learning, such as arts organizations, cultural and community centers, and schools as important and influential sites of curriculum, learning, and pedagogy; and the body and the senses as critical modes of mediation, communication, and representation of human experience and knowledge. She has authored several chapters and articles and served as a section editor for the *International Handbook of Research in Arts Education.*

Kavitha Rajagopalan is a research consultant in financial services and a senior fellow at the World Policy Institute, and has worked as a journalist in India, Germany, and the United States. She received a master's degree in international affairs from Columbia University, and a bachelor's degree in international relations from the College of William & Mary. She received a Fulbright scholarship in 2000 and the John J. McCloy Journalism Fellowship in 2004. She is the author of *Muslims of Metropolis: The Stories of Three Immigrant Families in the West.*

Kristine Rodriguez Kerr is a doctoral student in the communication and education program at Teachers College, Columbia University.

Margaret Beale Spencer is the Marshall Field IV Professor of Urban Education in the Department of Comparative Human Development and professor in the Committee on Education and the College. Her program of research stresses human resiliency, identity processes, and competence formation of ethnically diverse young people. Spencer's research, theory, evaluation efforts, and collaborative applications are based upon the perspective that all humans are vulnerable.

The work's resiliency emphasis is designed to communicate the importance of investigating children and youths' strengths, productive coping processes, as well as their capacity for constructing positive identities and healthy outcomes while developing under varying types and levels of challenging conditions. Spencer is the author of over 125 articles and chapters, has co-edited four volumes, and is the recipient of funding from over three dozen federal and philanthropic agencies. She has given major invited lectures and has been the recipient of numerous honors, including elected (2009) membership into the National Academy of Education. Her research has been featured by ABC and CNN.

Lalitha Vasudevan is associate professor of technology and education at Teachers College, Columbia University. She is interested in how youth craft stories, represent themselves, and enact ways of knowing through their engagement with literacies, technologies, and media. Her recent publications have appeared in *Digital Culture and Education, Written Communication, Teachers College Record,* and *Review of Research in Education,* and she is editor of a forthcoming volume on the use of digital media and arts-based literacy pedagogies to cultivate inquiry among court-involved youth.

Lauren Wells is a research associate and the director of the Broader, Bolder Approach to Education, Metropolitan Center for Urban Education. Before joining the Metropolitan Center for Urban Education, she was the project coordinator for the New Jersey Education Organizing Coalition, one of four national projects funded by the Communities for Public Education Reform (CPER) funders collaborative. Altogether, Lauren has over 10 years of experience in education program development, educational policy analysis, community organizing, and grant writing. Her research and practice centers around issues of educational equity and justice and is informed by her interests in the dynamics of race, class, and power in education, school reform, the social and political thought of historically oppressed groups, and community organizing and development.

Min Zhou is professor of sociology and Asian American studies and the Walter and Shirley Wang Endowed Chair in U.S.–China Relations & Communications at the University of California, Los Angeles. Her main areas of research include international migration, ethnic and racial relations, education and the new second generation, and Asia and Asian America. She is the author of *Chinatown: The Socioeconomic Potential of an Urban Enclave* (Temple University Press, 1992), *Contemporary Chinese America: Immigration, Ethnicity, and Community Transformation* (Temple University Press, 2009), and *The Accidental Sociologist in Asian American Studies* (UCLA Asian American Studies Center Press, 2011). She is coauthor of *Growing Up American: How Vietnamese Children Adapt to Life in the United States* (Russell Sage Foundation Press, 1998) and *Asian American Youth: Culture, Identity, and Ethnicity* (Routledge, 2004).

INDEX